New Life Clarity Publishing

205 West 300 South, Brigham City, Utah 84302

http://newlifeclarity.com/

The Right of Debra Jean Collett to be identified as the Author of the work has been asserted by her in accordance with the Copyright Act 1988.

New Life Clarity Publishing
name has been established by NLCP.
All Rights Reserved.

No part of this publication may be reproduced, distributed, or transmitted in any form or by any means, including photocopying, recording, or other electronic or mechanical methods without the prior and express written permission of the author or publisher, except in the case of brief quotations embodied in critical reviews and certain other noncommercial uses permitted by copyright law.

Printed in the United States of America

ISBN- 9781087926841

Copyright@2022 Debra Jean Collett

SOLDIER OF VALOR

By
Debra Jean Collett

DEDICATION

*Richard Dean Hobson
who is the inspiration for
this book, my brother,
my mentor, my hero.*

PREFACE

Nothing had ever come easily for Jackson Levi Montgomery, but he had character; which exhibited passion and drive that superseded even impossible accomplishments. He had spent a lifetime defying physical, mental, emotional and medical odds. When Jackson was born he required a long hypodermic needle to be shoved through the middle of his heart to get him to breathe and his heart to start pumping. Even as a young boy he faced challenges that were in need of undeniable perseverance and forward driving strength. At nine-years old Jackson catapulted from a backyard swing set and made a stiff, hard landing. This shoved the head of his left femur up into the hip socket causing excruciating pain. The injury required him to wear a metal brace on his left leg for a year. The brace was attached at the hip and had slabs of metal running down each side of his leg. Bending the leg was impossible. That made it so he could barely walk, let alone run; which completely halted his Little League career. Jackson was told that he would limp and probably not be able to run. Against all odds, and a year later, he threw the heavy, awkward brace into the river near his home and went on to play baseball with style. He took his team to the World Series of Little League Baseball and captured honors for his performance on the field.

Fighting with intensity became a pattern for Jackson. At the university, he was majoring in pre-med. Jackson had always wanted to become a doctor, but not just any doctor; a renowned neurologist or respected cardiologist. Nothing was done with mediocracy. Just getting by was not an option for Jackson, which always resulted in setting his goals higher than usual. He possessed an unwavering determination to be the best at everything.

And so it was as the Vietnam War broke out. The draft was instigated and he felt he was constantly looking over his shoulder in fear that his number would come up. Jackson had given a lot of thought to a decision he would soon be making. It was a dusky afternoon when he jumped into his 1964 Pontiac GTO. The car sported a metallic blue color with chrome fenders and trim. Brand new tires showed off the car's potential to be fast; which was one of Jackson's favorite characteristics about it. Jackson bounced into the front seat ready, but anxious, to fill out forms at the Marine Corps recruiting office. The destination was far enough away, allowing some time to contemplate the foreseen consequences of his next move. His father was a pilot in the United States Air force and Jackson had not discussed his decision with him at all. He felt there would be repercussions about him joining the Marines instead of the Air Force and carrying on the family tradition. Jackson felt his hands wrap around the steering wheel with a tense grip; his jaws ached from being clenched so hard. As he pulled up to the armed services recruiting office, Jackson hesitated. He thought to himself, "I don't know whether I am just an idiot, or a smart idiot." He next found himself signing the bottom line to join the United States Marine Corps.

Jackson Levi Montgomery was an exorbitantly decorated war hero, a renowned professional golfer, rich real estate entrepreneur, and happily married- or so he thought. He carried his six- foot-two stature with confidence and dignity. His appearance gave the immediate conclusion of success and once you met him the memory of his charismatic personality stayed with you. Jackson was living in a comfort zone and was totally unaware of what would follow.

TABLE OF CONTENTS

Chapter One: Rude Awakening ... 1

Chapter Two: Puzzle Pieces ... 21

Chapter Three: Keep Running The Race ... 41

Chapter Four: The Ravage Of War ... 61

Chapter Five: Uncommon Value A Common Virtue ... 81

Chapter Six: Love, Set, Match ... 101

Chapter Seven: Fame, Fortune, Family ... 131

Chapter Eight: Best-Laid Plans ... 165

Chapter Nine: Marriage And Mistletoe ... 185

Chapter Ten: Vengeance For Valor ... 203

Chapter One

RUDE AWAKENING

Slowly, Jackson opened his eyes and mundanely began counting the off-white square tiles of the floor. He was lying face down and quickly moved his eyes from right to left to increase his peripheral vision. Anxiety began to set in as he realized he could not turn his head. It was held stationary by some sort of brace. Memory failed him as he tried to collect his bearings. An annoying and excruciating headache was making his head feel heavy and the pressure was causing considerable discomfort. Time was a stranger, for Jackson had no idea how long he had been in this situation. His thoughts were interrupted as the sound of shuffling shoes entered the doorway and moved closer to his bed. From his side view he noticed two feet that were clad in expensive-looking, caramel-colored men's dress shoes. Suddenly he heard a clunking sound of metal and his bed began to vibrate. He felt the weight of his body as the bed turned him right-side up. He was now facing the ceiling where he found a predictably boring view of a simple light fixture and white cork-board ceiling tiles. His eyes moved to the left and he could see an average sized man with coal-black hair and dark skin standing by his side. The man wore business slacks, a pale-colored button-down shirt and a red paisley tie with blue background.

The white, crisp lab coat he wore appeared to be somewhat large on him and Jackson recognized that he must be a physician when he saw the stethoscope around his neck and the nametag on his chest pocket with the initials MD, after his name.

"Mr. Montgomery, I am Dr. Aziel Omar Zyaire". The doctor spoke with a heavy accent. "I am the chief Neurosurgeon at Denver's Veteran Hospital". And then motioning a few feet beside him he said, "And this is Nurse Trey Shepherd who has been caring for you." He briefly paused, turned his head and directed his gaze at Jackson. "Mr. Montgomery do you know where you are?" "Well, you just told me," Jackson sarcastically replied. "I am in the Veteran's Hospital in Denver Colorado". Dr. Zyaire continued with more questions. "Can you tell me your name and what you remember about how you got here"? "You also told me that. I am Mr. Montgomery. And I have no clue how I got here". "What is your first name?" the doctor asked. Jackson found himself extremely frustrated and began clenching his jaw tight. He took a deep breath and raised his voice, firmly replying, "I DON'T KNOW!" Dr. Zaire continued, "I know this must be very difficult and frightening for you, but your memory should improve now that you are conscious. Your memory will likely be regained with small portions at a time. You have been in a coma for three weeks and have just this morning returned to consciousness. There was a bad car accident and you were critically injured; receiving some significant and most prominent damage to the spine at T-8 and T-9. What this means is you have lost function and feeling in your lower body and legs. I am so sorry. We will, however, be giving you the best care available and you will have access to one of the top rehabilitation facilities in the country. We're going to take very good care of you, Jackson; that's your first name. If you need anything you ask Trey. He is an outstanding nurse. Or, you can talk to any of the staff and they would be more than happy to assist you with anything you might need. I will come by later to check on you". Dr. Zyaire turned and headed for the door. Now it was Trey's turn.

"You have a Halo brace bolted to your head to eliminate any movement until you have more time to heal. Right now, it is normal to feel some discomfort right above your temples where the titanium steel bolts are attached. Also, you are strapped to a rotating bed and your arms are temporarily restrained to also prevent movement. We will be turning you every two hours and taking your vital signs every three hours until you can get up, which will be some time in the future. There are two IVs in your arms, one in the left and one in the right. You'll be receiving antibiotics, fluids and pain medication through these IVs. We placed a catheter in you that drains urine into a large plastic bag that is hung on the bars at the side of the bed. The bag is emptied periodically when it is full. Do you have any questions? Are you comfortable?" There was an uneasy stillness that settled before Jackson could respond. Jackson felt a fever of rage overcome himself and thought, "If I wasn't in this bed I would deck you!" Finally, he said, "Trey? That is your name, right? I am lying in a torture chamber paralyzed from the waist down and barely can remember who I am; and you have the audacity to ask if I have questions and if I am comfortable"? "Well, what in the hell do you think? Of course I have questions! And I am certainly NOT comfortable. Are you an idiot?" Trey quickly responded, "I am sorry Jackson. I meant no offense. I just want to be able to do whatever I can to help you". Jackson barked his response, "You can help me by leaving. I want to be alone". Trey hesitated; something was compelling him to stay. He felt compassion for Jackson and truly wanted to help him. But he would respect his request. Trey turned around and as he headed for the door he called back over his shoulder, "I'll be back".

Jackson found himself blankly staring at the ceiling as tears trickled down his cheeks. They felt cool and slightly tickled. He couldn't even wipe them away. "Wow! So, my name is Jackson Montgomery," he thought. He closed his eyes trying to evoke more memory to the surface. Instead, he drifted off to sleep. He was mentally and emotionally exhausted. In his dreams, bits and pieces of scenes came to him about the accident. He kept seeing a red car that was totaled. He felt wet and realized it was rain pouring down, soaking him and giving him a chill. Jackson recalled a loud sound of a saw striking against metal and a boisterous call, "Is anyone in there?" His mind switched scenes and he was now driving somewhere. "But where?" There were dark forest-green pine trees everywhere and golden quaking aspen sparsely placed among the pines; he recalled the strong smell of pine as it rained. Windshield wipers were clomping back and forth at a rapid pace and still the vision was blurry. A warning sign was in view ahead and was intended to educate the driver of the upcoming curve in the road. The car began the descent into the curve. Abruptly Jackson came back to consciousness and it felt as though he was dripping sweat from his forehead. That annoying headache had returned. He tried to feel with his fingertips for a call-light but was unsuccessful. Jackson became increasingly annoyed as he realized pressing a call light for the nurse to get any pain medication was literally out of reach. Reluctantly he waited for the sound of someone entering his room.

"Can I get you anything Mr. Montgomery?" It was a different voice than he had heard. "Our shift has changed; and I will be your night nurse. My name is Carrie; Carrie Langston". "I am in pain," was his slow reply. "And, please, call me Jackson". "Okay Jackson, I'll go get you something for the pain and be right back". Carrie quickly whisked away. Jackson thought she was kind. He could tell by her voice and demeanor. He could see her braided, long blonde hair but was unable to see her eyes. "Eyes tell a lot about a person, he thought. I just imagine they are kind eyes and crystal blue." This was a pleasant thought for him to entertain. Carrie returned with a syringe of medicine. "What is that?" he asked. "It is Morphine. It should help in just a few minutes,"

Carrie replied. Jackson was glad to feel relief finally set in. As Carrie was giving him the Morphine, he seemed to have a Deja vu. Jackson saw himself getting Morphine through a similar IV for something else. He tried hard to focus and remember what he had done before that was so similar to this. "You should feel the effects immediately," Carrie said as she adjusted the IV pump. She paused when she glanced over at Jackson's facial expressions. His brow was furrowed and his eyes looked concerned. "Do you want to talk about it?" Carrie gently asked.

"I would if there was anything to talk about. Right now I just feel numb and I can't seem to put the puzzle pieces together", he responded. "I'm sure that will come in time, Jackson. Don't be too hard on yourself." Carrie continued, "You have just recently come out of a coma and already you are starting to get some of your memory back. It looked like you had a memory come to you when I was giving you the Morphine." "I did. But I'm not sure why." With that comment from Jackson, Carrie offered an explanation. "Maybe you were in another accident or perhaps you were in the military. You are an amputee. Your right leg is missing below the knee and I noticed the Marine Corps seal tattooed on your right arm." Jackson's face turned pale and his eyes widened in shock. He hadn't been able to look at his legs, so he hadn't noticed that he was missing one of them. Because he was strapped to the bed, movement was restricted to his arms. "I don't suppose I would have that tattoo if I wasn't a Marine. You know what they say: Once a Marine, always a Marine." Jackson produced a slight smile; which seemed to please Carrie. "Do you remember anything about the Marine Corps?" Carrie inquired. "No! I don't. I just don't!" Jackson became agitated so Carrie gently put her hand on his and told him that it was okay and they would talk later.

This was a lot to process and Jackson thoroughly went over it in detail. Time is something he seemed to have on his hands right now, but patience was scarce. During the next few days Jackson acclimatized to his routines that were consistently accomplished daily by the staff. This included one staff member he had become quite attached to and looked forward to her shift. Carrie was easy to have a conversation with and she made him feel comfortable, like he was talking to an old friend. There was a connection between them and he valued it enough not to question it. Carrie had made herself vulnerable by revealing to Jackson parts of her past and growing up. She had been raised in a small country town in Ohio on a family farm. She left the farm as a teenager to pursue a career in nursing at the University of Colorado. After graduation she was offered a job at the Veterans Hospital. Because the mountains and environment pulled her in, she accepted and decided to stay in Denver. Carrie's dad had just passed away from lung cancer a few months ago and she was now facing the dilemma of whether she should return to Ohio to care for her aging mother. Her older brother, Reggie, was running the farm and supervising the employees. He also had the finances under control. Carrie knew the affairs of her family were in good hands and that eased the urgency for her to return. Jackson had listened to Carrie express openly about her feelings for family, home and attachments. He enjoyed watching her expressions with her face and hands as she talked. Her voice was pleasant and she wore an amazing smile on her face. Listening to her talk melodically calmed Jackson. When she mentioned home and family, he began to wonder about his own. "Did he have someone; anyone that was worried about him; or for that matter missing him?" It had been six weeks since he had awakened from the coma. No one had been to see or even inquire about him. "I wish I had answers. What is going on? And, who am I?" These were repetitive questions that filtered through his mind every day. The CT scan that had been done on Jackson weeks earlier had indicated that there were no signs of trauma or injury to his head, only a slight concussion which resolved itself in a few days. This made him question his amnesia and exasperate about the length of time he would be trapped in this nightmare.

As the seventh week of his hospital stay slowly crept up, it produced a significant event. Jackson had just finished his morning therapy, which consisted of manual stretches of his arms and legs, fingers and toes. The worst of it was the spasms he experienced. Some were minor and others shook the bed violently. Trey was pulling the bedcovers up to his shoulders as they both noticed two officers at the door. The officers knocked politely and requested to come in. The taller man was huskily built, had a moustache, and was dressed in a highway patrol uniform. The shorter and smaller man was clad in a dark-blue police officer's uniform. Both men wore heavy black-leather belts around their waists that harbored secured weapons. After entering the room, each officer produced identification and their badges were clearly displayed. The taller man stated, "Mr. Montgomery I am Lieutenant Scott Reese of the Colorado Highway Patrol and this is Officer Vargas Gonzales of the Denver Police Department. We have been investigating your accident that occurred up in Aspen Colorado on March 17th of this year. I apologize for not getting to you sooner. Your vehicle was totaled and it took some time to salvage the license plate so we could determine to whom the car was registered". At this point in the conversation Officer Gonzales interrupted. "We ran the plates and found it was registered to a Jackson Levi Montgomery. We understand because of your injuries that you have had some memory loss, but does this name seem familiar?" "Oh, yeah. That's me; or so I'm told," Jackson responded. Then he asked the officers a question that had plagued his dreams for several nights. "You said it happened in Aspen, but do you have any idea how?" Lieutenant Reese took over the conversation. "According to information gathered by the highway patrol, firemen, and paramedics at the scene, it had been down pouring rain for hours before the crash. They estimated the crash took place approximately 1:00 pm the afternoon of the seventeenth. Dispatch received a 911 call from a passing driver just after 2:00 pm. The fire department and paramedics were first responders. It was described as a gruesome scene;

finding your car engulfed in smoke and unrecognizable. Looking in the window they saw no movement from the passenger, who was you. As they assessed the situation it was discovered that you weren't breathing. Someone cried out for help a few feet away and a couple of paramedics left your car to respond to his needs. They found the driver of the car lying on his back with blood covering his head and oozing through his torn pants on his leg. The medics said he had a compound fracture and possible head injury. He was taken immediately to the hospital by ambulance. While the medics worked on him, the firemen called into the car to see if they could get a response from you". "Whoa, wait a minute!" Jackson blurted out. "You're telling me that I was NOT the driver but the passenger? And, at first they left me for dead?" "Who is the guy that was driving my car and responsible for this mess?" Jackson demanded answers. Again, Officer Gonzales joined the conversation. "His name is Darren Mitchell. He told us that you are both successful real estate brokers. The company had sent the pair of you to Aspen to close a deal that was worth a fortune. He told us, also, that you asked him to drive while you filled out some paperwork." "Okay, go on." Jackson pleaded, "How did they get me out of the car if they thought I was dead?" Trooper Reese began, "The firemen heard a faint response coming from within and they immediately employed the *Jaws of Death* to cut you from the car. It took two hours of laboriously hard work to cut the metal that had been crushed against you and mechanically lift the engine off of your body. The medics were successful at administering CPR and getting you oxygen and starting an IV, or you wouldn't have survived. When they cut your suit and shirt off to be able to place the EKG leads, they saw your tattoo and assumed you were a veteran; so they brought you straight here." With soberness Jackson recollected some of the information he had received. He started to put pieces of the puzzle together even though they were still slightly foggy. "So, I now know my full name and that I sold real estate with some crazy idiot that doesn't know how to drive, but he is my partner and we make a lot of money. It happened in Aspen during a torrential rainstorm. Is there anything else?" "Yes, there is." Gonzales took the lead. "When we ran your plates for registration it not only gave us your full, name but it also gave us your address. Your home is located in a wealthy suburb of Littleton, Colorado. And something else, Mr. Montgomery; you're married. Your wife's name is Vanessa Noelle Remington Montgomery. Her family is very prominent in the area. We were able to notify her about the accident as soon as we received the information we needed."

Jackson had no words for a time. His thoughts raced to the dreams he had; and it was then he realized that they were part of his memory returning. Bits and pieces of the puzzle that he had seen in his dreams were verified by the officers' report. He felt relieved to hear he had family but questioned why his wife hadn't reached out to him. With that thought he asked, "Did my wife ask about me or seem concerned? It's been over seven weeks! Did she not realize I was missing? Was a missing person's report filed?" His questions were rapid and ran into one another with barely a break. "I'm sorry Mr. Montgomery. There has not been any kind of report filed on your behalf. Your wife's reaction didn't seem normal; in fact, it was quite casual. This concerned us but we were just there to report about the accident and give her your location. We told her you were in the Veteran's Hospital though, so she should know where to find you. Again, sir, we are deeply sorry about your accident and injuries," Gonzales finished off the conversation as he stepped over to the nightstand and left a card with his name on it and the Denver Police Department's number. "Let us know if you have any more questions." The officer and trooper tipped their hats and said to Jackson, "And Marine, thank you for your service."

The heavy silence was broken when Trey asked Jackson if he wanted him to stay but Jackson told him he was fine. Soon the room was quiet again and disturbingly empty. Jackson fought back tears. The more he thought about what he had just heard the angrier he became. He wondered about what kind of woman he had married, and what she was like to be able to completely ignore him like this. He recognized her maiden name as one of the wealthiest families in Denver. Eagerly he anticipated hearing her explanation, although he wasn't sure when it would come. Maybe he could get some answers from his real estate partner, Darren Mitchell, who had offered up some extremely useful information to the first responders. Jackson breathed in heavily and slowly breathed out. This was a lot to process and he felt abandoned and lonely. "If I was in a war zone, I certainly wouldn't be left behind." Jackson surprised himself with that thought. He was eager for the arrival of the night shift and found a quickened desperation to see and talk to Carrie.

Dusk was beginning to fall and several lights in his room came on automatically. Suddenly, he felt a heaviness come over him and he began to gasp for air. Glancing toward the windows he noticed they seemed higher than usual and he couldn't see out. It was the same with the windows near his door. Lights harshly glowed brighter and brighter and Jackson squinted hard to blot them out. The room walls were shrinking and closing in on him like a trash compacter. Flashes of light combined with loud explosions and sounds of gun fire overwhelmed him. He clenched his fists and pulled on the restraints. They cut his arms as he tried to fight off the perceived torture he was experiencing. "Medic! Medic!" he screamed as Jackson's whole body began to shake and tremble. Blackness and quiet followed.

"Jackson! Jackson! Wake up!" Jackson slowly opened his eyes to Carrie shaking his arm and simultaneously yelling at him. It was probably the first time he had heard her raise her voice. Her face was close to his as she spoke and he could finally see her eyes; her kind, crystal-blue eyes. "Welcome back. You've had a rough time," Carrie continued, "You were calling out for a medic, your fists were clenched tightly, and you were screaming. Jackson, can you tell me what you were dreaming about or thinking?" He rolled his eyes and looked at her, "I felt I was in a war zone and there were grenades going off and gunfire surrounding me. The Viet Cong were swarming around me like ants on an ant hill; trying to kill me. It was if I had a target on my back." Carrie listened intently and then commented, "I think you have been in a war zone at some time and you were reliving your experience. You're showing signs of post-traumatic stress. My shift has just started and I have a few minutes, so why don't you tell me about your day." Jackson began by recounting the conversations he had with the officers earlier. He recalled the devastating information that was given to him. Showing his emotions was not his forte and Carrie was quick to pick up on it. After a strenuous period of time had passed she suggested to Jackson that there were some positive facts revealed from the previous event: he had his identity, address, employment information and knowledge of family existence. Jackson reassured her about his feelings concerning the "family" information. He wasn't that happy about it. As usual Carrie was kind, a good listener, and understood Jackson more than anyone at this point in time. Carrie had to attend to her nursing duties. She was a responsible and dedicated nurse and also a compassionate person. She made time to check in on Jackson and give him opportunities to talk. The night crawled and time didn't seem to pass at all. Jackson couldn't sleep. His mind was bouncing all over the place from the accident to his work and war and then to his wife, Vanessa. Carrie gave Jackson something to help him sleep and calm him. Jackson winced at the thought of being dependent on anything, but especially drugs.

"Good morning, Mr. Montgomery!" Dr. Zyaire blurted out a crisp and cheerful greeting. Trey and two aides followed Dr. Zyaire into the room. Jackson sleepily opened his eyes. He realized he had slept undisturbed all night and was finally feeling rested. "We are going to release the restraints from your arms and remove the halo head-brace today. After we have finished the procedure these fine people will sit you up. We will be laying you flat to remove the brace. I will numb the area where the bolts are located so you will feel some discomfort but no pain. If you feel pain be sure to tell me. Any questions?" Dr. Zyaire tilted his head in order to see Jackson's mouth for the response. "No, I don't think so. Oh, wait! Maybe one. Will I be moved out of this torture chamber of a bed today, too?" His comment drew laughter. "Yes, of course. I am sorry I neglected to tell you that. Are you ready to proceed?" After getting Jackson's approval, the doctor motioned for a sterile tray of instruments to be brought into the room. It was covered with a blue sterile cloth and a syringe of medication and several instruments were precisely lined up. Jackson felt it was a daunting scene. The side bars on Jackson's bed were then lowered and a sterile blue cloth was placed under his chin and across his shoulders. Dr. Zyaire had ordered the nurse to administer IV pain medication to make Jackson more comfortable. The doctor donned blue sterile gloves and picked up the syringe from the tray. He proceeded to inject the medication into each of Jackson's temples, just above the bolts. Jackson felt the sting of the needle and was also feeling groggy from the pain medication he had just received. A few minutes passed and he could hear the bolts being removed from his skull. Dr. Zyaire carefully and slowly lifted the brace away from Jackson and placed it on the tray. "We are finished. You tolerated it well. You can have something more for pain in a few hours, but right now the nurse and aides will be removing your restraints and transferring you to a different bed. I placed dressings over the holes on each side of your head. When the dressings become soiled, the nurse will change them. You did well, Jackson. Good luck when you sit up. I'm sure you will be fine. I will check on you later this evening." "Thank you doctor," Jackson drowsily called out as Dr. Zyaire left the room.

Trey quickly removed the restraints so methodically that Jackson assumed he had done it many times. "Now, Jackson I want you to try and move your head from right to left. Slowly! Good, now up and down. Excellent. Next let's try raising your arms and wiggling your fingers." This required considerably more effort for Jackson but he pictured himself lifting weights in a work out session and began to lift his arms. They shook as he squinted his eyes and clenched his jaws. He raised both arms above his head in triumph and opened and closed his fists as a huge grin melted across his face. "That's fantastic!" Trey hollered. "One more milestone accomplished. You deserve a medal!" Trey stopped abruptly as he noticed Jackson glaring at him with disapproval. "I'm so sorry Mr. Montgomery." He timidly expressed. Jackson was sensitive about receiving medals.

The aides had acquired a new bed with fresh sheets and pillow. Trey and the aides acted with precision as they simultaneously lifted Jackson and transferred him to the new bed. The rotating turning bed was removed and Jackson settled back on his fresh pillow. "Oh, you're not through," Trey said in an ordering tone. Trey slowly raised the head of the bed until Jackson was sitting up. It was amazing that he had regained some muscle control in his chest and abdomen area. This enabled him to control his balance as he sat in bed. Jackson couldn't remember when he had felt such an overwhelming sense of accomplishment. He immediately defied the medical experts by mentally entertaining and envisaged walking again without help. In his mind he proudly walked out of the hospital and saluted the cheering doctors and staff members as he left. His thoughts were brought back to reality when the staff wheeled a dinner tray in and placed it over the bed. Jackson shook his head. "I am actually going to be able to feed myself." He enthusiastically thought. Jackson reached for the fork and as he placed the food on the utensil, he started the process of navigating it to his mouth when the tremors hit. Food flew everywhere and his plate flipped up in the air and crashed landed on the floor. Jackson blurted an obscenity and when the tremors stopped, he pounded his fist on the tray sending the rest of the glassware and dishes forward to grace his sheets.

"Oh, Jackson. Look at you! You look like a completely different person!" Carrie announced her arrival with surprise. She was full of questions for him but Jackson's demeanor revealed a distinct mood change that was not good. "You don't have anything to say about this incredible accomplishment?" "If you call sitting up and trying to feed yourself and spilling the crap all over yourself an accomplishment then, NO!" Carrie thought Jackson's reply was curt, but quickly brushed it off as she continued. "It won't be perfect at first, but you'll get better and better at everything. Just be patient with yourself. You've got this Jackson! Besides, Marines here persevere until their mission is complete. And I've been told you are an exemplary Marine soldier and maybe you have nothing to say right now but your friends, comrades in arms, and family have your back and have nothing but love and support for you." "I suppose my wife has so much love and support for me because of all the many times she has come to see me and been by my side," Jackson retorted. "I am sorry she hasn't been here. I can't speak for her and I truly don't understand why she hasn't come, but I'm sure she has a good reason. I do have some good news for you that might help to cheer you up. I looked into your background and demographics and I found you have a family living in Flagstaff, Arizona. Your mother and father are living there along with your youngest sister. You have another sister who is attending the University of Arizona. I took the opportunity to notify your family as soon as I discovered their whereabouts. I hope you don't mind. I updated them on your condition and they asked to have you call them as soon as you were ready," Carrie glanced at Jackson to receive his approval. "So, you told them I was paralyzed and a no good cripple." His voice lowered as he spoke the words out loud and then cleared his throat. "I wish they didn't know yet. I hate what I am! I wanted to let them know after I had recovered and was out of rehab." Jackson noticed Carrie directing her piercing blue eyes toward the floor. "It's okay Carrie, I know you meant well. How did they take the news?" "Your mother cried and your father immediately asked what they could do to help. I assured them you were getting excellent care and that you would contact them shortly." Carrie felt uncomfortable after she realized Jackson disapproved of her actions. She managed to divert the conversation away from family however, and shift the focus to Jackson's rehabilitation efforts. The next few hours were spent working on his upper body strength by lifting weights. This would prove to be invaluable as Jackson moved into the rehabilitation phase of treatment.

"Are you ready Jackson?" Trey enthusiastically thrust a wheelchair to the side of the bed. "This is yours and I will assist your transfer the first time, but then you will be on your own." "Where are we going?" Jackson inquired. "To rehab where the hard work begins. You will be challenged both physically and mentally, but you are strong and I have no doubt that you will conquer this task." Jackson looked at Trey with face drawn and eyebrows raised. "So, how do we do this?" Jackson anxiously wanted to begin more of his healing process. Trey demonstrated to Jackson how to lower his bed to the level of the wheelchair. First, he needed to make sure the wheels of the wheelchair were locked and the chair arm closest to him was removed. Then, using his upper body strength he was to move forward in his bed leaning and balancing with his straight arms, clenched fists and knuckles. Trey reached out to assist Jackson when he received a bold command from him. "I will do this! By myself!" Jackson announced. He held onto the opposite bedrail with his right arm and leaned forward to reach the side arm of the wheelchair. He jerked at the arm lifting the wheelchair slightly up and off the floor. Jackson then lowered his bed until it was level with the chair. Trey watched in amazement at Jackson's determination and grit. The tank and shorts he had changed into earlier revealed his bulging muscles and sculptured frame. Red-faced Jackson moved slowly down the bed inching his way into position. "Are you sure I can't help you?" Trey stated in an almost pleading tone. "No!" was bellowed out between catching a breath and slides. Jackson leaned over and locked the wheels which took all the stomach muscle control he could conjure. His face became pale as he placed his left hand on the left arm of the chair and then quickly pushed off with his right hand and arm to catapult himself into the wheelchair. Jackson replaced the chair arm, unlocked the brakes and announced, "Mission accomplished!" Trey, still trying to process what he had just witnessed, grabbed the handles on the back of the chair and quickly wheeled Jackson down the brightly-lit halls to rehab.

It was a room that was half the size of a basketball gymnasium. Several treadmills were lined up facing the windows to the left. The right side of the gym housed three weight sets with benches and spotting bars. In the middle was a wooden ramp that looked like it was covered with black sandpaper. It started at the floor level and gradually increased incline for two or three feet and then leveled off for several yards. The ramp made incremental declines at its end. At the beginning hung a hoist from the ceiling. It had canvas belts and straps with adjustable buckles. "We'll start with the easy stuff," said Trey. Jackson, with some help, found himself lying on a bench underneath a set of weights. The transfer had been hard because he wasn't used to trying to move dead weight, meaning his legs. One of the therapists approached him. He looked strong and built like a weight lifter. "How much can you bench?" he asked him. Jackson didn't hesitate, "Two-fifty, at my worst." The therapist smiled, "well, we will start out with less and then work up depending on how you tolerate it." This scenario felt comfortable and familiar to Jackson as he grabbed the bar and straight-armed it above his shoulders. He did it so quickly. Jackson made it look easy and done with little effort. More weight was requested by Jackson until he had exceeded expectations, close to 300 pounds. Conversation was difficult while lifting weights but Pete, the therapist, kept shooting questions at him expecting answers. Some, Jackson felt, were personal and none of his business. "I noticed your tattoo. What was your company in the Marine Corps? Where did you serve?" asked Pete. Jackson didn't answer for a few minutes and then placing the weights on the spotting bar, he drew a deep breath and heavily sighed, "I'm not sure I remember what company or battalion, but I was told I was an expert in marksmanship and one of the battalion snipers." Jackson had a sheepish look on his face. He didn't want to appear cocky or bragging. "You know, I'm not completely sure of where I heard that information. I'm not recalling very much about my life right now." Jackson replied. "I am a Marine. I served in the 2/5 E company of the 5th regimen of battalion snipers. I completed a tour in Vietnam for two years." Pete proudly stated these facts about *his* service, and continued, "We must have crossed paths, Jackson. I am proud to know a fellow Marine." As stimulating as this conversation was for Jackson's memory, he was becoming weary and called for Trey to return him to his room.

Jackson spent hours in rehabilitation five days a week. It would soon exceed six hours of grueling hard work daily. This would become a repeated ritual and wear on his perseverance. Today was just the beginning of unexplainable requirements and unforeseen challenges. Jackson didn't allow negative thoughts about defeat to cloud his mind. As he did his workouts, he focused on his family and the dim memories that had returned. He decided it was time to give them a call. Jackson looked for Carrie when he returned to his room. She was becoming more and more a staple part of his relationships. Jackson was troubled that he didn't have any guilt plaguing him about Carrie's friendship. He was so hurt, and anger seeped into his being when he thought about Vanessa. That thought quickly passed as Carrie entered the room. "Hello, my friend. How did it go in rehab today?" Carrie was always interested in the events of Jackson's day. He was in his bed and he leaned forward just a little to get closer to her. "I met a fellow Marine and found out I was a sniper in the same battalion as he. And, I bench press more weight than he can." Jackson's humor was shining through as the two of them talked. Jackson had a competitive nature and bragged about his bench-pressing skills. Carrie tilted her head back and cocked it to the side, "Of course you can bench press more weight than he can. I am not surprised at all!" Jackson exchanged thoughts about his memory return and Carrie followed by sharing more personal thoughts about her life. She divulged to Jackson some significant events that had taken place in her life.

When Carrie moved to Denver to attend nursing school, she met a handsome, outgoing young intern while working a night shift at a local hospital. Their dating was short and the relationship advanced at a rapid pace. Carrie became engaged a little over a year after she arrived in Denver. The two of them seemed perfectly matched. They had similar career choices and shared hobbies and interests. Carrie felt like their involvement with each other was magical. They were soon married in a beautiful, gothic-style church on the outskirts of Denver. An elaborate reception followed that accommodated hundreds of guests and the couple enjoyed a lavish honeymoon to Italy. Everything was secure and they were happy. One year later Carrie's new husband became controlling and abusive. She found herself becoming an abused wife with very little self-respect or identity. It was after three trips to the ER that she finally found the courage to remove herself from the situation and become isolated from him. Divorce came by necessity, and Carrie transferred hospitals for work. She eventually ended up here at the Veteran's Hospital.

Jackson's fists clenched tighter and tighter as he listened to this sweet woman reveal sensitive information about her past. Carrie lifted her head up and looked Jackson in the eyes, "I'm sorry Jackson. I probably shared too much. You have your own heartaches and challenges to deal with. I didn't mean to make it awkward." "No, don't be sorry. I'm glad you felt comfortable enough to tell me. But, I admit someone needs to clean that SOB's plow." Jackson stopped abruptly before he continued. "Oh, please ignore my bad language. I mean no disrespect." Jackson had a difficult time containing his anger. He felt that Carrie deserved better. "Well, if you want to talk more, I'm here for you." He smiled faintly, "I'm not going anywhere." He extended his words of comfort, "You have always been so kind to me and gentle from the first day I met you. You are one of the most compassionate people I know. Carrie, you deserve someone who treats you with respect and builds you up, not tears you down. You are a beautiful, intelligent woman with a successful career in nursing. I notice how you go out of your way to help people, especially me. I really care about you. This guy will get his karma, believe me. And you will find someone who is worthy of your love." Carrie reached over and squeezed Jackson's hand, "Thank you. That's sweet of you to say and I love you for it." Realizing what she just said, she stumbled over her words, "Uh, you know what I mean? Right?" "Of course," Jackson said as he tried to put Carrie at ease. The dinner tray was just arriving as Carrie stood up from the chair that was beside Jackson's bed. "I will leave you to your meal. And, thanks again." Carrie gave Jackson a big smile as she left to attend to her other patients

Chapter Two

PUZZLE PIECES

Jackson transferred himself to his bed after intense rehab and a long hot shower. Trey briefly dropped by his room to see if he needed anything. The halls were swarming and busy. And above all the regular sounds that he was used to hearing everyday an unusual one stood out. His mundane schedule and routine were suddenly accosted by the loud sound of high-heels rapidly clicking down the hall. They became louder and closer. "What…is…this?" He quietly thought to himself. In the doorway stood a live Barbie doll, at least that is how it appeared to Jackson when he first glanced over at the door. She was approximately five foot seven or eight, slim figure, and long blonde hair. Looking like she had just returned from a fashion show, she took a model's stance. A knee-length, yellow satin skirt showed her trim figure and revealed her long legs and curves. She wore a matching jacket on top with a lacy-collared white blouse underneath. On top of her head perched a wide circle-brimmed hat with wide black ribbon adorning its base. A small, tiny, black clutch occupied her right hand and both wrists were covered with shiny bangles. Jackson astutely concluded that she must not be married because he noticed no wedding ring or other rings for that matter on her fingers. He couldn't help but notice the heavy makeup on her face and the glossy, frosted, pink lipstick on her lips.

Jackson slowly directed his question at her, "Can I help you?" "Yes, absolutely!" she retorted. "You could have called me and let me know where you were." Her tone was demanding and Jackson winced before he could answer. "And, you are?" "This is unbelievable! You know perfectly well who I am; unless your little sweetheart caused you to forget." Now she was not only demanding but accusatory, too. "I am assuming that you are Vanessa, my wife. But as far as the 'sweetheart' goes, I don't know what you are talking about. I haven't called you because I have been in here for months. I just woke up from a coma with amnesia. I'm sorry, but I vaguely remember who you are." Vanessa stepped closer, "Isn't that convenient. Well, let me refresh your memory. We were married two years ago at the Lake Hills Country Club in Littleton Colorado. We live on a gorgeous estate in a ten-bedroom home that has a pool. Daddy gave it to us as a wedding present." Jackson inadvertently rolled his eyes. "You do remember Daddy, don't you?" She talked rapidly with few breaks and Jackson struggled to enter the dialogue. "Our reception was so grand and the best chef in Denver catered the event. Hundreds of friends, business associates, and family were there." She softened a little and giggled. "Daddy paid for a honeymoon to Europe, isn't that glorious?" "Sure," Jackson added. I can't imagine anywhere else." Vanessa didn't notice Jackson's sarcasm or his disinterest. "We live an upper society life-style Jackson; one that I have become comfortably used to. And, you were doing so well, even becoming famous, that is until you decided to take off and allow this to happen to you! You are such a disappointment. Golfing and selling real estate can't even make you money now."

"Golfing?" Jackson became curious. "Oh, yes. You are, or should I say were a professional golfer and became quite famous I may add. You were winning a lot of tournaments and bringing in buckets and buckets of cash." Vanessa sighed, "Jackson that just doesn't seem to be possible anymore. The doctors tell me that you are a paraplegic and chances are that you will not walk again or drive or golf or, let's see, be a real man." "What did you do Vanessa? Sell your wedding ring? I noticed you weren't wearing one." Jackson felt hurt and betrayed. "No, I haven't sold it yet, but I'm going to, soon." Vanessa seemed awfully cheerful for this conversation. "So why are you here, Vanessa?" Jackson impatiently replied. "Oh, yeah, that. You see Jackson you were great and we've had some fantastic fun together. You made a decent living and we were able to climb the social ladder. These are things to which I am accustomed. The life we were building together is no longer possible and I cannot endure being married to a cripple for the rest of my life." Jackson raised his voice and angrily asked, "I don't suppose that love has anything to do with this; it seems to be all about money?" "Oh, Jackson, sweetie you just don't understand. I'm not as strong and brave as you. We couldn't take of care of each other. I'm sorry, but I would not be happy. This is not going to work."

Jackson questioned her more through partially clenched jaws, "What now, Vanessa? What is it that you want, besides to end our marriage?" "I'm glad you asked," she frivolously replied. "Daddy had his lawyer draw up all the necessary papers. His lawyer and I will be flying to Mexico City in the morning to put the divorce papers through in a timelier manner than it can be done in the states. You will have the Mustang and the trust you have set up through the real estate sales. The house and all the furnishings are mine; and of course, my BMW. These papers won't require a signature from you so there is nothing to worry about on your end. My lawyer will notify you when the divorce is final." "It looks like you've got everything decided without any input from me. And, what if I disagree or contest it?" Self-control was getting harder and harder to portray. "Unless you have millions of dollars to fight Daddy and his lawyer, Jackson, I would just take this as it is and live with it. You don't really have a choice. Good-bye Jackson." With that last statement, Vanessa abruptly turned around and clip-clopped her way out much like she came in.

"Hey, what are you staring at? What's wrong?" The sound of Carrie's voice was a relief and gave Jackson a feeling that he was cared about again. His eyes were watering from staring without blinking. "Are you crying?" Carrie leaned down to look him in the eyes. "No, I'm not. But it's kind of strange that I'm not, considering the news I received today." Jackson's sad tone caused Carrie concern. "Do you want to talk about it?" "I don't know," he said as he fiddled with the bed sheet. "I am here for you. Take all the time you need." Carrie's concern grew deeper as she picked up on Jackson's distress. He began by telling her that Vanessa had paid him a visit and at first he didn't recognize who she was, but as the conversation grew pieces of memory came to him. "It didn't end well." Jackson went on to tell Carrie about Vanessa's plans and demands. He became more and more agitated. Carrie took Jackson's hand in hers. "I'm so sorry. I don't understand how she could do such a thing. If she truly loved you, she would stand by you no matter what." "Apparently, she didn't love me, only my money." "What's going to happen now? What are you going to do?" Carrie seemed anxious to hear Jackson's plans. "Vanessa's dad has everything legally done and processed. I didn't have a say in anything. Vanessa divided all our furnishings and belongings between us and of course she took three-fourths of everything. Right now, I'm just going to concentrate on getting healed and out of rehab. Then, I'll look for a house that is wheel-chair friendly and go from there. To tell the truth, I haven't really thought much about the marriage scenario or where I lived. My thinking hasn't been that forthcoming; it's only been on a day to day basis." Jackson went on to tell Carrie that he had decided to call his parents. He felt badly because now he had grimmer news to tell them.

As Vanessa was talking about their wedding, flashes of memory infused Jackson's mind about his family, especially his siblings. He had begun to recall life with his family, and this caused Jackson to yearn for conversation with them. He only wished it could be under better circumstances. Jackson was experiencing a cocktail-mix of feelings as he prepared to make the call home. His family, as he remembered, wasn't at all like Vanessa's, and Jackson had contemplated about the joining of these two families from the beginning. He wondered if it had been cordial or if there were clashes. It was more likely that there had been major conflicts considering the difference between the Remington's and the Montgomery's life styles. Jackson listened intently as the phone rang. A soft-spoken, pleasant woman greeted him. "Hello. Hello?" her voice brought familiarity to Jackson. "Mom? This is Jackson. I called because I have some serious news I need to tell you." He felt a lump form in his throat. In excitement she exclaimed, "Jackson? Oh, Jackson! It is so good to hear your voice." Then her tone became more somber, "How are you doing? We know about your accident. We were just waiting for you to call." His mother's voice sounded concerned. "I'm doing all right. I am going to rehab every day, and I have the wheelchair transfers down to a science. Mom, there is something else you need to know; something besides the accident. Vanessa has asked for a divorce. She and her dad's lawyer have gone to Mexico to finalize it. She took the house and everything in it. She did leave my Mustang and real estate trust to me. I checked on the amount that is in the trust and it is substantial. If Vanessa would have known, I'm sure she would have taken that also." Jackson's mother held the phone out so his dad could join them on the call. His dad bellowed in the background, "She always has been a selfish, high maintenance little diva. And she has never treated you or us very nice. Sorry Son, but it's true. She was soaking you for your money even when the two of you started dating. Never did like her! Don't you let her get you down or define who you are. In the meantime, keep working hard to get well. We are putting things on hold here and will be there to help with whatever we can in a couple of weeks. I just need to get things in order." "Listen Dad. I am grateful, but you don't need to do this. I can manage," Jackson insisted. His mother joined, "You've always been independent and strong willed. That's why you made such a good Marine. But we *are* coming and there is nothing you can say that will change our minds. We're family Jackson, and that's what family does for each other." His mother always had the last say.

Rehab became a time when Jackson could reflect on the puzzle pieces that he had received. He didn't have to concentrate when lifting weights as it came natural to him. So, he used the time to force his memory. Jackson kept reliving the scene of Vanessa's visit over and over in his mind. Disturbing as it was, he concentrated on the details of his relationship with her and allowed himself to be emotional as he experienced the return of memories. Jackson closed his eyes and was able to finally get a clear picture of life with Vanessa and how they met.

Vanessa Noelle Remington was raised by a nanny in the Remington dynasty. She had a fortunate upbringing which included private schools, riding lessons and frequent trips to Europe and abroad. When Jackson realized the extent of her family's wealth, it created more questions concerning the merging of the two families. He thought about how they met. A memory of being a professional golfer surfaced and he saw himself on the greens of several different clubs at various locations around the country. Jackson recalled it all: the long stretches of pristinely cut grass, a collection of sand traps sporadically placed, colorful flags and poles marking the hole, small ponds and pools intertwined, and beautiful foliage lining the courses. He could hear the crowds that were held back from the course by a small rope barrier cheering for him. Jackson had tremendous skills where golf was concerned. His scores were always under par and he had racked up a few tournament wins. He saw himself accepting large, shiny trophies that he held high to celebrate his victory. Flashes from the news cameras blinded him temporarily but didn't seem to faze him. Jackson enjoyed being in the spotlight. He had forgotten how satisfying it felt.

Jackson returned to the memory of the country club. Vanessa had told him that this is where they were married, and Jackson remembered that is where they also met-the Lake Hills Country Club on the outskirts of Denver. Jackson had been a member for a couple of years and was a regular attendee. He was found at the club only when he was not on tour. John Remington, Vanessa's father, had introduced Jackson to his daughter. Mr. Remington was an influential business czar who had acquired massive wealth by owning several corporations and a variety of real estate properties throughout the valley. He also, was an avid golfer. Jackson clearly recalled the day that he was introduced to Vanessa. He had just finished a round of eighteen holes and was headed for the clubhouse when Mr. Remington stopped him. "Are you Jackson Montgomery, the golf pro?" He led the opening of the conversation as if he already knew who Jackson was. "Yes Sir, I am." Jackson respectfully responded. "I hope you won't think I am being too intrusive, but I have followed your accomplishments in golfing, and I feel you have compelling motivation to reach goals." Mr. Remington continued, "I own several real estate companies that are involved in buying, selling and brokering. You could be a valuable asset to my company Mr. Montgomery. And, to make the offer more tantalizing, I will make sure you will have all the time you need to expand and promote your golfing career. Why, I would even be willing to be your sponsor. What do you say, Jackson?" "Mr. Remington," Jackson was interrupted. "Call me John." "All right, John, I am flattered beyond words. I don't really know what to say." Jackson's reaction was one of surprise. "Say yes!" Mr. Remington exuberantly replied. "Uh, yes! Absolutely!" responded Jackson. Mr. Remington then whisked Jackson away where he was presented as a new member of the company to colleagues of Mr. Remington. After business was concluded, his new boss gently took the hand of a beautiful woman who was standing nearby and pulled her closer to the two of them. "Jackson, I want you to meet my daughter, Vanessa."

The next few months were spent attending cocktail parties and dinner at Vanessa's home. It was an extraordinary mansion settled on ten acres of valuable land in the outskirts of Denver. The front acre supported the mansion and there was a mile-long road leading up to the front of the house. A half-circle of white pillars stood stoically on a porch that surrounded the front, double, wooden doors which were made of rich walnut. The large porch completely surrounded the front of the main house. Massive sections of the house were situated on angles extending from each side of the main part of the mansion. Each section had three floors of rooms with ornate windows. There were an abundance of trees and shrubbery and a white-marble fountain that was wrapped in exotic flowers. The fountain was located in-between the driveway in front of the house and the road leading up from the highway. In the distance were several horses in a green pasture and a state-of-the-art ridding stable was located nearby. The whole picture was daunting; especially to Jackson when he visited for the first time. Often, he would catch a glimpse of Vanessa riding the majestic stallions in the field, her long blonde hair being tousled in the breeze. The cocktail parties were a regular event at the Remington's; they entertained two or three times a week and Jackson felt compelled to attend every one of them. His exposure to Vanessa increased and his visits were often. Jackson started to take an interest in Vanessa and asked Mr. Remington for his blessing to pursue her. He wholeheartedly received that blessing and quickly, he and Vanessa became an item. Their courtship consisted mostly of attending corporate events and elaborate dinner parties. Occasionally, they enjoyed the symphony or ballet. Jackson loved the outdoors, so he made it his mission and challenge to get Vanessa involved in nature and outdoor activities. He tried taking her camping once and that turned out to be a disaster. Vanessa complained the whole time about the bugs, the dirt, the sleeping quarters, and the cold. She was annoyed that it lacked cold bottled-water and take-out service. She did enjoy Jackson's motorcycle, though. The two of them would often take the afternoon and ride up into the cool, refreshing air of the mountains to a small ski village where they shared a nice, quiet dinner and browsed the local shops. It was at this quaint little ski resort that Jackson proposed to Vanessa. It was simple, nothing fancy or elaborate but Jackson felt it was very romantic. Vanessa didn't appreciate the simple proposal but did light up when Jackson placed a five karat diamond ring on her finger. That's all she talked about for weeks.

The engagement was celebrated with an official announcement banquette. Vanessa's mother managed all affairs concerning the wedding. She hired everything done; money was no object. "Our little girl deserves the best!" was a phrase that Jackson's soon-to-be mother in-law said often. Vanessa came to Jackson periodically to announce the updates on the wedding and to assure him that "Daddy's paying for everything." Jackson found himself mesmerized with all the preparations and event planning that the wedding produced. He felt removed from it all and longed to feel some excitement, or at least be happy. "Something's not right, here," he thought. But, as soon as he began to doubt about his decision, Vanessa, her family and money maneuvered him to be compliant and play the game. That's what this was to the Remington's, a game; an expensive life-changing game.

Memories were now saturating Jackson's thinking. As the reflections of planning the wedding advanced, he became disturbed about the way his family was treated. Jackson had a recollection of his relationship with his family at that time; they were estranged. He remembered that he was angry at them for some reason, but couldn't pinpoint what.

His father was a middle-class working man who owned a restaurant in Flagstaff. Washing dishes and cooking was as glorified as his work got. The Montgomery's home was modest and they lived a moderate lifestyle. Jackson's mother was an elementary school teacher whose social life consisted of church gatherings. Past feelings of embarrassment surfaced and Jackson felt ashamed. He didn't want to be anything like his parents or live life the way they had lived. At the time he felt he was making a good decision for his future by moving to Denver and pursuing his golfing career. It didn't take Jackson long to build wealth and establish name recognition and prestige. All that existed were vague memories of Jackson involving his family in any part of his life. They were almost nonexistent. He grimaced when he recalled how he notified his family of his engagement and pending marriage to Vanessa. "A phone call! And a stupid phone call, after the fact!" Jackson was disgusted at his former self. His family had been notified by phone and then sent an invitation like a guest. Vanessa arranged for a seamstress to measure his sisters for bride's maid dresses and his mother for an appropriate dress to wear. She had also hired a professional tailor to fit his father for a tuxedo. The times and dates were all set up by Vanessa without inquiring if they were acceptable to the Montgomery family. Jackson was not aware of how insulting the Remingtons had been to his family. His family never complained. They were humble and grateful. When the wedding day approached, the Remingtons covered airfare, lodging and accommodations for Jackson's family. And the first time Jackson recalls seeing them for a very long time was on his wedding day.

The Montgomery family arrived at the airport and was met with a limousine and driver sent by John Remington. Quickly, they were escorted to their hotel where they were expected to ready themselves for the big event in an hours' time. Jackson's sisters complained about the dresses they were wearing; they made them feel uncomfortable.

One was dressed in a satin empire-waist yellow dress and the other the same pattern only a pale-green color. Floppy wide-brimmed hats completed the outfits. His mother was dressed in a similar style dress, only pale-blue and no hat. All the women wore matching high-heeled shoes. Jackson's dad completed the stunning group by proudly donning a black tuxedo with a black-satin lapel. The Montgomery family felt more like guests attending a royal wedding than the family of the groom. As they arrived at the country club their feelings of inadequacy emerged. It looked like a massive castle with all its magic and grandeur. Each one of them was escorted from the limousine up the two-tiered staircase to the front of the club. The doors were held open for them by ushers dressed in black suits with cumber buns, white shirts and black bowties. Jackson's family stepped onto the shiny, glass-like floor and simultaneously raised their eyes and tilted their heads upward. Gasps were heard as they surveyed the gold-trimmed, Victorian-style ceiling and several, massive, crystal chandeliers. On their right, a large dining area opened revealing tables covered with crisp, white, linen cloths. Comfortable high-backed chairs complemented the tables and were decorated to match with huge bows tied to the back of each chair. A waiter approached them holding a tray of goblets and offered them some champagne. They politely refused as they didn't drink alcohol. A woman in a sequined pale-blue evening gown motioned for them to proceed to their left where another grand hall opened. There were many guests mingling and they immediately spotted the bride and groom.

The ceremony was about to start. People were being seated when Jackson gathered his family and ushered them to their seats. His sisters were shown where to stand in the wedding line. Only moments passed before they heard music coming from the string quartette seated in the back. Jackson stood with his hands clasped in front of him and no emotion to his facial expression. The minister stood just behind Jackson and was holding what appeared to be a black Bible. The music suddenly changed to the wedding march and everyone's head turned and they stood up to acknowledge the bride's entrance. The couple spoke some of their own vows but other than that the ceremony was not heartfelt. Jackson could barely remember it with any feeling of dedication or joy. His mother cried, a lot. Jackson, looking back on this memory realized that his mother was crying because she had never met his bride, Vanessa, and was feeling so secluded and rejected. Everyone was being condescending to his family, including Jackson. The dancing and dinner concluded quickly after the ceremony. Jackson's family stood on the sidelines against the wall for a time during the dancing. His father and mother eventually danced with each other, but Jackson didn't even ask his mother for a dance. These memories were painful for Jackson and he tried to recall conversation with his parents and sisters, or sharing or something. But, he failed miserably. He couldn't even recall saying good-bye to them before they left for the airport.

Jackson's breathing was louder and heavier and his cheeks puffed out as he pursed his lips and exhaled. Sweat was beading on his forehead and temples. His hands encircled the metal bar holding 300 pounds of weight discs and he effortlessly placed it on the spotting bar above his chest. A heavy sigh was expelled as he struggled to push himself into a sitting position. "Welcome back, soldier. Where have you been?" Pete was standing near for support. He stepped closer and slapped Jackson on the back. Jackson transferred to his wheelchair as he replied, "You know, Pete, I was reminiscing about my past, my golfing career, my marriage to Vanessa, my family and what a stupid idiot I have been. You would think the Marine Corps prepared me to be smarter at life choices than I've been. I became so blinded by fame and fortune that I lost my identity. I don't even recognize the person that was living my past. Vanessa's a monster, and that's being polite. And her family is akin to the mafia, really! I bulldozed my own family out of the picture and treated them with contempt. There's no excuse for my behavior and I can't help but ask why my family would be so willing to now sacrifice for me and reach out." "It sounds like, from what you've told me, your family knows about unconditional love, hard work, humility and perseverance. Just be grateful that they are willing to reach out and make amends. You need all the help you can get, brother." Pete grabbed the wheelchair handles and proceeded to head back to Jackson's room. This time the halls were eerie and strangely quiet.

The shift was changing as Jackson re-entered his hospital domain. He was anxious to leave the hospital and buy a place of his own. Jackson quickly took a shower utilizing methods that he learned in rehab. This was one daily-living activity that he had taken for granted before his accident. It took time, patience and strength to accomplish something that used to be simple and a no-brainer. Now, he slowly grabbed his shirt, pulled it over his head and threw it on the floor. Then, one leg at a time, he turned his hips to one side and then the other and pulled his pants off. It was not easy. Jackson had prepared by having all his shower necessities available and within reach before he started to undress. He removed the side arm from the wheelchair and lifted his entire weight in a transfer to the shower chair. Jackson relaxed under the warm running water and for a few minutes felt a little sorry for himself. But those feelings were flitting. After a significant amount of time had passed Jackson composed himself and gathered all the strength he could to transfer back into the wheelchair, dry himself off, and then get dressed and transfer again into bed. He clocked himself after each shower so he could strive to beat the previous time. A few memories about the Marine Corps unexpectedly snuck into his thought process. They were expected to get things done with precision and expertise and do it in a timely manner. This training that Jackson received in the Marine Corps became a permanent part of his nature and character and assisted him with his daily routines.

There was a knock at his door. Carrie stood grinning and holding a sack of what looked like fast food. "I have a break and I thought I would have dinner with you tonight. I brought your favorite: double cheeseburger with fries and a chocolate shake, extra thick." She placed it on his hospital bed tray. "I never told you what my favorite fast food is." Jackson had a teasing tone in his accusation. "Oh, I know. But this is your favorite tonight." Carrie pulled a hamburger out of the sack for Jackson and one for herself. Then she pulled a large tray of French fries out and pushed them in front of Jackson. "Ketchup?" she asked. Jackson didn't realize how hungry he was as he quickly consumed the meal and conversed very little with Carrie. Carrie laughed and talked while eating and wiped her lips occasionally. She was comfortable around Jackson and didn't try to impress him with good manners while eating a burger. Carrie seemed relieved and stated, "I feel so much better now. How about you?" "Yes, that was thoughtful of you, Carrie. Thank you." Jackson faintly smiled and purposefully looked into her eyes. Those eyes spoke to him and they seemed to talk more than she did. Her eyes told Jackson of caring, kindness and interest. "Okay, I want to know all about your day." Carrie was never shy about leading the conversation. "So, you think you are going to find out more information about this soldier who can't seem to remember exactly who he is?" Jackson enjoyed teasing back. "Yup! Something like that!" Carrie always had a comeback. "I'm not sure where to begin." Jackson hesitated.

Jackson found himself unusually comfortable telling Carrie about his past. He felt she understood him and he found they had an unexplainable connection which made being vulnerable easier. "I called my parents," he slowly began. Carrie followed with, "And, how did they react?" "They surprisingly reached out to me. They even offered to come help me get settled after I am discharged." Jackson surprised himself because he seemed to be questioning their intentions. "Why was he tepidly acknowledging their response? Putting everything on hold to help family was actually expected considering their character and charitable nature," he thought. Jackson labored through telling Carrie everything that he had recalled about Vanessa and all the encounters he had with her and the Remington family. Carrie listened intently without comment or interruption. When Jackson came to the conclusion of his saga, Carrie firmly placed her hand on his arm. She sighed heavily, "Wow, Jackson, I can't begin to imagine the emotional pain you must have felt going through all of that. But it concerns me that you don't seem to show any emotion or feelings about your experiences. Did you love her, Jackson?" Jackson placed the palm of his hand over his mouth and squeezed his cheeks, then dropped his hand as he drew in a deep breath. "I don't know. When I look back on everything, I don't feel any emotion but disgust. I think I was in love with the idea of a lavish life-style and fame and prestige. Nothing about Vanessa or her family interlocks with anything in my life-at least as I see it now. This accident has brought an awareness to me of what is really important and what I want from life." Jackson took both of Carrie's hands, leaned into her and looked into her eyes. "You have helped me to rediscover who I am and who I want to be. I will be forever grateful and indebted to you." Carrie stood up and gave Jackson a big hug, catching him off-guard. She boldly and tenaciously stated, "I am so proud of you, Jackson. You truly are a strong, courageous individual. And I have no doubt that you will win this battle and go on to feel success once again." Acknowledging her compliment, he said, "Thank you, Carrie. That means a lot to me." "No problem." And then she quickly changed the subject. "I hear you have a big day tomorrow and it's important you get your rest. So, I am going to let you get some sleep. I'll talk to you after your therapy. Good-night Jackson." Carrie left the room and dimmed the lights on her way out. Jackson melted into his pillow and closed his eyes. He was feeling a peace and calmness that he hadn't been able to feel since before the war. His mind had corralled his thoughts and it was if a heavy burden had been lifted. Slowly his eyes closed and he drifted into an unfamiliar deep sleep.

Trey came by the next morning and had to coerce Jackson to get dressed and be in his wheelchair in thirty minutes. "Oh, yay. It's playground day." Jackson's flippant remarks did not set right with Trey. "Look, pal, you can be as sarcastic as you want, but if your goal is to get out of here any time soon, you will take this seriously!" Jackson covered his fear with sarcasm. He was having some apprehension about today's rehab session. His thoughts migrated to the hoist-sling located at the beginning of the walking ramp. Many times, Jackson had envisioned himself sitting in the canvas brace, grabbing the poles on each side of the ramp and triumphantly walking to the other side. He now feared his expectations might be too high this soon. Jackson shook the nervousness off as he usually did when confronting his fears and surged forward with determination. He greeted Trey, "I'm ready. Let's do this!"

Rehab seemed unaccepting today and Jackson didn't have the comfortable feeling that he usually had. He stared at the brace as he rolled his wheelchair closer. Suspended by massive, steel chains it gave the appearance of a swing, the kind you find at a children's playground. The canvas brace was resting on a chair. Jackson was instructed to pull his wheelchair next to the brace and prepare for a transfer. He had never transferred before without having a bar or rail to hold onto and briefly Jackson scanned the brace for a solution. Quickly he grasped the steel chain with his right hand. Pulling with his right and pushing off with his left, Jackson slid into the brace and onto the chair. "So far, so good," he said as he cracked a smile. Pete and another therapist strapped Jackson into the brace and asked him if he was comfortable. Jackson wondered humorously why everyone always asked him if he was comfortable when they should realize that he couldn't feel anything. He wouldn't know if he was comfortable or not. But he answered affirmatively.

"Are you ready?" Pete looked at Jackson, giving him time to think and then respond. "I've been ready for months!" Jackson had a compelling response. The loud mechanical sound of the hoist running and the brace jerking as it slowly lifted Jackson off the chair caused Jackson's heart to race and his breathing to deepen. "Now, Jackson I am going to raise the hoist and move you over to the ramp and when we get within reach, I want you to grab the walking bars on each side of you. Then, I will lower the hoist until your feet are touching the ramp floor. The more I lower you the more you will have to support your weight with your arms. This is where all those pushups and the weightlifting will come in handy." Pete was very thorough at giving instructions.

Before Pete started lowering the hoist he glanced over toward the door. "Hi, come in Carrie." "I'm just here for moral support. But if you would rather, I could leave." Carrie waited for Jackson to say something. He was surprised to see Carrie and had mixed feelings about her being there. He loved her having his back and at the same time he feared embarrassment and humiliation. But Jackson didn't have the heart to tell her to leave. "Sure, come join the party," he called to her. Jackson grabbed the bars on each side of him and watched the floor as Pete lowered the hoist until he could see his feet against the ground. Pete instructed Jackson further, "Okay, I am going to move your legs while you move your arms on the bars in a walking motion. Ready?" Jackson's face grimaced as he struggled to lift dead weight forward. It was harder than he thought it would be. Moving along the bars was like moving along the parallel bars in gymnastics, only unlike the gymnasts Jackson didn't have the luxury of his legs bearing some of his weight. He watched his foot bend backward and his toe drag along the ramp floor. Pete lifted his foot and placed it flat on the ground and then moved to the opposite side. This tedious exercise continued for about an hour. Jackson's arms bulged with pure muscle strength, his torso was dripping with sweat, and his jugular vein was noticeably distended through the whole process. When he arrived at the end of the ramp, he turned around and went back toward his wheelchair. Thoughts of walking again, playing golf and just being able to stand in a shower were what motivated him.

As he neared the wheelchair both of Jackson's legs began to violently spasm. Pete had to assist him into his wheelchair. The spasms shook the wheelchair and threw it off balance. "Don't worry, I've got ya." Pete reassured him. Jackson writhed in pain. His arms ached and they felt like needles were being jabbed over every inch of his skin. "Let me get you something for pain," said Pete as he disappeared into a room where they kept the medications. A clean white towel was dropped in his lap. "I thought maybe you could use this," Carrie said in a sympathetic tone. Jackson wiped the sweat from his face and neck. He merely said thank you and then he was quiet. Jackson awkwardly avoided looking at Carrie. Then she pulled his chin up with her soft hand so he was looking her in the eyes. "You did great. It will get easier. This is your first time and all those nerves have to adjust to being used again," Carrie tried to be supportive. Jackson was in a fog and his lack of attention was noted when she lightly punched his arm. "Hey! Did you hear me?" "Yes, I heard you. Don't worry, I won't quit until my mission is finished." Jackson swallowed a couple of pain pills and then told Carrie he would see her upstairs.

Dr. Zyaire had noted on Jackson's progress sheet that his pain was not being managed well and the spasms had increased. He also wrote that Jackson had received more feeling in his torso and legs. Dr. Zyaire doubled Jackson's pain medication and prescribed a muscle relaxer to help with the spasms. This pain regime would have sufficed for most patients, but it didn't seem to touch Jackson's pain. The pain he felt was excruciating and kept him awake at night. It was always worse after rehab and then on occasion when it did control his pain and he could sleep, he experienced disturbing nightmares about the accident and saw unexplainable explosions. Some nights he was abruptly awakened to feeling unbearable pain in the foot that was not there. These 'phantom pains' increased as he worked harder and longer in rehab.

As dictated by routine, Jackson had returned from rehab and showered. His attention was drawn to the hallway where he thought he heard the sound of a cane on the floor. It was a man maneuvering his crutches as he walked down the hall. He was wearing dress slacks, a belt, white shirt and a red-striped tie. "That's unusual," Jackson thought. The man moved into the room and out of the doorway. "Hi, Mr. Montgomery. I wasn't sure you would want to see me or talk to me," he sounded apologetic. "And why is that the case?" Jackson was trying to place the man somewhere in his past and remember who he was. "I am Darren Mitchel, your business partner. We sell real estate together and I was driving your car on the way to Aspen to close an offer. I am so sorry, Mr. Montgomery. It was my fault. I should have seen the curve ahead and slowed down. I really don't have words to express how badly I feel except to ask for your forgiveness." Jackson said, "You know I called you an idiot and wanted to deck you? The paramedics saved you from my wrath when they explained the details of the crash. You couldn't have prevented what happened and it certainly was not your fault. It was disturbing though how they left me for dead and administered aid to you. I was an afterthought until I managed to respond to firemen who cut me out of the car. My car exploded just after I was removed from it; I guess you can count me as lucky. I'm alive and that says something. Rehab is hard but worth every minute if it helps me to walk again," Jackson didn't really want to continue this conversation, so he changed the subject.

"Darren, why don't you tell me all about the real estate encounters we had. Maybe it will spark more memory. I know I was hired by John Remington and I made a small fortune, but my memory fails me about anything else. I just feel there is more to it." Jackson had suspicious feelings that kept gnawing at him about that part of his life.

Chapter Three

KEEP RUNNING THE RACE

Remington had built an empire long before Jackson came on the scene. Darren told him about the illegal activities that his ex-father-in-law had been involved in which included money laundering and tax evasion. Remington had become so big and powerful that it seemed he couldn't be touched by the law. His influence was tied to lobbyists in Washington D.C. and his money ran the political stage. Jackson was part of Remington's plans. Acquiring the influence and association of major professional sports, like golf, built his empire even stronger and he was able to control multimillion dollar corporations. It had been attested by local authorities that he formed a lucrative partnership with drug dealers both local and abroad. John Remington's dishonest character flaw was well hidden from the public. He carried a façade that fooled even the high level government officials that he dealt with weekly. An investigation surfaced when a whistle blower revealed and turned over physical proof of his corrupt dealings to the FBI. Darren went on to inform Jackson of Remington's indictment that occurred shortly after the accident.

Jackson sat stunned and stared at Darren. "I had no idea," he quietly responded. "I was being used all this time including the marriage to

Vanessa? I knew there was something more to the way he accumulated vast amounts of wealth so quickly. I definitely won't be going back to selling real estate which doesn't bother me that much, but if any of the golfing community finds out that I was involved and associated with him and married to his daughter, my professional golfing days are over! I need to talk to my lawyer, Richard Herchek. Maybe he can shed a light on what to expect. What are *you* going to do, Darren?" "I'm not going to count out selling real estate, and you shouldn't either. There are other companies that have great opportunities. Jackson you were so good at it. Within two years, you climbed the success ladder and made a name for yourself. You received multiple awards, certificates, and trophies for your outstanding accomplishments. There was one unique award that you received at a company party that I'll never forget. It was called 'The Shock and Awe' award and for a very good reason. Do you remember this?" "I'm beginning to," said Jackson. "I think. Go on." "You had been out selling almost all day and you had a scheduled dinner appointment with some corporate executive. Having one last real estate engagement to complete before the dinner put you into warp speed. The client was a sweet elderly woman who was doing quite well for herself. She lived alone. I believe you said she was a potential investor. Anyway, she loved you! All the women did. She opened her front door when she saw you pull up to her home, and stepped out onto the porch to greet you." Jackson remembered her stairs well. There were eight steps leading up to her porch. They were fashioned out of wooden slats and you could see through them. A three-inch space separated each step. Darren continued, "You bolted out of your car, grabbed your briefcase and began double-timing it up the stairs, skipping the bottom two. Suddenly, you caught the foot portion of your prosthesis leg under a stair. Your prosthesis leg separated from your body and slid down the stairs, clomping against the wood. According to Mrs. Thomasson, all you said was, 'Oops!' before she passed out. You managed to retrieve your leg and call the paramedics *and* get to your dinner date on time! You so deserved that award." Both of the men were laughing hard by the time Darren finished his rendition of the event.

Jackson started remembering more and more about selling real estate and his golfing career. "Hey Darren, where did we meet?" "I was working for Remington and he approached me about soliciting your expertise and influence to help his company. He hired me to make friends with you and gain your trust. Eventually, the plan was to include you in his real estate endeavors. And, we really did become friends; at least I still consider you my friend. You and I had a common interest, golf. We met at the country club and actually played many rounds of golf together. The first time I played with you, I could tell you were extremely skilled. You really intimidated me, especially when you kept dropping a hole-in-one almost every other time we played. I tagged along and watched you at some of the tournaments you were in. You worked hard Jackson, and it paid off. You were so close to participating in the PGA tour and then the accident happened." Jackson had more questions, "So, it's my understanding that we played golf with Remington and his cronies. Right? Do you know if any of the golf tournaments were sabotaged or were there bets placed on certain players, namely me?" Jackson wanted to know exactly the depth of his involvement with Remington's illegal activities. "There was talk about bets being placed but I didn't hear much. I didn't want to get more involved than I already was," Darren replied. Jackson was satisfied with the information that Darren had given him and the two of them parted friends.

Jackson had discovered from information that his lawyer provided that over 3 million dollars of Jackson's tournament money had been funneled through Remington's Charity Foundation and sent to the Cayman Islands. He thought it was being put in the joint account that he had with Vanessa. Because he trusted her, he gave Vanessa control over it. A large portion of the money was donated to the Remington Charity Fund and Jackson didn't see any of it. Financials for Remington were handled by his personal accountant and lawyer and they helped conceal the money laundering. Jackson was totally unaware of the other business transactions that occurred. Jackson shook his head, "What a miserable mess!"

Jackson Montgomery was an extremely intelligent man and usually nothing got passed him, except for this time. His pride was hurt and his ego burned when he realized how Remington had used and taken advantage of him. He hadn't been this angry since the battle fields of Vietnam. Jackson felt that he had to find a way to turn things around and do some damage control. In the meantime, Jackson proceeded to contact his lawyer, Richard Herchek. He wanted to make sure the real estate trust fund that he had set up was secured from Remington, any member of Remington's family, or business associates. Meanwhile, Jackson's other affairs seemed insurmountable and overwhelming. He was constantly dealing with Veteran Affairs to secure his benefits that he rightly deserved, but ran into mounds of red tape with the government. It frustrated him to know the government he proudly served and defended was consistently blowing him off. He embraced more pieces of his puzzle as life moved forward. Memories of The Marine Corps and Viet Nam periodically came into a dim view. Jackson wasn't sure yet if that was good or bad. Medical expenses were becoming astronomical and he needed help. Jackson was weary at battling life situations at every turn, so he purposely turned his focus back to rehab and was determined to make this battle end differently than had been predicted.

Days turned into weeks and weeks into months. Jackson could be consistently found in the rehab gym lifting weights and inching his way across the walking ramp. Increasing his weight-bearing capacity was a marked reason to celebrate. Carrie was partially right in saying that it would become easier. It wasn't exactly becoming easier, just more manageable. Physical therapy was a big part of his healing process. Jackson was faced with the daunting challenge of learning to walk all over again. Sometimes he felt like a helpless child and would briefly wonder if it was all worth it. Questions and doubt seeped in to his thoughts but he didn't allow them extended occupancy. He asked himself, "How can I feel so alone when I am surrounded by people every single day?" "Depression," he pondered, "makes you feel alone in a crowd." Jackson took handfuls of medication to manage pain, spasms, infection and depression. Right now, he wasn't concerned about becoming addicted; he just wanted some relief. The pills made him gag and stunted his appetite. Jackson didn't get in this kind of a slump very often, but even *he* had a breaking point. Jackson Montgomery was not only extremely intelligent but also incredibly sensitive and a down-to-earth human but he was subject to flaws and failures.

The next afternoon Jackson was about to leave his room for rehab when Trey looked around the edge of the doorway and announced, "Jackson, there is someone here to see you. He says he's a reporter. Should I have him come to your room?" "A reporter? What does he want?" Jackson had not experienced any dealings with reporters since the days of his golfing tours. "I guess; show him in." He tapped his fingers nervously against the wheelchair arms. Some anxiety was settling in as he waited for the reporter's arrival. Finally, a young man entered the room leaning in headfirst as if he was trying to get on the level of Jackson's wheelchair. "Hello, Mr. Montgomery. My name is Mark Buchanan. I am a reporter from the local newspaper and I am writing a column about inspiring sports figures. You are well known in your field for your determination, perseverance, and tenacity. I am interested in doing an interview with you, if you approve." "An interview? About what?" Jackson questioned. Mark flattered Jackson by reminding him of the strong influence he had on golf and his thousands of followers. "I don't see that I am inspirational but go ahead, ask all the questions you want." Jackson motioned for Mark to take a chair and sit beside him. Mark began, "Can you tell me what influenced you to become a professional golfer and how you overcame your handicap?" It took a few minutes for Jackson to respond. He hadn't given the fact that he was an amputee much thought. The word handicap was a familiar golfing expression and he hadn't really associated it with his amputation. Jackson could remember that he had always loved golf, from a young age. As he reminisced about the events that would answer Mark's questions, he was compelled to pause often to validate the memories he was experiencing. Jackson was able to return in time to when he was a young boy and walked several miles to the golf course near his home. He lugged a heavy, worn golf bag on his shoulders that carried two drivers, a putter, and four irons. The clubs were old and scuffed and a little too big for Jackson. He spent hours at the club house watching the golfers and hoping to get a glance at a professional now and then. Finally, after determining that his ability was sufficient, he scheduled a tee time and began his journey. Jackson was a natural and received many compliments from other golfers that were more proficient than he. Jackson remembered he could drive a ball for hundreds of yards, which surprised everyone. He went on to play for his local high school where he was able to secure himself a scholarship to the University of his choice. From there his dreams and career soared. It was amazing how Jackson managed pre-med classes and was still able to break into the professional community of golf.

Jackson was enjoying talking about his past but when he came to telling what happened after college he drew a blank and conversation came to an abrupt halt. "Wasn't that about the time that the Viet Nam War broke out?" he directed the question to Mark expecting him to know the answer. "Not my forte, sorry," Mark replied. Jackson thoughtfully continued, "I believe that was the time that I joined the Marine Corps." Mark ventured further with his questioning, "I am curious. What happened after the war, and what made you able to overcome having an artificial leg and still become a professional golfer?" "The word is *prosthesis,* and I don't remember getting from point A to point B or rather from after the war to touring with the PGA. I really wish I could. I do remember golfing for hours every day and miles and miles of walking. I would come home and take my prosthesis off only to find my stump sock soaked with blood." Jackson's brows furrowed as he recalled this particular memory. "I'm sorry Mr. Montgomery, but it's incredible how you pushed through all that!" Mark had slid to the edge of his chair.

"I understand you founded a charity and a scholarship fund. Can you tell me about that?" Mark was taking more and more notes as the interview continued. Jackson directed his answer to Mark's request, "I didn't have much as a kid and I was doing extremely well when I was on tour. I wanted to give back, so I started a scholarship fund for students graduating from high school and entering college. The charity foundation sort of evolved later. I donated half of my earnings, but I wished I could have done more." Jackson was feeling a little awkward; he didn't like to talk about himself. Mark kept going, "Wasn't it the PGA tour you were preparing for when you had your terrible accident?" "Yes, all my entrance fees had been paid and accommodations had been pre-arranged. It was to take place the following week." There was a long, silent pause. "If you don't mind, I think I am through answering questions. The interview will have to be over." Jackson shook Mark's hand as Mark reuttered his appreciation that he felt and the admiration he had for Jackson.

After the conversations he had with Darren and Mark, an overwhelming all-encompassing feeling of exhaustion settled in and prompted Jackson to retire early. He looked forward to quiet and letting his vocal chords recover. "I don't want to see or talk to one more person," he determined. Jackson let his tired body sink into the mattress and bedcovers and exhaled a sigh of relief. Startled by a knock on his door, he quickly opened his eyes. Dr. Zyaire entered the room. He had the appearance of determination, intent, and was professional in demeanor. "I am just making evening rounds, Mr. Montgomery. We have a lot to discuss. I have monitored your progress in rehabilitation and you are doing remarkably well. You are clear of infections and all of your major wounds from the accident have healed. Occupational therapy has reported success in managing your activities of daily living. How do you feel about these challenges?" Jackson wasn't sure how he should respond to that question because if he were honest he would scream, "I hate it." But, he realistically thought about it and said, "I am able to manage taking care of myself and cooking. I suppose all that is left is to have hand-controls mounted on my car so I can drive." "That sounds great, but a little ambitious with the car. Jackson, you must be free of pain medication before you can drive and then I will give the order for it to happen." Dr. Zyaire was always straight forward and bold. "I realize that," said Jackson. I'm working on it." "You also need to show some increased milestones involving your wheelchair transfers, particularly to a vehicle. And, the responsible ability to manage your medications," Dr. Zyaire concluded. The doctor went on with more instructions for Jackson: work hard for another week or two and then they would talk about a discharge date and make those arrangements. Future plans began darting through Jackson's mind as if there was a meteor shower going on inside his head. He thought, "What am I going to do? And *how* am I going to make this happen?" For the first time in what seemed like forever, Jackson felt alone and incompetent. He was used to being a leader, a forger and example. Now, he wasn't sure what or who he was. Silently he thought, "Come on, Marine! You don't quit until the mission is completed!"

Jackson was drawn into deep sleep by the exhaustion he felt. He didn't see Carrie until the following night. "I am so glad to see you," Jackson wore a huge smile as he greeted his favorite nurse. Carrie responded with a cheerful, "I dropped by to see you last night, but you were sleeping so soundly that I didn't want to wake you. I'm glad to see you, too." She paused to return the smile before continuing, "I looked at your chart and noticed that Dr. Zyaire had been to see you. What did you two talk about?" "Mostly about my progress towards accomplishing what I can and what I think I can't do. There's so much that still needs to be done; but he talked as if I could be discharged in a week or two." He looked at her with an apprehensive expression. "That's wonderful, Jackson! How come I get the feeling you are not excited about this possibility? I thought you wanted to get out of here as soon as possible. That's all you have talked about since I met you." Carrie patiently waited for a response. Heavy silence was what she heard and felt, not a response. After a few minutes she prodded him for an answer. "Jackson, talk to me!" "I'm not confident in my ability to do all this! Okay? Everyone expects me to be tough and capable of anything, but I'm not." Jackson hung his head. "Oh no! You are not going to feel sorry for yourself! You have worked too hard and come so far. You need to have that confidence and remember that you are not alone. Maybe the tough Marine can swallow some pride and ask for help." Jackson quickly sent a meaningful glare her way. "That's okay, I know that look. It means you're getting angry and that's good! You can get angry at the situation and fight to change it; not internalize it and direct it at yourself!" Jackson had never seen Carrie so committed to a cause-his recovery. Oddly enough, it was as if she had figuratively slapped him across the face to wake him up to reality. Jackson sheepishly looked at Carrie and said, "Yeah, you're right." "There's a lot of that going around lately," she rolled her eyes at Jackson. "What do you mean? Being right?" he questioned. "Yes! I'm right, you're right, sometimes, and there is so much in the world that is going right. Jackson, you need to focus on what is going right, not what you haven't accomplished." Jackson teased, "Me boldly admitting to you that you are right, isn't enough? You have to force your agenda on me too?" Carrie gently punched him in the arm, "I'm not trying to do that! I am only trying to help you!" She quickly retorted. "I know you are, Carrie, and I love and appreciate you for that, but this is something I have to do myself." Jackson became more insistent. That statement caused Carrie to bristle. She turned and walked toward the door and then turned around to say, "Jackson, I only feel sorry for you because you think you don't need anyone, not because of the accident or your leg. I hope you realize that everyone needs someone at some point in their lives. Good-luck." Jackson made an effort to call after her but she never turned around.

Jackson became distracted in the next few weeks with thoughts of Carrie. She had definitely gotten inside his head and his heart. He couldn't stop thinking about her and craved her presence. More and more determination surfaced as he thought about how he could make it up to her for pushing her away. Calls he made and messages sent were ignored. He asked about her every day and after several inquiries, one night he boldly approached the nurse's station in his wheelchair. He addressed the clerk behind the counter, "Excuse me. Can you tell me if Nurse Langston is working this evening?" "No, I'm sorry Mr. Montgomery," the clerk replied. "She hasn't worked for the last two weeks. She is on leave." Jackson quickly asked, "I don't suppose you could tell me where she is and if she's all right?" "No, Sir. You know I can't give out that information, but I can tell you that she left a message here for you in this envelope." The clerk handed Jackson a long white envelope with his name on the front written in black permanent marker. "Thank you." Jackson placed the envelope on his lap and wheeled back to his room where he could open it in private.

"Dear Jackson, I didn't want to leave things unsettled and was planning to come and talk the next day. I received word from Reggie that Mom wasn't doing well and he needed me at home for a few days. The message was urgent and unexpected. I'm so sorry that I didn't have time to see you before I left. I hope you are doing well and you are still 'fighting the fight' and 'running the race'. I know, old clichés, but they come from deep in my heart and I have certainly given a part of that to you! There are so many things that I love about you, Jackson. I love your loyalty and friendship, your integrity and determination, your strength and grit and your gentle kind heart. Don't give up or let up at all! Make me proud, Marine! Love, Carrie" Jackson folded the note slowly and placed it back into the envelope. He squinted both eyes shut to clear the moisture from them. His emotions had been on a pogo-stick, bouncing up and down and up and down again long before he read Carrie's message. Finally, he felt a portion of relief because he knew she was safe. At the same time, he was feeling excitement and boyish glee which caused some awkwardness about knowing that Carrie had feelings for him. Jackson had lingering thoughts about everything Carrie had expressed as he drifted off to sleep that night.

For the next few days Jackson's determination surged. He pushed himself in rehab to the point of exhaustion. Jackson was proud of his accomplishments and couldn't wait to show Carrie. Most afternoons were spent arranging for housing and securing his financials. He had a comfortable nest egg and was business savvy. Contact was made with Darren Mitchell for assistance in acquiring some real estate. Jackson needed something that was fairly near the hospital because he would be continuing therapy after his discharge. Darren agreed to do all he could to help Jackson. He even hired a contractor to make the house wheel-chair-accessible. As soon as Jackson closed on the real estate, construction could begin. Jackson's concern about finances grew as the mounds of expenses and bills accumulated. If he was still selling real estate, there wouldn't be a problem, but he wasn't. Eventually, he swallowed his pride and reached out to the Veterans Administration for help. Jackson was not treated like the decorated war hero that he was, or even thanked by his government for his service. He constantly had to send documents in to them to prove his service, his rank, his service awards and his military field. Jackson felt frustrated; the mounds of red tape and exasperating excuses were hard to track and process.

The positive things in Jackson's life didn't go unnoticed though, even amongst all the conflict and confusion. Jackson was extremely grateful to all who were offering support. His room was filled with vases of flowers, planters with greenery, and get-well cards. The flowers were refreshed on a weekly basis. Copies of news articles strategically lined a low shelf in his room. They told of his accident and reiterated many well wishes that came from around the world. The Magazine of Golf had a three-page feature of Jackson's golf career, his accident and the possibility of a comeback. Jackson stared at the photographs of himself in the magazine which varied from tee-off to the putting green. He soaked in every memory until he felt full and satisfied.

Jackson was startled to see Darren coming up the hallway and noisily barge into his room. Darren was off his crutches and was now capable of a full run. Out of breath he slid to a stop in front of Jackson's wheelchair. "Do you have anything scheduled for the next couple of hours? No appointments or therapy?" Darren excitedly asked. "Not a thing. Why are you so excited and in such a hurry?" Jackson was almost laughing. Darren exuberantly continued, "I have a surprise for you. I have already got permission from the medical staff so we're good to go!" Darren could hardly contain himself. Jackson on the other hand, grew cautious as a whirlwind of possibilities raced through his mind. He barely got the words "let's go" out of his mouth before Darren twirled him around and bounded out the door. Jackson instinctively glanced down to see if the safety belt was strapping him securely in the wheelchair.

The elevator seemed to be faster than usual and the situation was affected by Darren's excitement. The elevator doors slowly opened and Darren pushed out into the hall and made a sharp right turn. At the end of the hallway were two double doors that led to a rarely used hospital parking lot. There sat, in the middle of the bare parking lot, a brand new Mustang. It was a convertible and was painted fire-engine red. The shine of the chrome and the glistening of the paint beckoned the two men to advance closer. When they were beside the vehicle both men simultaneously reached out and gently stroked the car as if it were a new colt. No one said anything for a moment and then Jackson broke the silence. "When did you get *this*?" "Oh, this isn't mine, Jackson. This beauty is yours!" Astonished Jackson reacted, "What? How did you manage this? Did you rob a bank?" Jackson's eyes widened with excitement and approval. "Some of your golfing friends and associates and several of your Marine buddies wanted to do this for you and they pulled their resources together to make it happen. It is custom built with hand-controls, extra room between the front seat and back to allow easier access for your wheelchair, and it is built slightly lower to the ground to make it easier for you to get in." "This must have cost a fortune. How can I ever repay you?" Jackson sent a serious look Darren's way. "You don't get it Jackson! You already have. All of us are indebted to you. We are all better human beings for just knowing you." Darren made an effort to lighten things up, "I dib shotgun on your first drive." "You got it! Jackson replied. Oh, man. This is incredible!" He was wrestling with thoughts of processing the whole thing and accepting help of this magnitude.

A voice called from across the parking lot near the doors of the hospital, "And, I am the lucky one that has been assigned to teach you how to successfully drive it." Pete sprinted over to the car and slapped Jackson on the back. That seemed to be Pete's signature greeting. "Congratulations! We are all happy for you and pulling for you to succeed." Pete's eyes were moist and his expressions sincere. "Well, when do we start?" Jackson was like a race horse waiting to be released at the gate. It was determined by Pete that they could begin immediately.

Pete opened the driver's side of the car door and modeled for Jackson the correct way to transfer into the car, collapse his wheelchair and then lift it into the back. This was all done while the back of the driver's seat was pushed forward, crowding the driver against the steering wheel. Jackson sat in the passenger seat and observed intently as Pete went through the instructions several times. "Ready to give it a try?" Pete asked. "Ready as I'll ever be. You all know that I wouldn't be caught dead in a large green service van equipped with a lift for wheelchairs. This set up is perfect." Jackson made the transfer from the passenger seat to the wheelchair and then made his way around to the driver's side of the car. It took some practice to be able to open the car door while sitting in a wheelchair. He had to turn the chair so the edge barely cleared the door and then reach out for the car door handle to the right and behind his wheelchair. Awkward as it was for Jackson, his incredible strength made it look easy to onlookers. Once situated onto the car seat, he leaned slightly forward and collapsed his wheelchair. The seat and the back folded inward and the four wheels touched together. Jackson then quickly slid himself onto the console, precisely pulling the back of the driver's seat forward with one hand, and lifted his chair into the rear of the car with the other hand. His face was bright red and sweat was dripping down his temples onto his cheeks. Loud cheers erupted as he finished the first part of the process. Next came the most challenging part, actually driving.

Pete sat beside Jackson in the passenger's seat. He explained the functions on the steering wheel, which now contained hand-control levers, and how those functions were different from a regular vehicle. "Your hands will be doing all the work," Pete said. "But, don't worry. You'll get used to it." He went on to instruct Jackson about the hand controls and each of their functions. There were two controls on the left side of the steering wheel about the length of a ballpoint pen and the circumference of a skinny hot dog. They were horizontally placed two inches apart so the driver would have easy access to one or the other or both at the same time, depending on what action they were taking. There was another larger control on the right which housed functions that would only be used briefly, like the blinkers, lights, heater and radio. The right hand was used for most of the steering. The gear shift was located on the middle console in between the two front bucket seats. Driving with hand controls didn't necessarily demand strength but assuredly required coordination and alertness. The gas and brakes were maneuvered with the left hand by turning the left control or pushing or pulling it in a certain direction. The right hand put the car in gear and maneuvered the right control for everything else. Jackson began snail-pace slow and was limited to driving around the parking lot. Turning, acceleration, braking, and working the lights, heater and radio were all practiced extensively. It came easily to Jackson; he was a quick learner. Driving around the parking lot, however was one thing. It was a totally different scenario to contemplate driving out in traffic.

Every small thing that Jackson learned and tried made him appreciative of daily activities that he had taken for granted. When he thought about his future plans they always included Carrie. He envisioned taking her for a leisurely ride and ending the evening with a savory dinner at a fine restaurant. Sometimes he imagined himself driving to conferences where he was the keynote speaker and Carrie accompanied him. Oft times he would be driving to and from his office and occasionally out to the country club. Jackson's thoughts were filled with hope, the kind that gave him determination to win his battle and conquer his fears. So he dedicated long hours to practicing his skills. He carried a water bottle with him at all times so he wouldn't get dehydrated. The staff on occasion had to interrupt Jackson and remind him to eat. This is how Jackson spent his time for the next several days: bulldozing through rehab and relentless practicing of his driving skills. He anxiously anticipated Carrie's return.

Jackson's discharge was quickly approaching and he anticipated the completion of his new home. Pete and Trey had made arrangements with the hospital staff and Dr. Zyaire to allow Jackson personal leave, accompanied by Pete. The purpose: to select furnishings for his new home, and to get experience driving in traffic. That day didn't come fast enough for Jackson, and when it finally arrived he had butterflies like he was starting the first day of school. This was a big deal and he didn't want to blow it. Jackson arose extra early that morning to prepare for the day. He was dressed in dark brown suit pants, a plain brown sweater-vest with a buttoned down collared shirt to match. The outfit was complete with a beautiful, silk tie, and matching leather belt, shoes and brown socks. He had made arrangements to have his hair cut earlier. Jackson looked like he was going to an important business meeting, not to pick out furniture. It was definitely overkill but he was proud of himself for the accomplishment. It took Jackson three-and-a-half hours to maneuver taking a shower and getting cleaned up. He splashed some cologne on his neck just as Pete arrived in his room. Pete stood and stared at Jackson with his jaws clenched and a closed mouthed grin prominent. "Hey, Brother, I know we make a dynamic couple, but really? I am not your date!" "No one asked your opinion," Jackson blurted out. "Quit being such a jerk and let's just go!" "Okay, Bro, whatever you say." Pete grabbed the wheelchair arms as he pushed forward out of the room. You could hear his deep, heavy laugh as they ventured down the hallway.

As they pushed through the double-doors to the parking lot bright warm sunlight hit their faces. Jackson was definitely dressed too warm for the occasion, but proceeded forward as if he didn't notice the weather. He focused on the shiny-red Mustang sitting in front of him as he rolled up alongside the driver's door. Jackson began his transfer and when he was finished and back in the driver's seat, Pete jumped in the passenger side of the car. Jackson's transfer was flawless. They both snapped their seat belts on and Jackson started the car. "You'll have to tell me the directions to the furniture store Pete," Jackson excitedly said. Pete turned his head toward Jackson. "Are you ready?" Jackson nodded his head up and down. "Yeah, it can't be much worse than driving a tank!" Both of them laughed slightly as Jackson made a right turn onto the boulevard by the hospital.

Jackson pulled into the parking lot of the furniture store, parked and turned off the engine, and exhaled deeply with relief. He began his transfer out of the vehicle as Pete stood by and watched with concern. As they both approached the glass doors of the store, Jackson looked up and gasped with disbelief. "Surprise!" There stood Carrie with her blonde hair flowing over her shoulders and her infectious grin welcoming them. She was dressed in tan slacks and a patterned feminine top that loosely hung over her hips. As Jackson came closer, she broke out in a run and wrapped her arms around his neck. Pete stood by with his arms folded and a sly grin on his face. He had previously notified Carrie about the shopping spree and invited her to attend with them. "You look great!" Jackson felt that was an understatement. "Thank you. So do you." Carrie and Jackson couldn't take their eyes off each other. They exchanged some small conversation and then Jackson suggested they all go inside and buy some furniture.

The two of them acted like newlyweds, selecting the furnishings as if they were in their own little world and there was no one else around.

Having similar tastes enabled the process to go quickly. Jackson leaned toward a Spanish-look of rustic dark wood and rod iron. Tables he selected were covered with black or grey slate. Color-scheme became a consistent mixture of red and black. Carrie enjoyed acquiring artwork for decoration. Paintings of old Spanish town buildings with worn brick and cobble-stone streets were a favorite and a few smaller paintings were of the Spanish countryside, particularly by the ocean. As they glided through the process, Carrie and Jackson envisioned together what it would be like to visit Spain and marvel at its beauty. They ended the afternoon with Jackson insisting on treating Carrie and Pete to a fine dinner at a restaurant that he frequented often before his accident.

The maître d' welcomed them. "Good-evening Mr. Montgomery, sir. It is so nice to see you again. Would you like your regular table?" "Yes, please. There will be three of us and I will need accommodations." "Absolutely, sir that will not be a problem." The maître d' then showed them to their seats and introduced their waiter. Jackson positioned himself alongside Carrie's chair and insisted on pulling it out for her. He was a gentleman in every way. Jackson proceeded to order an expensive bottle of wine and appetizers. This restaurant was known for their steak and lobster, and each of Jackson's guests enjoyed their succulent steaks cooked to perfection. A final glass of wine ended the meal. Jackson resisted because he was driving. He lavished the waiter with a very large tip and the waiter thanked him and told them all to have a great evening. Carrie and Pete couldn't help but notice how everyone knew Jackson and was drawn to him. The staff treated him like a king.

Carrie had taken a bus to meet them at the furniture store which opened an opportunity for Jackson to drive her home. Pete just patiently sat in the back with the wheelchair and silently observed and listened to the couple's interactions. Neither of them stopped talking the entire way home to Carrie's apartment. As the car came to a stop,

Pete jumped out to open Carrie's door so Jackson wouldn't have to make several transfers. "I got this Jackson." Pete uttered suddenly. In one smooth motion Pete quickly stepped out of the backseat and opened Carrie's door. She then whisked by Pete and walked briskly to the driver's side of the car. "Thank you Jackson. I had a great time and the dinner was wonderful." She leaned down to give Jackson a peck on the cheek when intentionally Jackson turned his face toward her, cradled the back of her head in the cup of his hand and pulled her close. Jackson tenderly and slowly kissed her and then gently pulled slightly away. "Thank *you*, Carrie." Jackson stared at her as she pulled her fingers away from his, gave him a warm smile, and turned toward her apartment door. He protectively watched until she was safe inside. Pete jumped in the passenger seat and after fastening his seat belt, he slapped Jackson on the back. "You owe me one, buddy." Pete chuckled as they drove away.

The next few days consisted of moving into Jackson's new home. Friends and coworkers helped; and Jackson hired the heavy lifting to be done by a moving company. He was anxious and mildly intimidated by it all. Pete and Carrie helped box the things in his room up and load them in the car. The discharge nurse came in and went over instructions for Jackson to continue rehabilitation several times a week, follow-up appointments, and managing his medications. The time finally came for Jackson to sign the discharge papers and be officially released from the hospital's care. Pete and Carrie, the discharge nurse and Dr. Zyaire were all there to shake hands, give hugs and voice congratulations to Jackson. He had made some wonderful, everlasting friendships and was a little melancholy about leaving them behind. "Okay! You're out of here. Let's go!" Pete was his exuberant self. As they rolled down the hallway to the elevator, Jackson pondered on the memories of being here and the care he had received. Strips of light passed over him from the reflections of the ceiling lights in a mesmerizing way. He heard the small ring of the elevator doors opening and took in the sights and sounds that he had lived with for months for the last time.

Jackson had closed his eyes and when they reached the main lobby and exit, the doors opened to a startling surprise. The hallway from the elevator to the glass doors and lining the entrance up to his car was filled with hospital staff, friends, colleagues, Marines and reporters. Jackson was overwhelmed by the support. The five Marines present saluted him as he passed by and the crowd cheered. People were waving their hands and shouting "Good-luck, Jackson!" Jackson became emotionally touched and again squinted and rubbed the moisture from his eyes. He looked up as several cameras flashed repetitively, temporarily blinding him and a nearby engine backfired. Jackson's heart raced and he started to hyperventilate. Suddenly, he found himself on the battlefields of Vietnam. Terror surged through his entire body.

Chapter Four

THE RAVAGE OF WAR

The ground was wet and the air hot and moist. There was a distinct smell of foliage and damp dirt. Black silence was Jackson's companion as he lay belly first with his chin resting on his M40 sniper rifle. A blanket of stillness covered him and he could barely hear himself breathe. Loud explosions were heard in the near distance and periodically bullets whizzed by his ears sounding like mosquitoes. Jackson was still and didn't flinch a muscle. His eyes were focused ahead and he was waiting for his target to come into the range of his scope. An enemy machine-gun bunker was just ahead, and Jackson watched the flashes from the popping gunfire emerge. His mission was clear: to destroy the bunker and all NVA, (North Vietnamese Army). Jackson had scant backup and had come to the conclusion that he was going to be somewhat on his own. He didn't have time to contemplate anything. Quick, accurate and precise decisions had to be made. His survival depended on it.

Slowly he exerted even pressure on the trigger and fired into the bunker with dead-point accuracy. The machine gun firing temporarily stopped. But, rapid return gunfire soon accosted him. Jackson reacted by quickly changing his position and not breaking his camouflage. He belly-crawled into a trench close to the bunker, pulled the pin on a grenade and threw it over his head, landing a direct hit on his target. Two Viet Cong soldiers flew out of the bunker on the impact of the explosion. Jackson muffled their screams by his desperate and intentional strategic thinking. With remarkable speed he was able to move around the bunker. Jackson moved with precision and the quickness of a jaguar. He hurled more grenades and assaulted the enemy with raped rifle fire. After several minutes that seemed like an eternity, the black silence again settled in. Jackson patiently leaned against the dirt of the trench, shallowly breathing in silence until he was sure there wasn't a threat. When enough time had passed, he realized that he had accomplished his mission. He had single-handedly taken out at least 20 Viet Cong and eliminated the threat for his battalion. Jackson again laid back on the dirt of the trench and signaled his commanding officer that the way was clear for the battalion to fortify their position. His eyes stung from the smoke and the smell of death haunted him. Jackson made his way back to his battalion and joined his fellow Marines in combat. He had saved a lot of lives, but he had sacrificed lives to accomplish it.

Back at base camp the exhausted soldiers rested wherever there was a clearing, whether it was foliage or dirt, it didn't matter. Jackson was always hungry and rations were scarce. "Montgomery. You've got mail!" A young, dirt-covered Marine reached into a canvas bag and handed Jackson a letter. It was from home and momentarily took him away from this horrible war and let him bask in memories of family and friends. Jackson had time to read and savor the letter. He had received a gunshot wound to his right thigh and was in the Medical corps barracks recuperating. The doctors had removed a bullet and patched him up. They wanted him to rest, but Jackson was determined to get back into battle with his company. For his valiant efforts taking out the bunker and being injured, Jackson received a Purple Heart and a Silver Star Medal. The Silver Star was a coveted medal but the medals didn't mean much to Jackson at the time. He just wanted to complete his mission and stay focused on his duty as a Marine.

Jackson's thoughts took him back to when he joined the Marine Corps, which was just after graduating from high school. He was majoring in pre-med at a local university. Jackson knew the Vietnam War was extremely unpopular and controversial, but he felt a strong sense of responsibility to serve his country and a patriotic duty to volunteer. His schooling was put on hold and Jackson remembered donning the Marine Corps uniform of crisp, blue dress pants and jacket, a white hat with a black shiny brim, and gloss-shined black shoes. He wore it proudly as he was sworn into the Marine Corps at Camp Pendleton, California. Vowing to defend his country and the constitution of the United States made Jackson take on a serious demeanor. He was an expert marksman and later received the Distinguished International Shooter medal. Consequently, because of his expertise in marksmanship, Jackson became a member of the 2/5 F Company 5th Regimen of Snipers in the Marine Corps. His regiment would eventually become the most decorated regimental sniper platoon in the Vietnam War.

While in Vietnam, battle fatigue was the norm. The constant sound of explosions and rapid popping of gunfire never ceased. The sounds of war were as consistent as the rain fall. Jackson and his fellow Marines were found digging trenches every day. Sleep was a stranger and only indulged in on occasion while deep in the trenches. The counter offensive campaigns that Jackson participated in were brutal. He witnessed villages massacred and women and children with grenades strapped to their bodies used as weapons against the Americans and their Allies. It sickened him to realize that the Viet Cong had no regard for life.

One campaign became his biggest nightmare. The horror he witnessed could not be erased from memory. Again, Jackson was sent ahead as a scout sniper. The Viet Cong had overcome a small village and were torturing the villagers. Jackson had made his way to the top of a hill that looked down on the village. He saw several Viet Cong in a group pulling at a young woman's arms and maneuvering her toward two ropes that were tied to two different trees. She was pregnant and looked terrified. Charlie, as the Viet Cong were called, tied the ropes to the woman's ankles and strung her upside down. They then graphically tortured her by splitting her from end to end. Jackson lost his cool and temper. Rage filled every cell of his body to his core. The rage provided the energy and motivation he needed at that moment. He burst into the village with his rifle blazing and rapid gunshots pulverizing the entire group of Viet Cong that had carried out this distaining act against humanity. A few Marines followed Jackson and within minutes they had secured the village. The women and children were terrified and there were screams and wailing for their dead. It was a site that should have never been and one that no one should ever have to witness.

After securing the village, Jackson and a handful of Marines ventured forward into a rice paddy field where his men were receiving heavy fire from the enemy. Several Marines had been injured and a Medivac Helicopter had landed to pick up the wounded and the dead. Soldiers were fighting off the enemy gunfire that was directed at the copter. Jackson saw this as his chance to make a rescue effort and ran toward the enemy fire; jumping over mounds of dirt and dodging bullets. Artillery was being launched from every direction. Jackson spotted three Marines that were on the ground and calling for a corpsman. The men behind him had his back and protected him as he lifted one of the Marines up, put his arm over his shoulder and ran to the Medivac. Then, without hesitation, he repeated it for the second Marine. Counter firing increased and the artillery launches grew closer. All he could concentrate on was the wounded. The thought "No man left behind" felt like a brand in his mind. Jackson started to retrieve the third Marine when orders were shouted from the copter for him to pull back. Jackson ignored the order and took off on a full run to the last Marine. He lifted his whole body over his shoulders and carried him to the Medivac with popping of rapid fire and bullets racing past him. Jackson could hear the loud pings the bullets would make as they grazed the ground close by. Safely, they arrived at the copter and soon they were in the air headed for the Medicorps camp. Jackson's commanding officer immediately yelled at him over the sound of the spinning helicopter blades. "Damn it Marine! I gave you a direct order. Do you understand what that is?" "Yes, Sir!" Jackson retorted. "Sorry, Sir!" His commander just shook his head and then sat down on the floor of the helicopter. The sound of the blades whipping around at a phenomenal speed reminded Jackson of the sound of the wings of a large flock of birds in migration. It became mesmerizing. Jackson briefly nodded his head in sleep that was justified after his valiant rescue.

Jackson wasn't disciplined for his actions, which was a little surprising for him, but rather he was awarded another Silver Star and promoted to Lance Corporal. Slowly he gained the respect of higher ranking officers and became a leader to those under his command. His reputation was well-known and his charismatic personality drew everyone to him. Jackson used his sense of humor to lessen the anxiety he was feeling on a daily basis. His sensitivity made him many friends and his humility brought admiration from almost all who knew him. He tried to write home as often as he could, but never mentioned his awards or medals. Jackson didn't want to worry his family, especially his mother. Most nights and days were spent in the trenches, digging the trenches or shooting at Charlie camouflaged by surrounding foliage. Scarcely did he receive a break from combat to write family or just a reprieve. But every once in a while Jackson got the relief he craved, rarely, but it did come.

Battles were raging in every direction. To the north the siege of Saigon became a nonstop brutal carnage. Planes constantly flew over Jackson's head venturing into enemy territory to drop their devastating bombs. Sometimes he could see the results of those bombs forming black cones of smoke in the air preceded by a loud sonic-like boom. Medic helicopters landed and took off every hour loaded with wounded and the dead. This never-ending nightmare continued day after day. Jackson was back at base on occasion where he witnessed the arrival of new recruits. It saddened him to know that a large percentage of them would not return home and many would be maimed by the ravages of war. Jackson was given responsibility to prepare some of those new arrivals for a reconnaissance mission to the north of them. They were to survey and fortify a way for a battalion of soldiers to be sent toward Saigon and provide reinforcements for the troops. It became increasingly difficult for Jackson to motivate his men when he was feeling demoralized from the effects of the anti-war demonstrations and protests that were occurring at home. It was hard to fight a war when you didn't feel supported. Too often Jackson had to brush off the feeling of abandonment and betrayal he felt after receiving that kind of news from home. But Jackson was strong and a brilliant leader. He cared deeply for his men and made sure they were prepared physically and mentally for battle.

A Private boldly approached Jackson and saluted, "Sir, the Commander wants to see you immediately in his quarters." Jackson returned his salute, "Thanks Private." As Jackson drew near the Commander's quarters, possibilities of the reason for the summons went through his head. He thought he had a pretty good idea of what was ahead. Jackson gave a salute to the Commander and said, "You wanted to see me Sir?" "Yes, Corporal. Your reconnaissance mission leaves at 0500. Are your men ready?" "I believe they are, Sir," Jackson replied. "You *believe* they are Marine?" The Commander glared at

Jackson. "They *are* ready, Sir." "Make sure you follow orders precisely this time, Montgomery. No acts of heroism. Understood?" The Commander stood up and leaned forward resting his knuckles against the surface of his desk. "Sir, I understand, Sir" was Jackson's purposeful reply. "Dismissed." The Commander gave his last order to Jackson. Lance Corporal Jackson didn't realize at the time that this would be the last order he would officially receive.

Five a.m. came quickly and Jackson gathered his gear, his rifle and put his helmet on his head. He walked to a small clearing where his men were gathering. After calling the soldiers to attention Lance Corporal Montgomery proceeded to review their mission orders with them. He emphasized the importance of staying alert and paying attention to details at all times. He cautioned them to not get too confident and to make sure each of them had each other's backs. "Good-luck Marines. Semper Fi!" A boisterous "Ooh-rah" was returned and the Marines were put at ease. "Head out!" Jackson pointed with his hand in the direction of travel. He was located near the middle of the group.

In Vietnam the "gooks" as the enemy was also called, used clever but dirty warfare. They positioned booby-traps along the hundreds of trails leading through the jungle. Some consisted of spikes that would shoot into the pathway when a trip-wire was launched. Others were grenades ready to explode when a soldier pulled a nearly invisible wire that was attached to the pin. The Marines had to be hyper alert at every turn; watching every step they took because the traps were hidden by the thick foliage of the jungle. This was difficult when they were on the run; which is what they were at this moment in time. Jackson had a young green marine in front of him and in a split second he noticed the pin from a grenade dangling across the pathway. He reacted quickly and shoved the Marine Private off the path in the opposite direction. "Grenade!" Jackson screamed as he kicked the grenade away as hard as he could and dove to take cover as it exploded.

Dirt was raining down on Jackson and his ears were ringing. He could not hear a marine yelling at him to respond to see if he was all right. His head pounded and he realized he had lost his helmet during the explosion. The smoke was thick and choking him. Jackson was laying on his back and he attempted to raise up onto his elbows to get up when he felt an excruciating pain shoot up his right leg and sharp pain in his sides. Time seemed to stand still for Jackson as he peered over his stomach and saw his right foot was missing. He slowly turned his head to the right and saw his boot with his foot still inside it lying a few feet away. He was bleeding profusely and feeling weak. "Medic! Medic!" Jackson weakly yelled, barely having enough breath to voice his urgency. He again turned slightly to see a Corpsman rushing toward him holding his helmet on as he dodged gunfire. As the Corpsman drew close, Jackson belted out, "I think I need a needle and thread over here!" That was the last thing Jackson remembered. Everything went dark as he passed out from the loss of blood.

It only took a few minutes for the Medivac helicopter to arrive and Jackson was loaded onto the copter. The Medics went to work on him immediately. They started IV fluids and put several compression bandages on the end of his right leg to slow the bleeding. His vital signs were unstable and the Medics weren't sure Jackson would make it. Several minutes went by before landing at the base camp and Jackson was rushed into surgery. The doctors removed six pieces of shrapnel from his ribs and chest and cauterized the end of the stump on his right leg. He received several blood transfusions before he was stable.

Jackson woke up a day and a half later lying in a hospital bed in DaNang. He was in critical condition and had been transferred from base camp in order to receive better care. His head was still pounding and he rolled his eyes up toward the ceiling and saw two bags of IV fluids hung on a pole next to his bed. The fluids were running down plastic tubing and into a vein in his arm via a good-sized needle that was taped securely to his arm. Jackson again raised up on his elbows to catch a glance at his right leg just to check and see if the nightmare was real. Doctors and nurses attended to his needs and he was given IV Morphine to help with the pain. Jackson couldn't understand why he was feeling horrible pain in the foot that was not there. The Doctor explained that it was called a phantom pain and that it was very common among amputees. Just using that word sent chills down Jackson's back. He was in shock and woke up frequently startled out of sleep. He knew this was something that would eventually send him stateside.

Anger set in as Jackson felt he had let the Marine Corps down by not completing his mission. Jackson wasn't able to accept his circumstances and fought reality viciously. He had been in the hospital a few weeks when his commanding officer payed him a visit. Reality set in when the Commander told Jackson that his family had been notified and that he would be transferred stateside to a Veterans Hospital near Camp Pendleton, California. When Jackson heard that news, he felt he was going around in circles, ending up at Camp Pendleton. Then the Commander stood at attention, saluted Jackson and proceeded to award him with several medals. They included another Purple Heart, a Silver Star, a Bronze Star, a Navy Commendation Medal, an Expeditionary Medal and the Vietnam Distinguished Service Medal. The Commander saluted Jackson again, "Thank you for your distinguished service, Marine. You fought valiantly for your country and we are very proud of you. Semper Fi." With that the Commander told Jackson good luck and sharply turned away from him and exited his room. He was told his medals would be shipped stateside. Jackson stared at the ceiling in disbelief.

Back home Jackson's mother had awakened from sleep when she saw the blast that took Jackson's leg. Immediately she knew something was wrong. A few days later her fear was confirmed by a visit from two Marines to their home. The family waited in fear and with hearts pounding as they watched the Marines in full uniform, slowly and soberly walk up the Montgomery's driveway. Jackson's mother began screaming "No!" over and over. His sisters started to cry. The whole family knew what this meant. There was a distinct possibility that Jackson had been killed. That was their biggest fear. The doorbell rang and Jackson's mother answered the door. One officer asked, "Is this the residence of Jackson Levi Montgomery?" "Yes," she said and she invited the two officers in. She took in a deep breath as the officer began, "Ma'am, we regret to inform you that your son, Jackson has been critically injured in battle. He will be coming stateside to Camp Pendleton in a few weeks." "He's not dead?" she blurted out and began sobbing. "No Ma'am but he has lost the lower portion of his right leg. It was touch and go for a while but he is a tough Marine and he has pulled through it. He is facing more surgery but is expected to recover well." Then they asked if they could sit down and talk to Jackson's parents for a minute.

They all settled in the living room as the officers began telling Mr. and Mrs. Montgomery about Jackson's selfless service and why he deserved all the medals he was awarded. They showed them the citation that Jackson received for the Navy Commendation Medal which was signed by the highest ranking Marine Corps officer. They also shared some comments from some of his men and the medics that rescued him. "Your son has quite a sense of humor." The officer had just told them about Jackson's comment to the Medic about "needing a needle and thread". "Jackson is a good Marine and an honorable man who has served his country with distinguished valor." The officers handed Jackson's parents some papers and told them who to contact about Jackson's arrival at Camp Pendleton and then they both gracefully exited.

There were mixed feelings at the Montgomery home that night. The whole family was elated at the news that Jackson was alive and at the same time extremely concerned about the state of his health. They began making plans for a trip to California as soon as Jackson arrived. The time went by quickly and they were notified of Jackson's arrival four days after the officers' visit. Immediately, a call was made to the hospital where Jackson was staying. Jackson's mother frantically asked him if he was okay and how he was doing. "Don't worry about me, Mom. I'm fine. I'm excited to see all of you," Jackson replied.

The trip to California was hot crossing the desert and somewhat boring. When they arrived, the Montgomerys made their way to a specified building to acquire passes to get on base. Then they navigated their way to the hospital to see Jackson. The hallways of the hospital were light green and for the most part empty. It echoed as they walked toward Jackson's room. The floor tile was checkered white and black and didn't seem to match the color of the walls. Hospital personnel were disciplined and wore crisp white uniforms and lab coats. A clear plastic envelope-like structure was fastened to the right wall of each room beside the door and held the patient's chart. There was a round light placed above the doorway that lit up when a patient needed help.

Jackson was asleep as they entered his room, so his parents quietly asked the nurse if it was alright to wake him. She said that was fine but to not stay too long because he needed his rest. The family entered the room only to discover that it was a hospital ward. Jackson's bed was separated from two others by curtains hung with metal clips between each bed. The bed was mostly round tubular metal that was painted white. There was a half-circle at the head of the bed. It had vertical bars coming down to the edge of the bed, resembling half of a wagon wheel with spokes. Another shorter version was at the end of the bed. The bedspread was a white chenille and the sheets a starched crisp white.

Jackson's mother stood by the side of his bed and noticed the bed covers were neatly pulled up to his armpits. She was trying to imagine the extent of his wounds while covering her mouth to muffle the sound of her crying. Jackson must have known they were there. He slowly opened his eyes. "No matter how much you water my leg, it won't grow back." He managed to grin at his family and they all leaned down and hugged him being careful not to brush up against his wounds. "Looks like you still have your sense of humor, Son," Mr. Montgomery, Sr. stated. "Tell us about what happened," he continued. "I really don't want to talk about it." Jackson was quick to respond. "How about you tell me what I have missed." That seemed to be his compromise. The family pulled up chairs next to his bed and began telling him about the events and happenings that he had missed while being away. Jackson was relentless in avoiding talking about the war and after some time he showed signs of fatigue. Jackson's family said their good-byes and Jackson drifted into a foggy sleep.

The next few months were spent healing and going to rehab. Jackson eventually was strong enough to navigate crutches and then the most important day arrived. He was fitted for his prosthesis. The hard plastic, flesh-colored leg and attached foot slipped over his stump like a boot. When Jackson stepped down suction held the prosthesis in place. He didn't have to wear a strap over his leg above the kneecap thanks to modern technology. As Jackson began to walk without assistance of any kind, he had to adjust to the awkward feeling he had of balance. It was off. Jackson was a fast learner and a determined man. He wanted to get out of the hospital at Camp Pendleton as fast as possible. He attended counseling therapy three times a week and Jackson managed to charm the therapist into allowing him a short leave of absence to go golfing. He coerced one of the male aides at the hospital to take him. Jackson's friends and associates would do anything for him.

Jackson became a regular at a near-by country club. He found that even with a prosthetic leg, he had not lost his abilities to golf like a professional. He improved every time he graced them with his appearance and he was recognized by several pro-amateur golfers. They encouraged Jackson to line up a sponsor for when he was out of the hospital and discharged from the Marines. They felt he had a bright future ahead of him in golf. Jackson started making big plans for when he went home.

The arrival home wasn't as easy as Jackson imagined it to be when he was in Vietnam. He felt awkward staying with his parents and seemed to always be jumpy and agitated. Jackson stood in the middle of the room where he was sleeping. It was the room he grew up in as a child and teenager. Slowly he turned from wall to wall, taking in all the pictures and trophies that hung on the walls and adorned his dresser. Memories of being a star athlete came to mind as he glanced at the ribbons that hung on the trophies. He took a deep breath, shrugged his shoulders, and sauntered to the living room to watch television. Jackson sunk onto the couch but he didn't relax. His thoughts were racing about getting a job, arranging for a sponsor for golfing, and acquiring a vehicle. Several times Jackson abruptly stood up and paced in front of the TV.

The employment he desired finally came. It was a construction job where he had to wear a neon vest for safety and a hardhat. Jackson again found himself digging trenches only this time he didn't have to dodge bullets. The work was hard and hot, but Jackson persevered as if he felt he had something to prove. He bought an old used car to help him get to work. It was rusted and painted different colors when a fender had to be replaced by the previous owner. It didn't start all the time but it was transportation and Jackson couldn't complain. Often he would return from work and go straight into his room. Slowly he pulled the prosthesis off his sweaty leg only to find the bottom of it was filled with blood. He quickly cleaned it up and took a shower and acted as if nothing was awry. Jackson quietly ate dinner and rested on the couch while he watched some television. This seemed to be the routine day after day. On one occasion, Jackson's mom slipped up behind him while he was on the couch. Her intentions were to give him a big hug and tell him how much she loved him. She bent down and placed her arms around Jackson's neck. Instinctively, Jackson grabbed his mother's arms and flipped her over his shoulder before realizing who it was behind him. "Are you okay? Damn it, Mom I could have killed you. Don't you understand? I am trained to kill! Especially when someone sneaks up behind me." Jackson was visibly upset and concerned about his mother. "Just don't ever do that again. I need some air." Jackson briskly walked out the door to his car and drove way.

The next day Jackson was down in another trench digging and keeping to himself as much as possible. A large, sweaty man approached Jackson displaying a confrontational swagger. He had a dark yellow hard hat on and his long hair was in a ponytail at the base of the helmet. His reddish brown beard was brushed with dirt and he clenched a shovel in his right hand. "Are you the soldier that I've been hearing so much about?" he gruffly asked. "Depends, who wants to know?" Jackson was being cautious with his reply. The man scuffed dirt onto Jackson's back. "Ain't you got nothin' to say soldier boy?" Jackson bristled, "First of all, I am a Marine in the United States Marine Corps and I'm not a *boy*. I am not looking for any trouble so why don't you mind your own business?" Jackson was trying hard to contain his anger. The man shot his reply back at Jackson and it hit him like a dart. "You mean mind my business like you did over in that unwanted war? You're nothin' but a monster and a baby killer!" With that remark, Jackson leaped out of the trench just as the man raised his shovel to hit him. Jackson grabbed his arm and twisted it so the man writhed and dropped the shovel. "Do you want to say that to my face?" The man didn't say anything.

"I thought so. At least I am not a coward." Jackson replied. The dirty, sweaty man then threw a punch at Jackson hitting him in the face. That was a big mistake on his part. Jackson clenched his fist and returned the punch with a major force that knocked the man to the ground. "Don't ever cross me again." Jackson started to walk off when his supervisor arrived on the scene. "What's going on?" he yelled. "Nothing, it has all been taken care of," Jackson told his boss as he wiped some blood off of his mouth. "Yeah? It looks like it. You both are fired!"

Jackson found himself at a local bar, downtrodden and feeling a bit sorry for himself. "Give me a beer." He said to the bartender. "What does the other guy look like?" The bartender motioned toward Jackson's black eye and bloody mouth. "I don't know. I didn't pick him up off the ground to find out." Jackson's arms rested on the bar and his hands wrapped around the bottle that was in front of him. His Marine tattoo was visible on his left arm. "In the service?" asked the bartender. "Marine Corps." Jackson sat up straight to respond. "Served two tours in Vietnam fighting for my country and came back to this crap load of disappointment." "Is that what the fight was about?" The bartender was full of questions. "Yup. And I lost my job because of a fight that I didn't start!" Jackson set the bottle of beer down hard against the counter. It was empty and Jackson stood up, reached into his pocket and threw several bills on the counter. "Thanks," he said as he started to turn around to leave. "Hey Marine. I appreciate your service." The bartender called out to Jackson as he approached the doorway. Jackson had one hand on the door handle and turned his head toward the bar and gave a nod to acknowledge the comment. Jackson drove the long way home. He needed some time to think and process what had just happened. His thoughts kept bringing him back to the idea of pursuing golf as a career. He had already lined up several sponsors and all he needed to do was move to Denver where the hub of golfing seemed to be and where he had good chances at a productive start.

Weeks later Jackson received an official discharge from the Marine Corps. Jackson teared up as he read the certified letter instigating an honorable discharge from the Marine Corps and thanking him for his distinguished service. Jackson felt a void hit as he realized he was no longer on active duty, or even involved with assignments or orders. A feeling of loss came over him and he suddenly lost his bearings. Jackson just realized how much the Marine Corps meant to him and how much it was a part of his life. He read the letter while quietly sitting at the dinner table. There was no one around and the room was dimly lit. Jackson abruptly yelled a profanity and slammed both his fists hard against the table top. He then sobbed for several dragged out minutes.

Jackson had to take out a loan to acquire descent transportation that would make it to Denver, Colorado. He purchased a two-year old Pontiac GTO that was a bright royal blue with black interior. Funds from his Veterans benefits would carry him financially for a while until he was more established. Jackson started to look forward to his road trip and his future. His spirits were lifted as he entertained hope and positive thinking. With a loaded vehicle and plenty of cash in his wallet, Jackson hit the road. Destination: Denver, Colorado. Jackson personalized his new car by hanging his dog tags around the rear view mirror and placing a Marine Corps decal in the back window. He even had a Marine Corps license plate. To Jackson, these small things were sweet reminders of a part of his life that he cherished and loved, not to be forgotten. The items drew attention and brewed mischief whenever he was driving. The reactions ranged from a short honk and thumbs up to a long hard honk and an obscene hand jester. After a while it became mundane and Jackson ignored all of it. Negative public reaction about the war became less and less. Once in a while Jackson would be watching the news and protests were pulled up on the screen. He watched for a few minutes and then sharply turned the television off and threw the remote angrily at the TV. Jackson went for days without watching the news or tuning in to updates about the war. He couldn't stomach how the war was being handled by politicians here in the states when the real battles were being fought by soldiers who were held back from doing their jobs. It nauseated Jackson. As the war started showing signs of retreat from the American forces and Allies, he was horrified to think that all those brave men died and sacrificed for nothing. And then to have the ones that made it home treated like criminals and scum was unbelievable. Sometimes he felt he was having nightmares about two different wars: Vietnam and the homeland. Black stillness and loneliness invaded his environment often and Jackson fought off urges to drown those thoughts in liquor and drugs. It became increasingly more difficult to resist.

Jackson settled into his new apartment and took care of the mounds of paperwork that had to be signed and given to the Veterans Administration. He arranged for follow-up visits with an orthopedic specialist at the VA. Jackson had to be extra careful to watch for infection in his stump. While in Camp Pendleton recuperating from the loss of his leg, he had acquired a bad infection that took an additional two inches of his leg. Now, Jackson was vigilant in watching for signs of infection or unusual trauma. But this didn't slow him down. One of the first things he did upon his arrival was make an appearance at a local Pro Shop to purchase a new set of golf clubs. No expense was spared for the purchase of the clubs or the three packs of Spalding golf balls. Jackson then purchased a membership to a prestigious country club. He figured he might run into someone there that could help him find a job.

Most of Jackson's money was spent on rounds of golf at his new found home away from home, The Lake Hills Country Club. Jackson had just taken a hot shower and was leaving the locker room after a long hard day. He stopped at the front desk to make sure his tee-off time was scheduled for the following morning. A voice came from beside him,

"You wouldn't happen to be Jackson Montgomery?" Jackson put his wallet in his back pocket and turned toward the voice. A man close to his age stood next to him. He wore nice slacks and a golf shirt to match. Golfing shoes were on his feet, so Jackson assumed he was a pro or a pro-amateur golfer. "That would be me." He continued, "What can I do for you?" "Let me introduce myself. My name is Joseph Fielding, but everyone calls me Joe. I am one of the golf pros here at the club and I have been looking for some new and fresh talent to accompany me on the PGA tour coming up. I have asked around and been to several clubs. I have also talked to several of the local pros and your name kept coming up. I have been watching you on the course and you are miraculously talented. Wonder if you might be interested?" "I am definitely interested," Jackson excitedly responded. "Let me buy you dinner and we can discuss the details." Joe shook Jackson's hand. This was the beginning of a long friendship and the start of Jackson's successful career as a professional golfer.

He made several tours on the PGA circuit the next few months and quickly soared to the top, winning a couple of prestigious tournaments along the way. Jackson and Joe became the best of friends and they didn't always spend all their time golfing. Jackson went dancing at some local clubs and attended many galas and sporting events. His social life was soaring right alongside his golf career. One afternoon, Joe approached Jackson with an invitation to go to his cabin and go boating at Crater Lake near Aspen. Jackson eagerly accepted, even though he had not been boating since before Vietnam. He wasn't sure how it would work with his prosthesis, but Jackson never turned down a challenge.

They arrived at the cabin in the evening and settled in with their belongings. There were a total of four men in the group. They all eagerly ate dinner and then crashed under the thick quilts that were on the cabin beds. The quiet mountain air was relaxing and Jackson slept well. This was the first time in a while that he didn't wake up during the night with a nightmare. The next morning was brisk and a little on the cool side. After gathering all the gear and equipment, the group piled into the massive truck that was pulling a brand new ski boat on a trailer behind it. The marina was 15 minutes away and Jackson's excitement made those miles shorten. Joe was driving and was very experienced in launching a boat. He stopped at the water's edge to give the other's instructions as to how they could help. One of Joe's friends would back the trailer with the boat on it down the launching ramp and into the water until the water covered the front trailer wheels halfway. Jackson was to climb into the boat before launching. Another friend was to back the boat off the trailer as Joe unlatched the chains and the gear lift that held the boat secure. It went smoothly with Joe barking instructions to everyone. The truck was driven to the parking lot with the trailer and parked. The boat was maneuvered to the side of the dock, where the driver of the truck and Joe were picked up. Jackson marveled as he witnessed the launching. It was quite a process!

They stayed most of the time in the middle of the lake. All on board had taken their turn at slalom water skiing; which is using only one ski. Jackson carefully observed each of them position the ski just right in the water by using one hand to keep them upright and afloat, and grasping the ski rope with the other. He could tell it took uncommon strength to resist the pull of the boat and lift themselves up and glide to the top of the water. They controlled the ski by using the edges and were able to zig zag to one side of the boat's wake and then the other. Body control played a big part in being successful. The skier would go as long as he had energy and then drop the ski rope which signaled to the driver that he was finished. The boat would then circle around and pick the skier up. Most of the time it took a few minutes for the skier to catch his breath. He sat on the bench inside the back of the boat dripping water and breathing heavily. The last one to ski was Joe. As he sat in the back of the boat catching his breath and drying off he immediately turned to Jackson. "What do you say? Are you ready to try water skiing?" Joe was a little hesitant to ask, but blurted it out anyway. "You think I can do that? You're crazy!" Jackson half-heartedly laughed. The last time he had been water skiing was during his college years. He momentarily got a lump in his throat and a little bit of fear and uneasiness set in. "Hey, no pressure my friend, but if anyone can do this with one leg, you can!" Joe was trying to be sensitive yet encouraging at the same time. "Why not?" was Jackson's meager reply.

Jackson found himself in the water behind the boat. He had managed to take his prosthesis off and pull the water ski boot onto his left foot while sitting on the edge of the boat before he jumped in the water. Jackson was a confident swimmer. He had been a lifeguard and taught swimming lessons in his earlier years. But this was out of his comfort zone. Once in the water, he used all his strength to keep his balance and reach the ski rope which had been tossed to him and was barely within his reach. Swallowing a lot of water, he leaned forward to grab the handle of the rope and then whipped onto his back to rest. He took a few minutes to prepare himself and then he lifted the tip of the ski up as he shouted "hit it!" which was the signal for the driver to pull the throttle to full speed enabling the skier to raise himself out of the water to the surface. Jackson watched his water ski wobble back and forth as he desperately tried to steady it with one leg. And then he face-planted directly in front of himself gulping down water as he fell. He coughed and sputtered as he dropped the rope and saw the boat begin to return to pick him up. "Do you want out?" Joe screamed over the sounds of the motor. "No way! Again!" Jackson repeated the process at least ten more times when on the eleventh try he felt himself triumphantly gliding to the top of the water, his wobbling ski steadying and his arms grasping the rope with renewed strength. Boisterous cheers were heard from the boat and Jackson felt the feeling of a job well done. He had accomplished the impossible and experienced pushing himself to his limits. This extraordinary feat gave him courage to discover other areas for him. Some areas of which no one else had ventured.

Chapter Five

UNCOMMON VALUE A COMMON VIRTUE

Whirlwind experiences and sharp turns at every bend became Jackson's life style. He drove himself to exhaustion every day. It was worth it to him to feel the emotional high that he felt when he accomplished something that no one thought he could. Some days were filled with reporters wanting interviews and paparazzi tailing him to every destination. He was regularly featured in the local newspaper and the coveted Magazine of Golf. Jackson was still alone and although he dated, he preferred it that way. Often he would be seen at expensive restaurants downtown and on the outskirts of the club, alone. Jackson was known wherever he went. Maître d's, valets, and owners of the restaurants he frequented knew him on a first-name basis. He was treated like a king and the red carpet was rolled out to greet him. His favorite places to dine became those that served steak and lobster. The waitresses remembered how he liked his steak, the kind of wine he drank and what salad dressing he preferred on his salad. Jackson always left a hefty tip, most times more than the going amount.

Jackson felt a void in his life and he struggled to find out what that might be. Often, he thought it might be that he hadn't dealt with the memories of Vietnam, or the homesickness he felt when he thought of his family back home in Arizona. He couldn't quite put his finger on it and it developed into a dark cloud that followed him around like the pesky paparazzi. Jackson still took medication for pain and the spasms that he felt in his amputated leg. The more this void haunted him, the more he became distressed. His drinking increased and it became noticeable to all his friends and colleagues. It was really surprising that he was able to stay on top of his game and continue winning on tours and at the course.

Joe walked up to Jackson. They were at Lake Hills and had just completed an eighteen-hole course. "Feeling a little off?" Joe asked in a concerned voice. "It's nothing." Jackson took a drink of the cold cola he had retrieved from the bar. "Come on Jackson, talk to me. I'm your best friend and I feel like you haven't been yourself lately." Joe put his arm around Jackson's shoulder. "I just have this emptiness inside, and it seems to fill up with nightmares. That's all I have is nightmares, every day and every night. I close my eyes and all I can see are explosions, my friends being killed, and people being tortured. It's like I never left Vietnam! I drown them with booze. That seems to help temporarily. But as soon as the hangover is done doing what it does, they are right back. I'm a mess." Jackson hung his head and rested his hand against his forehead as he leaned on the table where they were sitting. Joe tried to comfort him. "Look Jackson, I don't even pretend to know what you went through in Vietnam, but you're my friend and clearly you could use some direction and help. Have you considered seeing a therapist? You know, someone who could counsel you?" "Been there. Done that when I was at Camp Pendleton. I just need to find a reason to be motivated to pull myself out of this dark place. Good talk!" Jackson stood up and said his good-byes to Joe, leaving Joe bewildered at the way the conversation had concluded.

Jackson felt like he had finally found the motivation he needed when he met a stunning woman at the country club. She was introduced to him by her father, John P. Remington, a well-known real estate tycoon. Jackson will never forget how she mesmerized him at first glance. He looked deeply into her green eyes as he took her hand and kissed the back of it. Her name was Vanessa and she affectionately smiled at Jackson. She carried herself with poise and grace and wore her expensive clothes as if they were tailor-made just for her. Jackson pursued a courtship with Vanessa that was blessed by her father. Mr. Remington had invited Jackson to work for him in his real estate business. The meeting of Vanessa, and the offer of a real estate business venture had turned out to be huge blessings to Jackson at that time. Jackson was able to feel the emptiness disappear and the void filled. It didn't take long before the couple began planning their lives together.

Jackson saw another explosion of bright lights and was suddenly startled by someone shaking his shoulder. "Hey, Jackson! Are you still here with us? Are you okay?" Jackson looked up after being in a daze to see Carrie standing next to him. He was abruptly brought back to reality by the cheers of the crowd, the camera flashes, and the dozens of balloons that lined the sidewalk and exit leading from the hospital. He realized his thoughts had been briefly elsewhere and seemed relieved to be where he was at that moment and not in his past. "We love you, Jackson" was sung in unison by the hospital staff. Feeling an overwhelming sense of gratification, he made his way to his car, transferred into the driver's seat and lifted his wheelchair into the car like he had done many times. He bent down to tell Carrie good-bye and frantically looked around. She wasn't there. The passenger door slammed shut and Carrie bounced onto the seat. "Oh, here you are!" Jackson said with a big smile. "What are you doing?" "I am going with you and we are going to host *the* best house-warming party!" Carrie reached over and gave Jackson a kiss on his cheek. "Let's go Marine!" Carrie softly chuckled as she snapped her seatbelt on and settled back into the bucket seat of the car.

Jackson's new home was a few miles away, deeper into the country than the city. There were beautiful homes spotted in clearings along the way. The small road leading to his home was lined with fragrant pines and rich foliage. Small spots of wildflowers checkered the fields and the sun was shining down warming the inside of the car. Carrie had her window down and wind was tossing her hair back. She had sunglasses on, but Jackson imagined her eyes twinkling because she had such a big smile on her face. In the distance you could see the Rocky Mountains with their snowcapped splendor. Jackson was not feeling any emptiness or void, rather he was happier than he had ever been. Occasionally, he glanced at Carrie and grinned as she danced with her arms in the air to the music on the radio. Jackson's driveway soon came into view and he was taken back by the scene. Banners were strung over his garage that beckoned a welcome home. Bundles of helium balloons that were tied to stakes lined the driveway. Dozens of people, some he didn't recognize, crowded around his porch and front yard. The theme was patriotic with red, white, and blue colors dispersed, and stars and flags sporadically placed. Jackson slowly pulled into the driveway and just stared at the picturesque view in front of him. Carrie took off her seatbelt and turned sideways to face Jackson. "Are you surprised? Everyone felt that since you didn't get an appropriate welcome home when you got back from Vietnam, we would do 'double-duty' and give you a combined welcome home from the hospital and Nam today." Carrie beamed with excitement and Jackson sat shaking his head in disbelief.

After transferring from his car, Jackson was escorted by Pete and Trey up the ramp that led from his garage to inside his house. There were several photographers snapping shots at his every move. Jackson opened the door, wheeled just inside, and gasped in amazement. The door opened to a large spacious living room with beautiful wooden flooring and light yellow walls. A massive window looked onto the street in front. A wheel-chair adapted recliner sat off to one side with plenty of room for Jackson to maneuver around. A small sofa sat next to the recliner that was raised up so he could transfer to the sofa if he chose. In front of the sofa, with space enough in between, was placed the dark grey slate table that he and Carrie had selected from the furniture store. Several framed Spanish art pictures adorned the walls above the sofa and an up to date television and sound system aligned the wall across from the recliner. The television sat next to an exquisite rustic fireplace with a large dark wooden mantel. Lights and television turned on remotely by a control that Jackson held in his hand. He wheeled around the recliner and turned into another spacious room, the kitchen. Pete showed him how the cupboards were designed to lower to wheelchair level at the push of a button that was located on the countertop. Everything from food to pots and pans was at Jackson's reach. The low refrigerator was fully stocked with food and drink. One of the nurses that he recognized from the hospital said, "All these dishes and silverware on the cabinet are waiting to find a home. We thought it would be nice if you put your personal touch to it." "Absolutely. Just let me finish the tour of this magnificent structure and then I'll be right there." Jackson turned to his right and wheeled down the hallway where he saw a guest bathroom and a guest bedroom located across the hall. All of it was wheelchair accessible. The bathroom was done in rich dark browns and rod iron and took on a renaissance castle look. The bedroom across the hall was decorated in a similar fashion. There was a double walk-in closet against one wall and two single beds covered with dark red and black Spanish designed quilts and shams were against the other.

Jackson's heart raced as he entered the master bedroom. A king-size bed was off to the right and included a massive wooden headboard, dresser and armoire to match. A black and red velvet quilt covered the bed that was low to the ground to make it easier for Jackson to transfer. To his left the wall housed a triple-sized walk-in closet with low shelves and adjustable racks for hanging his clothes. Then he saw it, the unbelievable shower in the corner of the room. It was large enough to fit three wheelchairs in it. Lined with soft brown tile it gave off a warm feeling. The floor was covered with a slip guard surface for safety. Built in shelves were on the left side and a comfortable smooth granite bench was placed just inside where he could transfer using the grab bars that had been provided. The floor slanted toward a drain which was at the front of the shower and the opening to the shower was even with the bedroom floor to allow his wheelchair to get close enough to transfer onto the bench. The faucets and shower head were placed on the side where they were reachable and the shower head was hand held when not resting on a hook. Frosted glass sliding doors enclosed the shower to allow privacy. Jackson had positive comments at every turn and felt like he couldn't thank everyone enough. He was overwhelmed by it all and felt very fortunate.

The next few hours were spent organizing the kitchen. Take-out was ordered and plenty of drinks were available. It was more like a party than work. There was a lot of laughter and storytelling, which is just what Jackson needed. About an hour into the project, Pete pulled Trey aside into the living room where they couldn't be overheard. "Do you know anything about what happened here two weeks ago?" Pete questioned. "No, I don't know what you're talking about," was Trey's response. Pete continued, "Two weeks ago someone broke into the house and trashed it. They pulled everything out of the cupboards in the kitchen, breaking the dishes all over the floor and spilling food everywhere. They even pulled all the sheets and quilts off the beds and left all of the towels that were on the towel racks on the floor. A couple of lamps were broken, too." "Who discovered it?" Trey was shocked to hear about this from Pete. "Some contractors went in to tie up some loose ends and they found the place a mess and called the police. The police notified me because I'm the contact number. I was able to get some people over to clean up and we replaced the broken dishes and lamps. An investigation is underway. I haven't told Jackson and I don't feel he needs to know yet. I'm just going to tell him that there were indications of some robberies locally and I think it would be wise to change his locks, replace his garage door opener, and put in a security system. What do you think?" "Oh yes, absolutely. He should definitely do all that. Do they have any idea who might have done this?" Trey was very worried. "The officers are still investigating, but I have a pretty good idea who it might be. I think it was Vanessa. I overheard Jackson and Vanessa having an argument on the phone a few weeks ago and I heard Jackson say, 'Go ahead and try! You've already taken everything and tried to make my life miserable.' He seemed to feel threatened. He was extremely uneasy when he finished the phone call." Trey countered, "But if Vanessa did it, how would she get a key or access to the property?" "I'm sure her daddy could take care of that." Suddenly Pete quieted down as he was being summoned to the kitchen.

Everyone was so kind and Jackson settled into his home with all of his friends' help. Carrie lingered every day for a few days, but eventually had to return to work and her busy schedule. Jackson went to rehab regularly, only to come home to a lonely house with no one around. He started eating out more and more just to expose himself to socializing and the company of others. Wine was always his beverage of choice at dinner, but Jackson didn't stop there. He would have a late night cocktail before bed and a handful of pills. Waking up with night terrors came more often during sleep and he began to slip into a deep depression.

Pete managed to get Jackson to talk to him when he was at rehab. "Do you remember the saying the Marines had about value?" "Not really." Jackson rolled his eyes at Pete as if he was expecting a lecture. And he got one. Pete went on, "uncommon value a common virtue." "Do you know what that means? It means that you and every other Marine has proven their worth or their value by their service; that develops into valor, a common virtue amongst Marines. Jackson you have value and you have proven your worth! Let your valor shine through during hard times. You will never lose your worth and you need to go forward with valor." Jackson peered at Pete and was quiet, but he was thinking about what he had said.

Jackson *did* doubt his worth and that was evident by the way he took care of himself. He frequented the club less often because he felt it was no place for a cripple in a wheelchair. Jackson became more recluse and solitary. His drinking graduated to an early morning start and continued throughout the day. Carrie checked on him often and realized from her daily calls that Jackson was in a dark place. Carrie was in love with Jackson and she couldn't stand idly by and watch him deteriorate in front of her eyes. She made a call to his family to let them know about the seriousness of the situation. Her call was answered with plans for a visit from Jackson's sister, Samantha. Sam, as she was affectionately called, was training to be a nurse at The University of Arizona and she had some time for a break coming up. Jackson's whole family had been there for him when he was first discharged and came home from the hospital, but they had business to attend to back in Flagstaff and couldn't stay as long as Jackson needed. So, Samantha's visit would be good for Jackson.

Plane tickets were booked for the following weekend and arrangements were made for Carrie to pick up Sam at the airport. Carrie was anxious about this visit. Jackson was unaware of their plans and she was worried about his response. Nevertheless, the time came for

Carrie to retrieve Sam and all her luggage from the airport. Carrie had previously described her vehicle and personal appearance to Sam. She drove a black, Jeep four-wheel-drive which had an American Flag decal in her rear window. Carrie wasn't really into politics that much but she was extremely patriotic, especially since she met Jackson. Carrie took comfort because she knew what Sam looked like from pictures that sat on Jackson's fireplace mantel, but Sam had never met Carrie. Carrie's vehicle slowly pulled up to the curb of passenger pickup. The traffic was bumper to bumper and lots of angry drivers were present. She frantically began looking for Sam because she only had limited time for parking. Both of them spotted each other at the same time and Sam waved, followed Carrie's gesture and then hurried to the car's trunk. She lifted her luggage, which consisted of a medium size blue canvas bag, and a carry-on bag that matched, into the trunk. Carrie had stepped out of the car to help. She gave Sam a big hug and rushing she said, "I'm *so* glad you are here. We have lots to talk about." Both women jumped into the car and fastened their seatbelts. Brief, short honks could be heard coming from vehicles behind Carrie that were waiting to park and pick up passengers. She put her blinker on and waited patiently for a clearing in the lane. Then she sped off quickly, took a deep breath and settled into the seat. Carrie glanced at Sam, noticing her striking beauty. Long blonde hair cascaded over her shoulders and her skin was kissed brown, evidence of the Arizona sunshine. "How was your flight?" Carrie gave a huge smile to Sam. "Tell me everything that has been going on with you."

Carrie and Sam visited nonstop during the hour and a half that it took for them to arrive at Jackson's home. Sam told Carrie all about nursing school and how much she loved it. She expounded a little on her social life, which seemed to Carrie to be somewhat short and brief and then Sam turned the subject to Jackson. Carrie told Sam in detail about the last few weeks since Jackson had arrived home. She told about all the support he had received and how well he was doing and then she ended by mentioning the break-in. Carrie cautiously told Sam not to mention it to Jackson just yet. They were discussing Jackson's health both mentally and physically when they arrived and pulled in to the driveway. The garage door was open and Jackson's red Mustang was parked inside.

"Wow! Is that Jackson's?" Sam pointed to the Mustang. "Yes, it is *and* it is equipped with hand controls and it is custom made to fit Jackson perfectly. It gives him a sense of independence to be able to drive himself to destinations and freedom to leave anytime he chooses." "That's amazing!" said Sam. Sam and Carrie made their way to the front door, dragging luggage behind them. There was a small ramp leading up to the front porch, in place of any steps. Carrie motioned for Sam to ring the doorbell. A couple of minutes went by and then the door gradually opened. Jackson sat in his wheelchair and held the door open. He had a blank expression on his face. "Surprise!" said Sam. "I would have warned you ahead of time, but I wanted this to be a surprise and spontaneous. Carrie helped me with all the arrangements. She's great by the way!" "What are you doing here?" Jackson furrowed his brow as he asked the question. He didn't look too pleased. Sam replied, "I thought you could use some company and I have a few days off from school. Besides I miss my big brother." Jackson cocked his head and looked over at Carrie, "So you're behind all this? And you went behind my back?" "I'm guilty. I knew you wouldn't agree to get some help unless I arranged it without you knowing. I'm sorry Jackson. It was done out of love, from both of us." Carrie turned to Jackson with a pleading look on her face as if to say, "Please let it be alright and just accept the help." Jackson let out a long, dragged-out "Ohhh… come in." He opened the door wider and pushed his wheelchair back to clear the way for Carrie and Sam to enter. Jackson showed Sam to the guest room and gave her time to settle in while he talked to

Carrie. In a low voice Jackson confronted Carrie, "What are you trying to do?" "I'm concerned about you and I am just trying to help." She retorted. "I don't need any help, not from you, not from anyone!" Jackson raised his voice slightly and then calmed himself. "Well, you do need help. You just don't realize it right now. So, swallow your pride and let me and Sam help you." Carrie put her arm around Jackson, but he flinched. She bent down to give him a kiss and smelled alcohol on his breath. "How much have you been drinking Jackson?" Carrie's worry deepened. "Not enough. And it is not your concern or any of your business." Jackson bellowed out his response and Carrie knew he wasn't himself. Carrie didn't want to make matters worse by further conversation, so she leaned down and quickly gave Jackson a peck on the cheek. "I'll talk to you tomorrow. Call if you two need anything." Even as she said it she knew that Jackson wouldn't call.

Sam woke up the next morning and fixed breakfast for herself and Jackson. She made his favorites, at least what she remembered to be his favorites-pancakes with lots of butter and syrup. To Sam's disappointment her brother didn't eat much but went straight to the bar and fixed himself a drink. Sam began asking questions: "Why do you drink so early? What kind of alcohol is it? Do you mix your medications with it?" Jackson stopped her in mid-sentence, "Enough! I drink early because I can. It is called a Moscow Mule and it is made with Vodka. And no I don't take my meds at the same time that I'm drinking." "Are you deliberately trying to kill yourself Jackson? I know you and this is not like you at all. What is going on? Please talk to me." Sam teared up as she pleaded with her brother. "Well, little sis, I am really not much use anymore and you're right; I'm not myself. I'm a has-been failure. I drink to cover up the pain and take meds to treat the effects of amputation and war injuries. And then, I go to rehab over and over to try to obtain an impossible goal, to walk again." Jackson tipped his head up and finished his drink. Then he sat the glass down hard on the counter. "Any more questions?" Jackson started to put his hands on the wheels of his chair as if he was getting ready to retreat to the other room. "Yes, one more. You know I love you Jackson, right? And I know you love me. I read every one of the letters you wrote to me while you were in Vietnam. I know you sacrificed for your country and your family, but you're home now and you don't need to sacrifice anymore. You have no more debts to settle. Teach me how to make a Moscow Mule and let me be in charge of your drinks and when you can have them. Please! If you love me, you will let me do this for you." Sam was becoming desperate. "Are you kidding? What's in this for me?" Jackson replied. "Uh, one less thing for you to worry about?" was Sam's sheepish response. They finally reached an agreement just as the sun was setting. "Do you want to grab something to eat?" Jackson smiled at Sam. "Yes, but you're going to have to teach me how to drive your car. Especially when you've been drinking." "I think I can manage that. Let's go!" Jackson picked up his keys and they ventured into the night. Everything was new and exciting to Sam. She gathered each experience and put them together to make a bouquet of memories.

They arrived at Jackson's favorite restaurant. It was a little pricey, but he wanted to show his sister a good time and spoil her during her visit. Jackson ordered for Sam, steak and lobster of course. Jackson laughed as he watched Sam struggle to crack the lobster shell to get to the meat. Sam ordered a cola and Jackson had his regular, red wine. As they were finishing their dinner, Jackson went to pour himself another glass of wine when Sam covered his glass with her hand and said, "You've had enough." "Have you ever had wine? And how would you know if it was enough?" Jackson seemed annoyed at her actions. "I have never had wine. Besides, I don't think I would like it. And you've had enough because you're driving and you had a drink before you left home." Sam was determined to hold Jackson accountable for their agreement. "How do you know you don't like it, if you haven't tasted it? Here, taste it." "No thanks Jackson. You know that I don't drink. Can we just go home?" Sam was anxious to leave and remove herself from the awkward situation.

Sam was sound asleep when she was awakened by several loud screams coming from Jackson's room. She ran to his bedside to find the bed violently shaking and Jackson yelling "Medic! Medic!" She stood by his bed and kept trying to verbally wake him up. Sam was cautious to not make the mistake of touching Jackson when he was having a night terror. The whole family learned about this right after Jackson came home from Vietnam. "Jackson! Jackson! Wake up. You're home. Come on Jackson!" Sam forcefully kept yelling at him until he finally responded. Jackson was breathing hard and rapidly and his shirt was drenched in perspiration. He punched the bed with his fist as he slowly woke up from the nightmare. "Sam? What are you doing in here?" Jackson seemed to be disoriented. "I heard you screaming and came in to check on you. Are you okay?" Sam's voice sounded a little fearful. "Yeah. Yeah. I'm fine. Go back to sleep. Sorry I woke you up." "That's okay Jackson. I'm here for you. Can you tell me what your nightmares are about?" "They're about Vietnam, people dying and me feeling helpless to do something about it. I constantly see women and children being tortured." He then cautiously told Sam about the pregnant woman that was brutally murdered in front of him. "And then I see explosion after explosion and relive losing my leg over and over." Sam fell silent for a moment and then with tears in her eyes she looked at her brother with more respect and love than ever. "This is horrific that you had to experience all of the carnage. No wonder you have nightmares and terrors. Anyone would! But Jackson none of this was your fault and you did your very best to right some wrongs in people's lives. You're not only my big brother but also my best friend and my hero." "I'm nobody's hero, but thanks for the compliment. I love you, too." Jackson fell back onto his pillow and brushed his fingers through his damp hair. Sam returned to the guest room. This would not be the only time this scenario would play out while she was there.

The breakfast aroma coming from the kitchen allured Jackson there. Sam talked him into eating more than he usually did and then he complimented her on the meal and headed to the dining room. It was late morning and he was accustomed to having his drink about this time. Sam was in the kitchen and cleaned up the dishes from breakfast. She went to the refrigerator and pulled out a bottle of Ginger Beer and three limes. Then she went to the liquor cabinet and grabbed a bottle of Vodka. She took note that it was half empty. Carefully Sam cut the limes on a clear plastic cutting board into wedge shapes. She poured the Ginger Beer in the glass, added a fourth of a cup of Vodka and squeezed the lime juice into the glass. After placing ice in the drink and one lime on the top she carried it into Jackson and waited for him to give his approval. When that was verified, she told Jackson that she and Carrie were going shopping while he was in rehab.

This routine was repeated daily on a regular basis. The activities that Sam and Carrie would participate in varied, depending on their moods. Most of the time they would go on shopping sprees; other times were spent in a salon getting pedicures and manicures. The three of them became really close and spent a lot of time together. Some evenings were spent having a game night or making chocolate-chip cookies. Jackson became the expert in cookie making. They popped popcorn on his new air-popper and watched movies on other occasions. Carrie and Sam noticed that Jackson's mood was changing significantly. He was more positive and cheerful and laughed much more than he used to laugh. His desire to drink decreased and he worked on breaking his smoking habit, one he had picked up in Vietnam. Sam and Carrie had a huge secret and they were waiting for the right time to tell Jackson. Sam told Carrie earlier that she had made an agreement with Jackson about his drinking and that she had been mixing his drinks for him.

Reluctantly Sam let Carrie in on her sneaky strategy. Every time she made his Moscow Mule, she decreased the Vodka just a tiny amount until he was getting a good fresh lime made with Ginger Beer. Carrie laughed so hard when she heard this but she added. "Jackson is going to have your hide!" "Probably." Sam said. "But it was totally worth it. He is so much healthier and happier now. He's even been able to decrease his pain medication." Both of them hugged each other and quietly celebrated their success.

It soon came time for Sam to return to school. Good-byes were difficult for both Carrie and Jackson. Carrie shouted good luck to Sam when she dropped her off at the airport. Sam waved as she entered the glass doors leading to the plane departures. The trip had been productive and helpful to Jackson, even though he had a hard time admitting it. Carrie found her way back to Jackson's home and was excited to spend some time alone together. She slowly opened the front door. "Hello? Hello, Jackson?" Carrie called out as she scanned the living room and kitchen trying to locate him. "I'm back here. I'll be right out." Jackson's voice came from the back bedroom. Carrie put the bags of take-out on the kitchen counter just as Jackson appeared in the doorway leading into the kitchen. She noticed he had taken a shower and was dressed up more than usual. "What's the occasion?" she asked. "Nothing. I just wanted to be at my best for you." Jackson grabbed her hand and pulled her close. "Come here," he said. Carrie found herself comfortably sitting on Jackson's lap. Jackson took her face in his hands and gave her a passionate kiss. Carrie softly rubbed the back of her hand and fingers against Jackson's cheek. She stood up and took her jacket off and placed it over one of the dining room chairs. She turned around and paused before she asked, "Are you hungry?" Carrie didn't want to take away from the mood. "I am starving." Jackson looked at Carrie to see what the menu might be. "Good! I got take-out from this little Chinese restaurant just down the road." Carrie was perplexed by Jackson's reaction. "Chinese? Really? Chinese Carrie? For me? You know how I feel about Chinese food, especially rice." "Oh, no! Oh. My goodness. I do know that. What was I thinking? Obviously I wasn't, thinking that is!" Carrie's face turned bright red and she began apologizing profusely. Jackson bellowed out a big hearty laugh and said, "That's okay. I'll order a pizza." His eyes were watering from laughing so hard.

Good times came and went for them. Routines lingered and were stretched out to last. Carrie took up where she left off at work and Jackson attended rehab. They were able to catch a few private moments here and there that helped to quench their desire to be together. Jackson was down in rehab with Pete and he had just finished 'walking the walk' which he sarcastically called walking along the ramp using the bars to steady himself. He was feeling physically good as he approached the end of this exercise. Jackson was sweaty and a little out of breath, but not feeling anything out of the ordinary. Everything went dark.

Suddenly Jackson found himself above the ground looking down on his own body. Pete was urgently administering CPR and a doctor was placing defibrillator paddles against his chest. He saw his body wrench and lift upward as they shocked him with several volts of electricity. Jackson wondered if he was dead and then thought how stupid that question was because if he wasn't dead, he wouldn't be in this predicament. Jackson became engulfed in a blinding bright white light. He looked up to see a horse, carrying his grandfather in the saddle, standing nearby. The horse was a majestic white stallion that was still and silent. His grandfather then pulled the reins and guided the horse toward Jackson. Before Jackson realized what was happening, his grandfather reached down and with one arm swooped Jackson up and onto the back of the stallion. Lights went flashing by in silence and traveling was unexplainable, but Jackson could feel them moving at a fast pace.

What seemed like minutes passed, but were actually seconds. His grandfather pulled on the reins and brought the horse to a complete stop. A few feet in front of them a waist-high white altar was placed. It was surrounded by beautiful greenery and flowers. On top of the altar laid a very large white leather book and a personage who Jackson didn't recognize stood behind it. He was dressed in white robes and seemed to glow. He motioned for Jackson to come. Jackson threw his leg off the saddle and used the stirrup with his other leg to dismount from the horse. It was then that Jackson noticed he had both of his legs and could feel and walk normally. Cautiously he approached the altar. The personage motioned for him to kneel. Jackson had never been very religious, only when he was young, but now he quickly reacted and knelt beside the altar.

Communicating in a way that was foreign and unexplainable, the personage began to speak to Jackson. Jackson understood every word. He instructed Jackson about the book that was before him. It was his book of life. The book slowly opened to a place that was about three fourths finished. The pages were thin and gold leafed and the writing was unrecognizable. Jackson was told that this was a record of his life, but his life was not over. He must return and finish his mission. The use of those exact words took Jackson back and he was startled. The environment here was peaceful and serene, he felt whole and complete. He didn't want to return to his life and so Jackson resisted the personage's instructions. Jackson's experience with the here-after was brief, but he must have agreed to comply because he began experiencing excruciating pain, none like he had ever experienced.

He felt his spirit combine with his physical body and he slowly opened his eyes. "Oh, Jackson, welcome back my friend! You really had us scared." Pete was tearing up as he spoke. There were IV's and monitors attached to Jackson and he was really disoriented from the dream or phenomenon or whatever it was that he just experienced. Jackson desperately wanted to tell Pete, but felt Pete would think he was crazy. Jackson actually wondered if he was crazy, but this experience was so real that it assured him he was sane and very much alive. Dr. Zyaire entered the room where Jackson had been transferred from rehab. Jackson had fond memories about Dr. Zyaire and considered him not only an excellent doctor, but an amazing friend. "You know, Mr. Montgomery, you are constantly defying medical standards and norms. It seems to be your expertise. You were recorded to be medically dead for seven minutes. They usually call the code to be finished at five, but your colleague, Pete insisted on continuing. It was explained to him that you could possibly have brain damage from the lack of oxygen, but he was persistent and determined to prove them wrong. And I might say, he succeeded." Dr. Zyaire was proud to give Jackson the information. He continued, "All tests show that you are within normal ranges on your blood work and your EEG is normal, no brain damage. Congratulations Jackson, you've broken the odds again. Once more, it's good to see you, just not under these circumstances."

Another person of interest emerged from the background. As soon as their eyes met, Carrie gently threw herself on Jackson's chest and began sobbing tears of relief and joy. "Awe, be careful," Jackson grunted. "My chest is really sore from CPR. I feel like my ribs are broken." "I'm sorry," Carrie said and she raised off his chest but still managed to smother him with kisses. "What happened?" Jackson inquired. "I was feeling just fine." "They don't know the particulars but classified it as a cardiac and respiratory arrest." Carrie was perplexed about the cause, though. She and Pete proceeded to tell Jackson the details of when he collapsed down in rehab and how Pete did continuous CPR and another nurse bagged him while he was transferred to another treatment room. "They used the defibrillator four times and they were just about to call the code when Pete seemed insistent on giving you a few seconds more. And then on the fifth time, they shocked you into a normal sinus rhythm and you began to breathe on your own." Carrie retold the incident with intensity. Jackson was stabilized now and everyone left his room but Carrie. She cemented herself next to his bed and didn't budge.

Jackson insisted that Carrie take breaks and get herself something to eat and drink. But she wholeheartedly stuck with Jackson by his side. She brought her food into his room and occasionally snuck Jackson's favorites into him to replace the hospital food that he was tiring of quickly. "Remember that night that I brought you a hamburger and a chocolate shake and we shared dinner together when you were hospitalized before?" "Yes, I definitely remember that." Jackson squeezed Carrie's hand. "Well, that's when I first began to fall in love with you Mr. Montgomery." "I'm sure I didn't notice," Jackson teased. Carrie blurted out an exasperated "Oh, you!" "But," Jackson paused. "It was because I was so caught up in my feelings for you that I couldn't concentrate. I love you Carrie Langston and I am so glad I am still here to show you how much!" Jackson clasped her hand in his and raised it to his lips. He gently kissed her hand while he lovingly gazed into her soft blue eyes. Throughout the evening Jackson tried to gain the courage to tell Carrie about his dying experience but every time he was really close, he talked himself out of it. Then after Carrie had been giving him some prolonged looks, she broke the ice. "Okay, marine, something is bothering you. Let it out! Talk to me. Jackson I hope you know you can talk to me about anything." "Yeah, I know." Jackson took a deep breath and thought to himself "Here goes."

He began, "Carrie you have always been a devout Christian and come from a religious background. You've always made religion a big part of your life, right?" "Yes, that's true. But that doesn't mean that I haven't had my struggles and questions." Carrie was beginning to wonder where this was leading. "Just bear with me for a minute."

Jackson leaned onto his side so he could talk more directly to Carrie and see her face. "I haven't always been a religious man. My parents raised me in the church but I fell away when I went to Vietnam. It was a Godless war to me and I stopped believing in Him. I wondered if heaven existed for the many soldiers that were killed. And, I knew for sure that heaven didn't exist for me; I was a killer and had done things I felt God, if there was a God, could never forgive. I have remained with that point of view from when I returned from the war, through the marriage to Vanessa, the accident and divorce. That is until last week when I had that dying experience. It has completely changed me Carrie. What I am about to tell you, I have told no one else."

Jackson took a good hour and a half telling Carrie about what he had seen and heard when he was 'dead'. His face lit up as he spoke about his grandfather and the stallion. He admitted how disappointed he was when he was given the instructions that he had to return. "The personage said I had to 'finish my mission'! Finish my mission Carrie! That's what I've been trying to do since I joined the Marine Corps. Who would have known that I had a mission to complete here? And I truly believe that God, had me experience this event to show me what that mission is. I don't expect you to believe me, but I hope you do." Carrie was not dry-eyed when she responded, "Of course I believe you, Jackson. I have my Christian faith that witnesses to me that what you have seen and heard is true. The bigger question I think, is what do you think? And how do you feel about all of this?" Jackson took a few minutes and then looked Carrie directly in the eyes, "I can definitely tell you it has changed me and given me a different perspective on life. I feel more worth and value as a human being. I want to do more and be a better person. I realize how short life can be, and I want to live the life I have left to the fullest. And, I'm hoping you will share that life with me." Carrie lightened the conversation, "Why, Marine, are you asking me to marry you?" The room became silent and they both decided that was a subject for another time.

Chapter Six

LOVE, SET, MATCH

The doorbell rang and Jackson hurried from the kitchen where he was fixing himself a turkey-club sandwich. He opened the door to find two police officers standing in the doorway. Jackson recognized one of the officers, Officer Gonzales who was one of the law enforcement personnel who investigated his car accident. "Hello, Mr. Montgomery. I don't know if you remember me but I am Officer Vargas Gonzales and this is Officer Liam Jenkins. We were assigned to make an inquiry about the break-in you experienced a few weeks ago. May we come in?" Officer Gonzales was doing all the talking. "Sure. Come in and sit down." Jackson made a motion toward the living room sofa. "May I get you something to drink, a soda or water?" Jackson was anxious for them to get right to the point and answer the questions that he had lingering in his mind, but he didn't want to appear unhospitable. "No thank you. We're fine," replied Gonzales. The two officers settled on the sofa and Jackson pulled his wheelchair close. They politely removed their hats and set them on their laps. Gonzales began, "We understand there was property destroyed but nothing of value was missing. Is that correct?" Jackson nodded his head with a yes reply. "We want you to know that a person of interest was apprehended just shortly after the incident. A passing jogger reported a man dressed in a black hoodie and a black ski mask exiting your front door. Our witness said the man seemed to be in a hurry and kept looking around as if he was expecting someone. When the jogger heard about the break-in on the news, he came forward with his information. The man that broke into your residence has a record and fortunately, did not cover his tracks very well. He left fingerprints and we were able to pull up a match in our system. We can't release his name yet because of the ongoing investigation, the upcoming court appearance, and charges that are pending against him. But we can tell you he was hired to do the job." "What? Who hired him?" Jackson became more perplexed as the story grew longer. "I'm sorry to tell you this, sir, but it was your ex-wife Vanessa Remington." "Do you know this for sure? How did you find out it was her?" Jackson sounded desperate. This time Officer Jenkins continued, "We followed a paper trail from the money the suspect was paid. It led to a large deposit of five thousand dollars made in his account the day after the break-in. When he was officially arrested, he gave up your ex-wife as the one who hired him. We got a warrant to seize her bank accounts and found a five-thousand-dollar withdrawal the morning after the break-in." "It seems odd that you keep calling it a break-in, said Jackson "because there was no sign of forced entry." "You're right." agreed Officer Jenkins. "The suspect was given a key to your home by Vanessa Remington." The facts remained that Jackson's home had been broken into, whether by forced entry or the use of a key. It didn't really matter to him at this point. His insides were festering up a sick feeling and thoughts of betrayal in the biggest way. "Sir, we just want you to know that a warrant for her arrest has been issued and the other suspect is in jail awaiting trial." The officers concluded, "If you have any questions or you need anything you let us know immediately. I'll leave my card with my number on it." Officer Gonzales leaned toward the coffee table and placed the card so it was in plain sight. The two officers stood up, put their hats on and walked toward the door.

Gonzales turned back as they left, "We're so sorry for your misfortune, Jackson. We will do everything possible to bring you justice." Jackson sat in the doorway and watched the two of them get into their patrol car and drive slowly away. He heard the loose gravel that was at the end of his driveway pinging against the patrol car.

Jackson slammed the front door. He glanced at the lock and recalled getting all his locks changed just after the break-in; which now caused him to have retrospective thoughts about why he changed them. Pete had suggested it and Jackson felt relief. He clenched his fists and hammered the arms of his chair. Verbal expressions of disbelief and anger were spoken out loud as if someone was there to hear. "Why would she do this?" he yelled. "This is unbelievable! I really don't know for sure that this is where it stops, or if there is more to come." Jackson had a tinge of fear come over him when he thought about Mr. Remington and his illegal dealings. Jackson had a gut feeling that Mr. Remington thought he knew too much about his operations. He wasn't sure what Remington was capable of when it came to protecting his business ventures and his daughter. Jackson had a strong urge to get himself a drink to help calm his nerves, and then he remembered that he had dumped all of his liquor out and trashed all of his cigarettes. So he fumbled for the phone.

"Hello, Jackson? Are you alright?" Carrie was concerned hearing from him this early in the day. "Not really. Do you think you could get off work a little early and come grab some dinner with me? I'll tell you all about it then." Jackson waited for her response. "Sure I can do that. You sound upset? Do you want to talk now?" Jackson assured Carrie that he would survive until he saw her. He told her that he would pick her up at eight. Jackson wanted to give her time to change and freshen up after work. "I'll see you then. I love you Jackson." It was just what he needed to hear from her. Jackson ended the call with Carrie and immediately dialed his lawyer. He wanted to be one step ahead of the Remingtons and protect himself, if that was even possible. Jackson contemplated confronting Mr. Remington at the club, but his lawyer gave strong instructions to not do that. He advised Jackson to lay low and not be confrontational. Admonishing Jackson to be patient just irritated Jackson more. His lawyer told him to let the police do their jobs and let the detective handle it. Jackson wasn't so sure that they would be able to do what it would ultimately take to defuse the situation. He resolved, against his lawyer's advice that, he wasn't going to sit idly by and do nothing.

Time dragged, like trying to walk an unwilling dog, while Jackson waited for his and Carrie's date night to arrive. Jackson pulled up in front of Carrie's three-story apartment building and signaled with a special honk. It was customary between them that when Jackson picked her up that he honked a signature honk that only Carrie recognized and let her know he was out front. Carrie's apartment building had several sets of stairs which made it impossible for Jackson to go meet her at her door. This way he was at least able to watch her come down the stairs and reach the car safely. Jackson looked up and enjoyed watching Carrie descend. She was so beautiful and graceful. Delicately she floated down each step, occasionally tucking her long blonde hair behind one ear. When she reached the last step she grinned and vigorously waved at Jackson. "Hi!" She said as she opened the passenger door and softly slipped into the seat. "You look stunning. Are you hungry?" Jackson waited for a slight minute before pulling onto the street. "Thank you, and yes, I am starving." Jackson suggested to Carrie a fine Mexican restaurant that served superb food located on Colorado Boulevard. They both agreed on the destination. Jackson impatiently pulled out onto the street as if he was in a hurry. "Jackson, what's the hurry? I am hungry, but not red-flag hungry. You can slow down." "I can, but I'm not going to just because you told me to." Jackson's tone was rude and disturbing. "Sorry," was all Carrie said. Not much conversation took place between them after that, and the drive was silent and mentally exhausting. When they arrived at the restaurant, Jackson and Carrie exited the car and the valet parked for them. Jackson took Carrie's hand and looked into her eyes. "I am so, so sorry. Please forgive me. I was a complete idiot and very rude. I apologize. It's no excuse, but I am extremely stressed right now and I shouldn't have taken out my frustrations on you. Please, let's just have a nice dinner and I promise that I'll behave." "You better!" Carrie countered. She leaned down and gave him a quick kiss. "You're forgiven."

The hostess seated the couple at a table in the back, which Jackson preferred. Carrie grasped the back of her chair and started to pull it from the table. Jackson put his hand up to signal her to stop and then *he* pulled out Carrie's chair for her and seated her like the gentleman he was. Jackson pulled his wheelchair up to the table and picked up the menu. Carrie had looked over the menu and decided what she was going to order. The entire restaurant was designed with a South-of-the-border flair, including the menus. Bright colors of turquoise, red and yellow were cheerful and inviting. The environment was calming yet enticing, and lights were dim and romantic. The waiter approached and asked if he could get them anything to drink and Jackson quickly responded with, "I'll have a Coke, please." "I'll have the same." Carrie chimed in. All the employees wore a dark red polo shirt with the restaurant's name embroidered on the left chest just under the left side of the collar. A black cotton apron was tied around the waiter's waist and they all wore black pants. Their waiter eventually brought their drinks and then took their order. Without talking to each other beforehand, both Carrie and Jackson ordered the exact same thing. Their minds seemed to be synchronized in their thinking processes. They laughed about it and finished one another's sentence. "Wow! That was..." "Weird," Carrie finished Jackson's thought. Then she became more serious. "What is bothering you, Jackson?" Carrie started to quiz him about half-way through their meal. "I had two officers come to my home this morning."

Jackson proceeded to tell Carrie all the details of the officers' visit and how upsetting it was to hear the vital information that they brought with them. He was compounded with the emotions of disappointment and anger during the whole conversation. Carrie listened carefully and reached over and clasped Jackson's hand. She could tell he was fighting back emotions and tears as he talked. "What are you going to do?" Carrie asked. "Well, I called my lawyer to see if there were any legal ramifications and he told me there wasn't much that I could do more than what was already being done by the police. I don't know Carrie. I just don't trust the Remington family. I am afraid that I am in danger and I feel you are, too." Jackson was sincerely concerned. "How can that be?" Carrie added. "They don't even know who I am." "Oh, yes they do! They know all about you, where you live, our relationship, and probably more." Jackson expressed his worries forcefully, hoping he could get her to understand the seriousness of the situation. He also suggested to Carrie that she should change her locks like he had done. "Don't you think that's a little over-kill?" Carrie's brows furrowed and she tilted her head to emphasize her question. "No, I don't. I really don't! I just have a gut-instinct that we should be extremely careful. I don't know if I would survive if anything happened to you. I love you and I don't want to lose you." "Awe, now you're getting gushy." Carrie giggled and that seemed to spark a reaction from Jackson that was unexpected. "Carrie! Will you please take this seriously? I feel responsible for putting you in danger!" Jackson's voice raised enough that it drew attention from other patrons in the restaurant.

The drive home was mending and cathartic. Dinner hadn't exactly been as calming as Jackson would have hoped, but the drive home made up for any gaps that their dinner conversation had. Carrie took on a more serious approach to listening that enabled Jackson's anxieties to flow from him and dissipate. He relaxed more but didn't dismiss his valid concerns. Carrie broke a long pause, "Maybe you should go to the police with your feelings of being threatened?" Jackson grunted, "They won't do anything. I'll have to handle this myself." Jackson pulled up to Carrie's apartment building and you could hear the sound of gravel against his tires as he slowed down and then came to a stop. He leaned over and gave Carrie a kiss on her cheek and then a passionate kiss on the lips. "I'm sorry I burdened you with all of this tonight. I really needed you, especially you. I want you to be safe. I need to keep you safe." "I understand." Carrie placed her hand on Jackson's cheek. "We're in this together Jackson. I am not going anywhere. You can't scare me away and neither can the Remington family!"

Against all the advice that Jackson had received the day before, he defied it completely and went to the club the next day. His plans were to confront Mr. Remington and try to reason with his ex-father-in-law. As his car approached Lake Hills Country Club, his stomach began churning. He was bombarded with memories of his golfing career, the many tours he went on, good friends made and of course his marriage to Vanessa. One of the golf caddies recognized him and Jackson tipped him for parking his vehicle. Jackson made his way to a wheelchair ramp located to the far side of the main stairway entrance. Finding himself inside the massive lobby, he directly went to the front desk. "Mr. Montgomery! It's great to see you again, sir." The desk clerk had a huge smile on his face and seemed eager to help Jackson. "Is Mr. John Remington around today?" "No, sir. Mr. Remington has been gone for a while. I was told that he is staying in the city to do business. I'm sorry. Can I help you with anything else?" "No, that's okay. I'll just have to catch him another time." Jackson was about to leave when he felt compelled to wander over to the Pro Shop.

He sat by the door and scanned the inside of the shop reminiscing about the times he had spent there. Abruptly, he stared at the isle where the golf balls were. There stood Joe looking professional and sharp as ever. Jackson knocked on the door and waved to get Joe's attention. Joe immediately dropped what he was doing and opened the door. "Jackson! Get in here. It's been too long!" Joe's excitement thrilled Jackson and the two of them started an immediate conversation. After a bit of catching up, Joe leaned down to ask Jackson an important question, "How would you like to come help me at the shop? I am the athletic director here and I have become greatly involved with the tennis program. I'm behind on racket stringing and could sure use your help." At first Jackson was offended, "Is this glamourized basket weaving, Joe? Because I'm not that hard up!" "No, no! It's a legitimate, complicated process and I need you. Besides, I think you would enjoy it and it would bring you back to the club. Jackson, you belong here." "Show me this process." Jackson reluctantly replied.

The two of them made their way to the back of the shop where a large room opened up and looked more like a machine shop rather than a pro shop. There were four racket stringing machines that took the appearance of a metal work bench with a vice located at each end. Several levers and a wheel that held bolts of tennis string were strategically placed on the bench. A tennis racket was secured to two of the benches. Joe walked over to the closest one and Jackson followed. Joe slowly and carefully demonstrated to Jackson each step of the process. It took about forty-five minutes to string a racket. When it was finished Joe grasped the handle with one hand and bounced the fatty part of his hand against the strings to show Jackson the importance of the tension placed on them. He explained that the string tension makes a huge difference in the racket's performance. The players depend on it. Joe went on to explain that some of the more experienced and professional players request a particular string tension for their personal rackets. Jackson was enticed and asked a lot of questions that surprised even himself. "Here, hold this." Joe handed the newly strung racket to

Jackson. "Swing it! How does it feel?" "A little awkward, but kind of good." Jackson smiled as he swung the racket back and forth alongside of his wheelchair. "Why don't you think about it and come over to the club in the next couple of days and you can hit some balls with me." "Joe, I am in a wheelchair, in case you haven't noticed!" Jackson felt like Joe was appeasing him. "And since when should that stop the infamous Jackson Levi Montgomery?" Joe laughed and reminded Jackson of the alleged impossible water ski run and eventually a snow ski run that he had accomplished just a year ago. "Okay. You win. I'll come by tomorrow." Jackson shook Joe's hand and they both grasped each other's forearm.

Jackson was up earlier than usual and met Joe at one of the tennis courts at the club. Joe provided him with a strong but light tennis racket that had a handle to fit his grip perfectly. He placed a square wire box with two long handles attached to it next to Jackson. The handles came together to form a way to carry it in one position and when the handles were pulled to the bottom of the box they formed legs for the box to stand on. It was filled with bright yellow brand new tennis balls. A wire lid opened on top to allow the player to reach in for a new ball when needed. Joe explained that it was called a "hopper" and was essential for tennis practice. "After you empty the box you can retrieve all the balls by pushing the wire box down on top of a ball hard. This is done while holding the two wire handles together at the top. The ball is pushed through the wire at the bottom and placed back in the box." Joe watched Jackson's reaction. It was one of surprise, with a little bit of disbelief.

Jackson started off his tennis skills by learning the elements of the backhand swing and the forehand swing. Joe would throw balls at him and have him return them over the net. Jackson was amazing and caught on really quickly. His strength was an advantage for his returns but especially helped as he began to maneuver his wheelchair around the court as Joe increased the difficulty to return by throwing the balls just out of Jackson's direct reach. It was an indoor court so they didn't have to battle the heat and sun and there was plenty of water for them. Jackson was relentless and soon became obsessed with the newfound sport and challenge. His occasional visit grew into a daily occurrence, and when he wasn't stringing rackets, he was playing tennis. Jackson was able to pick up a little extra cash from the racket stringing that he did but he immediately spent it on tennis supplies. Eventually, he purchased his own racket and strung it himself. Jackson worked so hard on the court to maneuver his wheelchair quickly that he developed calluses and blisters on the palms of his hands. Tight, light-weight leather gloves were the solution. They reminded Jackson of the golf glove he used to wear on his left hand.

Jackson quickly mastered most of the skills that Joe had taught him. The next challenge was the tennis serve, which proved to be more difficult. To serve Jackson had to wheel his chair into place at the back of the court on either the right or left side, depending on the serve status. In one motion he was required to toss a tennis ball with his left hand straight up over and barely behind his head. Then as it descended he brought his racket, held by his right hand, in back of his shoulder and raised it over his head to come in contact with the ball at exactly the right place and time. The racket would hit the ball sending it scaling over the net at tremendous speed and he finished the serve by sweeping the racket in front of himself. Vision had to be focused on the ball and placement was crucial. Jackson then, with a lightening reaction, wheeled himself into the middle of the court just a few feet away from the net to ready himself for the return. If he intercepted the ball before it got too far over the net and was able to forcefully slam it back into the opponent's court, he usually gained a point in his favor. Jackson spent hours upon hours practicing and lifting weights to increase his strength and power. He shared his whole experience with Carrie, every detailed step. For a brief moment, his concerns about the Remingtons were put on the back burner and he rarely gave them any thought.

"Carrie, why don't we go out and celebrate tonight?" Jackson was having his nightly conversation with the love of his life. "Celebrate what?" Carrie was curious. "Celebrate my accomplishments with tennis. Besides, I have a surprise for you." "You're always full of surprises, Jackson. You keep life interesting and exciting. Actually, a big juicy steak sounds perfect!" "Okay, see you at seven." Jackson hung up the phone with a big grin on his face. Life was going well for him right now and he felt he had a lot to celebrate.

Jackson and Carrie settled in to their dinner easily with the usual red-carpet treatment and celebrity service. When the waiter brought them refreshment he casually asked, "If you don't mind me asking, sir, I was wondering if the rumor was true, that you've taken up tennis?" "News travels fast, I see. Yes. The rumor is true, but it is wheelchair tennis, not regular tennis." Jackson felt somewhat uncomfortable with the conversation. "That's incredible sir! How do you do that? I've never heard of wheelchair tennis." The waiter couldn't seem to pull himself away from the table and the conversation. "It's a fairly new sport and you might say I'm one of the pioneers in this area. I find it extremely challenging but also very rewarding." "Well, I plan to follow you in this sport like I followed you in golf. It's been a real pleasure speaking with you. Thank you." Leaving the conversation at that, the waiter returned to his work. Jackson turned to Carrie, "How did he ever find out about this?" "When you're famous, Jackson, your life is no longer your own. Besides, I find it endearing that so many people know who you are and follow you." Carrie raised her coke glass for a toast. "Here's to you Jackson. New beginnings again!" They put their glasses together causing a faint clinking sound and then they finished their drinks. Jackson motioned for the waiter to bring refills. "What is the surprise? The suspense is killing me!" Carrie rapidly rubbed her hands together above the table so Jackson could tell she was anxious. "Oh, yeah. That. I have bought a brand new wheelchair that has wheels that are designed to turn rapidly and quickly with very little effort. It will be amazing and help me so much with my game." "That's great!" Carrie then leaned in and asked, "When do I get to see you play?"

Joe brought some unexpected news to Jackson the following day at the club. "You won't believe this." He started out. "I was contacted by the newly formed Wheelchair Tennis Association. They are interested in promoting wheelchair tennis nationwide and they asked for my expertise *and* they want to meet you!" "That's crazy!" Jackson lifted from the seat of his chair slightly because of the excitement. "Why do they want to see me?" Joe went on, "Well, I sort of told them about how phenomenal you were and I sent a copy of your serving speed to them. They were impressed to say the least. They want to set up some tournaments, and the first one will be hosted by Lake Hills." Joe could not hardly contain himself. "You mentioned my serving speed. What's that?" Jackson was really interested now. "It's the recorded speed of the ball you serve. I recorded you at 147 mph. It's one of the fastest ever recorded and new to wheelchair tennis." "I don't know what to say. When is all this going to take place?" Joe answered, "In two weeks. We have two weeks to whip you into shape. Are you ready to become famous all over again?" Jackson shrugged his shoulders. It wasn't about being famous for him. It was about going forward with valor.

During the weeks that Jackson spent perfecting his tennis skills, there were questionable events taking place. One evening Jackson came out of the club after a long and hard work out. He was tired and wanted to go home, shower, call Carrie and crash. Jackson closely approached his vehicle, when he noticed his rear tires had been slashed. Suspecting someone was waiting for him, Jackson spun his chair around to be able to scan the parking lot of anything suspicious. He headed back to the club where he called the police and then the roadside service he had with his car insurance company. The police were there in a matter of minutes and questioned Jackson about his association with Mr. Remington. Jackson told them that he had been threatened indirectly by him, but he couldn't prove it. The police responded to Jackson's statement with, "Sir, do you have anyone else that would want to harm you or someone who might be considered an enemy? The reason I ask is because, and I didn't know if you knew, Mr. Remington is in prison. He was convicted and sentenced last week. It's very unlikely that he had anything to do with this." "With all due respect, that's where you are wrong. I worked for him for a couple of years and he has unbelievable connections all over the state, everywhere! He hires people to do his dirty work, just like his daughter did when my house had a break in. I believe that was a warning from him then and I feel this is too. For some reason he thinks I know his business secrets or too much about his dealings because I worked for him and I was once married to his daughter. But, I don't know anything. He just doesn't know that. Still, he is trying to warn me to not say anything or I will face consequences. There is literally no one else that could be behind all of this." "That's quite a theory, Mr. Montgomery, and I am not doubting that theory could be right, but it does need some extensive investigation. Right now we don't have any evidence leading toward a suspect in this particular case. I'm sorry. We'll get back to you if we have anything." With that comment the officer tipped his hat at Jackson and left, just as the tire repair company arrived.

Jackson was mentally and physically exhausted when he arrived home. He barely had the energy to shower and fix himself something to eat. He transferred into the recliner in the living room and almost fell asleep before he remembered to call Carrie. "Hello, beautiful! How was your day?" Jackson felt a renewed energy as he anticipated hearing her voice. "It was really good. Today was a descent day for a change. How about yours?" Carrie anticipated a positive response. "Oh, life has been exciting again, today. Someone slashed my tires. They were flat when I came out to the parking lot. I didn't notice anyone around so I went back into the club and called the police and somebody to come repair my tires." "Oh, Jackson! This is scary. Did the police know who had done this?" "No. They actually asked me who I thought had done this and when I told them Remington, they treated me like I was paranoid or crazy. They said he couldn't have done it because he is in prison, which I didn't realize at the time. But, I still strongly feel that Remington had something to do with all this." "So, they didn't believe you? Are they even going to check out the possibility?" Carrie's voice was anxious and her speech more rapid. "They appeased me and said they would look into it, but I have my doubts. I am calling my lawyer tomorrow and he and I are going to pay Mr. Remington a visit in prison." "Jackson! That's crazy! What are you thinking? That could make things worse and put you in more danger. Promise me that you'll be careful." Carrie was almost tearful sounding because she knew that she couldn't talk Jackson out of this ridiculous idea. "I will and I'll call you as soon as I get home. I'm really tired now so I am just going to crash for the night. I love you." Jackson barely heard Carrie respond with "I love you, too." He fell asleep in the recliner with the phone still in his hand.

 Jackson contacted his lawyer, Mr. Richard Herchek, the next day and gave him his proposal. Reluctantly, his lawyer agreed and told Jackson he would meet him at the prison. The heavy metal doors of the prison made a banging sound that echoed in the hallway of the entrance. Mr. Herchek greeted Jackson and they briefly sat down to discuss the conversation that Jackson would have with Mr. Remington. "Remember, don't offer any information that he doesn't know and ask questions, don't accuse or he will shut down and might not talk to you." Mr. Herchek was precise about what Jackson was to say. "Yes, okay I've got it." Jackson tried not to show his nervousness. Jackson was practiced at controlling his facial expressions so his lawyer didn't suspect anything awry. Both men produced identification with picture ID and proof of citizenship. Their bags were searched and they were asked to leave them up front. They were told they could retrieve them later. Jackson passed through a special metal detector that accommodated his wheelchair and Mr. Herchek was searched by a security guard. This last procedure brought the reality of what he was about to do to Jackson in an abrupt way. He swallowed hard as he wheeled himself behind the prison guard that was showing him the place where he would be able to speak with the prisoner. Mr. Herchek followed close behind. Loud buzzers went off as they passed from one corridor to another. They eventually came to a large room that had cubbyholes partitioned and spaced with dividers between them. In front was a shelf to lean your arms on and a phone on the wall to the right. You looked through thick, clear shatter-proof plastic. Jackson pulled his wheelchair up to the shelf as close as he could and locked the wheelchair brakes. A prison guard on the opposite side of the plastic leaned down, picked up the phone and motioned for Jackson to do the same. "Are you ready?" he asked. "This is how you will communicate with the prisoner. You will have thirty minutes, unless the visit needs to be cut short. We will be behind the prisoner and monitoring the situation at all times. Any questions?" "No. I have no questions. I am ready." Jackson said it with a tone like he was trying to convince himself that he was.

    The guard turned and opened a door that had a loud buzz precede it. Another guard ushered Mr. Remington into the room. He was dressed in an orange jumpsuit and looked scruffy, as if he hadn't shaved in days. His face was expressionless and dark. The guards removed his handcuffs but not his ankle chains. Remington slowly settled into the chair provided and lifted the phone to his ear. "Well, what a surprise Jackson. To what do I owe the privilege of this visit? Is it because you missed me, Jackson?" Jackson knew right then it was going to be a challenge to talk to Remington, but he took a deep breath and proceeded. "First of all, I want to clear some things up with you. The whole time I was married to your daughter I concentrated on my golfing career and selling real estate. I never was involved in any of your business dealings. I had and have no knowledge of what led you to here and to be arrested. I had absolutely nothing to do with it. I am still trying to put my life back together and I don't think about anything else. I am not interested in what goes on in your life at all! I'm asking you to call off your people and stop threatening me. I have nothing to tell the authorities. Please be reasonable Mr. Remington." There was a long silence as Remington leaned forward and directly stared into Jackson's eyes. He finally responded but with condescending sarcasm, "Well, Jackson I'm glad to see you are putting your life back together. Good for you! You do owe me for some of that success you have enjoyed. But you see, I discovered rats in my organization. Rats are an unwanted pestilence. They're nothing but trouble and can cause rapid infestation, and that is why one has to stop them immediately and eradicate the rodent. I don't like rats, Jackson. Some big rat knew enough to put me here and now I have to take care of business." Jackson's lawyer stepped into the conversation. "Mr. Remington, I advise you to not threaten my client. These threats can be used against you in a court of law if you decide to make an appeal." Mr. Remington sing-songed his reply, "Relax. I'm no threat to Mr. Montgomery. Why I am here and he is out there. I think he is being a little dramatic and paranoid. I suggest, Jackson that you concentrate on your new tennis career and your beautiful girlfriend, Carrie. Is that her name?" Jackson lost his cool and became defensive. He slammed his fist on the shelf and uttered his own threat, "Don't you dare hurt her or I'll…" "You'll what? You're pathetic! Guard! We're through here." Remington hung up the phone and flashed a condescending grin at Jackson and his lawyer. Mr. Herchek took hold of Jackson's arm, "Come on; let's get out of here."

Jackson and his lawyer spent the most part of the next day trying to put forth a plan of action against Remington, but seemed to keep hitting a dead end. Frustrated, Jackson blurted out, "So, I just do nothing? What am I supposed to do? Wait until I get killed or worse, Carrie gets hurt?" "Be extra diligent with precautions. I don't think Remington wants blood on his hands. He just wants to scare you." Mr. Herchek was trying to calm Jackson and at the same time give him some solid advice. "I guess you're right. I plan on being extra careful but mark my word. He *will* slip up and when he does, I will be right there to catch him. He's not going to negatively affect my life anymore." Jackson left his lawyer's office more determined than ever to silence Remington's threats and dissolve any association with him at all. He put his thoughts deep in his mind. He had an important meeting at the club with Joe and an official Wheelchair Tennis Association representative. It felt good and Jackson was relieved to think about tennis once again. He felt he was right in his element when he was on the tennis court.

Jackson took some extra time getting ready for the meeting at the club. He wanted to make a good impression. As he approached the ramp leading into the club, he hesitated. Jackson briefly thought about his dying experience and his second chance at life. He anticipated this opportunity with hope and gratitude. He silently bowed his head and gave thanks to God for all his blessings. Jackson had never prayed before, but felt this was a good time to start. He pushed his wheelchair up the ramp with ease. Jackson's arms had become massive with solid muscle and his bench pressing of weights had skyrocketed. He could now bench press more than 350 pounds. Jackson straightened his tie and made sure the knot was centered before he entered the foyer of the club. He thought to himself, "Here's to going forth with valor!" Jackson approached the desk and was greeted by a cheerful clerk. "Mr. Jackson. Welcome. Mr. Fielding said for you to meet them on tennis court number three." Jackson acknowledged the instructions with a polite 'thank you'. The distance from the front desk to the entrance to the courts seemed to be longer. Then Jackson realized it was just his nerves.

Jackson swung open the huge doors that led to the court. Bright lights and the faint smell of a locker room greeted him. He glanced to his right and saw Joe motion to him. "Come over here Jackson and let me introduce you to our guest and future partner." Jackson drew near to the two men and Joe reached out his arm and waved it in Jackson's direction. "Jackson Montgomery, let me introduce you to Mr. Robert Cornel. He is one of the Wheelchair Tennis Association's CEOs." Mr. Cornel shook Jackson's hand and said, "Glad to finally meet you Mr. Montgomery. I have heard so much about you. I hear from several sources, and not just Joe, that you are an up and coming star in wheelchair tennis." Jackson humbly responded, "I am enjoying it very much and I look forward to playing in some tournaments." Jackson always felt awkward when people complimented him in public. "We are going to try and make that happen right here at The Lake Hills Country Club. We are planning on sponsoring tournaments for wheelchair players nationwide, starting here. The idea has been in the process for several months and all the tournament particulars are ready. We just needed a place to start. I contacted Joe and now we are here scheduling the first wheelchair tournament. It's a great thing that there are enough players who want to compete and we can accommodate them now," he added.

The meeting was cordial and went smoothly. Mr. Cornel explained the rules of wheelchair tennis to Jackson. Jackson was relieved to know that the only difference in wheelchair tennis and able-bodied tennis was the amount of bounces the player was allowed before having to return the ball to the opponent's court. Wheelchair tennis players were allowed two bounces instead of one. The tournament would be played by bracket elimination with a consolation bracket available. Jackson's excitement grew as they discussed more details about the event. The tennis tournament was scheduled for two weeks, beginning on the Friday and Saturday of that weekend. Jackson left knowing that he had a lot of preparation to do. Thankfully, Joe took care of all the logistics and all Jackson had to worry about was playing well. Information about the tournament spread fast and in no time there were surprisingly thirty players registered.

The next entire week found Jackson practicing at the club from sunrise to sunset. He purchased another racket for himself in case he broke strings in the tournament, then he would have a spare. He also invested in some sharp-looking tennis attire, and even though he wouldn't be standing on his feet, he made sure they looked good in new sneakers. His shirt, shorts, shoes and socks were all white. There was some narrow blue trim around the collar and sleeves of his shirt, but that is all the color he wore. He made a special effort to check the tension on his rackets to make sure they were set in the range that allowed optimum performance. Jackson checked and re-checked his wheelchair. He wanted to be prepared. He was ready for this! Jackson's relationship with Carrie had not suffered through this whole ordeal, but rather had become stronger. Carrie supported Jackson in every way that she possibly could. She was almost more nervous than Jackson.

The big day finally arrived. Jackson had retired early to bed the night before and arose extra early to a carbohydrate-loaded breakfast. He was more excited than nervous. He checked to make sure he had all of his equipment in his tennis bag and both rackets. Everything was accounted for and Jackson grabbed his tennis bag and placed it on his lap. He wanted to be independent with everything, especially this. Jackson pulled his wheelchair up to his car, opened the door and threw his tennis bag onto the back seat. He then proceeded as usual to transfer into his vehicle. Jackson left forty-five minutes early so he could pick up Carrie on his way to the club. He pulled up to her apartment and gave his signature honk. Carrie bounced down the stairs with an energized run and jumped into the car. "Ready?" she asked, and before Jackson could answer, "I sure am! Ready to see you crush this!" "Well that makes one of us." Jackson smiled at her in a way that made her realize that he was teasing. Carrie knew how important this tournament was to Jackson and how serious he was about succeeding. She also knew that Jackson was a strong and confident individual who sometimes knew no boundaries.

Somehow, today the club looked different. It had shaken off some of its excellence and snobbery and had taken on a friendlier and welcoming look. There were colored small flags lining the stairs leading up to the entrance. A gigantic banner hung from the roof and draped over the front of the building. It was printed with bright letters: *The Lake Hills Country Club welcomes the Wheelchair Tennis Association and tournament players*. The crowds were larger than usual, and Jackson noticed a slew of photographers on the steps and filtering through the entry way. The parking lot was full but Jackson found a handicapped parking stall near the front of the club. He pulled into it with obvious excitement showing in his facial expression. Carrie offered to take his bag for him but Jackson insisted on taking it into the building himself. That didn't surprise her at all. "Are you nervous, Jackson?" Carrie raised her eyebrows to emphasize her question. "A little, I guess. Honestly, I'm trying hard not to think about it very much." Jackson finished his sentence as he and Carrie arrived at the bottom of the ramp. Instantly, a barrage of reporters was shoving a microphone in his face and flashing pictures. They shot questions at him so fast he couldn't answer any of them completely. Jackson was relieved to finally push through the entrance and enter the lobby.

Registration took place at the front desk and a schedule of the games to be played was listed bracket-style on a large bulletin board located just down the hallway toward the courts. Jackson completed his registration and payed his entry fee and then he anxiously rolled over to the schedule. There were three columns of brackets with ten players in each column. Jackson was in bracket 'A' and was the first player listed. He would be playing an opponent named Bradly Parkston. Jackson checked his watch and noticed he only had thirty minutes before game time. He gave Carrie a kiss and showed her the direction to the observer stands. "Good-luck Jackson! You've got this! I love you!" Carrie called to Jackson as he hurried down the hallway to the tennis courts. He looked for the third court which was the one he was scheduled to play on and when he found it, he froze at the entrance. It had big glass doors that gave him an overview of the court, the net, the boundaries, line judges and everyone in there. Mostly he focused on a player who was warming up. It must have been Parkston. Jackson watched him for a few minutes, trying to grasp an idea of his strength and player style. He really didn't even know if that was possible, but taking some time before he entered the court helped to calm his nerves. Jackson played game strategies over and over in his head and mentally prepared for the match.

Jackson pushed through the doors and they closed behind him. A man who looked like an official approached him. "Mr. Jackson Montgomery, I presume?" He was polite and friendly and after verifying Jackson's identity he showed Jackson to a side bench where he could leave his bag and gear. "Grab your racket and I'll introduce you to Bradley Parkston, your opponent." The man motioned for Jackson to follow him as he walked onto the court and up to the other player. "Mr. Jackson Montgomery meet Bradley Parkston." They both shook each other's hands and turned their attention to the officiator. "I will be one of the line judges for your match. I assume you both know the rules? Remember in wheelchair tennis you have two bounces of the ball before you have to return it rather than the traditional one bounce that you see in able-bodied tennis. Scoring will be exactly the same and we will start the match off with the traditional racket spin. Are you ready?" Jackson listened intently. He had done a lot of studying about scoring and the rules of the sport months ago and felt confident with his knowledge. Both men acknowledged to the officiator that they were ready to begin the match. Jackson scanned the observer stands until he caught a glimpse of Carrie. She gave him a big smile and a thumbs up.

Jackson conducted the racket spin because he was first on the roster. He stretched his arm out holding his racket by the tip of the handle. He set the top of the racket on the ground and gave the handle a fast spin. The racket spun around two times and then lost velocity and wobbled to the ground. It was lying still with the handle pointing toward Jackson. There was some light applause heard from the stands. Jackson briefly remembered instructing Carrie about 'Tennis Etiquette'. This included: No loud or boisterous cheering or yelling, no yelling at or taunting the players during a serve, no loud verbal criticism directed toward the line judges, no applauding a player's serve no matter how good you think it is, and only applaud after a point is scored or after a great return. Jackson's thought process was abruptly drawn back to the decision he had to make. Jackson had three choices because he won the spin. Number one: he could choose whether he wanted to serve or receive first. Number two: he could decide what side he wanted to start from. Number three: he could defer the choice to his opponent. Jackson chose to serve first and his opponent had the option to choose either two or three. He chose two and opted to receive from the far court side.

Both men proceeded to the back of the courts on the deuce side or right side of the court. Jackson carefully positioned himself to make the serve, knowing that he could not use the wheels on his chair or any part of his lower extremities to stable himself. Jackson picked up the brand new tennis ball from his lap. It had a strong smell of rubber and felt fuzzy to the touch. He called out the beginning score, "Love-Love". Jackson watched his arm toss the ball directly above and behind his head. Still having his eye on the ball he forcefully swung his racket and made contact with it. His vision followed it as it whizzed over the net and bounced once in the service box in front of his opponent and spun off to the right of his opponent out of his reach. Parkston was unable to return Jackson's serve. Jackson went over to the left side of the court and called out the score, "15-Love." This was repeated one more time and the score soon became 30-Love. On his next serve Jackson was challenged as Parkston returned his serve with vengeance. Jackson hit the ball back over the net and so did Parkston. The men volleyed for about ten minutes. The room and stands were quiet with the sound of the bounce of the ball hitting the court echoing throughout. Jackson was maneuvering his chair back and forth across the court to reach his opponent's returns but missed hitting the ball before the third bounce on the last volley. He lost a point and the score was 30-15. Parkston still had the service and Jackson prepared for his opponent's best. The ball came blistering toward Jackson and bounced once. He effectively returned it so it landed just barely over the net and bounced away from Parkston. His opponent scrambled to get to the ball but was not successful. Service came back to Jackson and the score went up to 40-15. Jackson was now at an advantage. He just had to win one more point and he would win game one. Concentrating on his serve more than ever, he called out the score and then delivered a blinding unreturnable serve. Cheers arose from the stands and Jackson was pleased that he had won this game. He didn't dwell on his victory too long because he also knew he had to win five more games.

    Per the rules of the game, the players switched sides after game one. Jackson again had service because he won the last point of the previous game. The next three games were intense. Parkston adjusted to Jackson's monster of a serve and there was much more volleying observed. The players seemed to be equally matched in skill and talent. It was anyone's guess how this match would turn out, but Jackson thought of nothing but success and to complete his mission. Jackson won the next two games and on game three they switched sides again. Jackson had incredible endurance which was another advantage that he had. Game three had an increased amount of volleys and Jackson had to stretch out of his comfort zone several times. But Jackson slammed a lob over his head back into Parkston's court and took the winning point. This put Jackson up three games to zero. He was half-way there. The two players fiercely battled each other in the following games, with Parkston winning game four and Jackson winning games five and six. This gave the first set to Jackson. He tried not to think about the future sets that were to be played. His strategy was to take everything slowly, one step at a time.

That is exactly what Jackson did the rest of the day. He played with vigor and intensity, each game and each set, one at a time. His strategy paid off. Jackson was victorious in his first match. Reporters were close by to tell the story of Jackson's remarkable success. Jackson recalled what his opponent said to him after they shook hands at the end of the match. "Congratulations Jackson! I've never seen quite the serve that you have, even in able-bodied tennis. You have great potential." "Thanks, Mr. Parkston. That means a lot coming from you." Jackson raised his racket in triumph. Jackson continued on to win another match that exhibited equally as nail-biting of situations as the last match. Tomorrow he would play two more matches and if he won both of them he would be the tournament champion. Now he was winding down and getting ready to head home to eat and rest and prepare for the next day. Carrie had run hastily down to the court after the end of the matches to meet Jackson. She ran over to him and threw her arms around his neck, approaching Jackson from the side so as not to startle him. Jackson was hot and sweaty but Carrie didn't seem to mind. She gave him a big hard kiss and expressed her excitement about his wins. "I am so proud of you! I love you so much!" Jackson returned the sentiment and rolled over to the bench where he loaded his gear and retrieved his rackets. He placed his tennis bag on his lap, again resisting any help, and looked at Carrie with a huge grin that covered his whole face. "Let's go! I'm done here, for now." Carrie walked beside Jackson as they exited the club. As soon as they opened the outside doors, cameras began flashing and reporters crowded around blurting out questions directed to Jackson. This time he stopped and answered a few. "Mr. Montgomery how does it feel to make a comeback in tennis instead of golf?" was one question and another, "Would you say your training that you received in the Marine Corps played a big part in your success?" They were great questions and Jackson could tell they were heart-felt, so for the sake of his loyal followers, he answered them the best he could. He posed for a few pictures and then was off down the ramp to his car. Jackson propelled his wheelchair faster than usual and Carrie had to slow run just to keep up. They both laughed all the way to the car.

Carrie had left her vehicle at Jackson's the night before the match and Jackson took her back to her apartment and picked her up the next day for the match. So, she had transportation already at Jackson's. Jackson pressed his garage door opener and watched his double car garage door slowly and noisily open. He drove the car into the garage, turned off the ignition, and threw his head back on the headrest to give a huge relieved sigh. "I'm so glad that is over." Jackson turned his head toward Carrie and smiled, "But I enjoyed every minute of it!" "You look tired. Are you hungry? Carrie asked." "It seems you are always asking me that," Jackson laughed. "That's because you are always hungry and I just happen to have impeccable timing. Why don't we go inside and you can take a shower while I order take-out? And, I promise no Chinese!" "That's a great plan," Jackson said as he began the transfer from his car into his wheelchair. He noticed his arms were more sore than usual and his shoulders ached. He thought he would ice them after his shower.

Jackson headed straight to his bedroom and Carrie called for Mexican take-out. She knew Jackson would take about an hour and the take-out wouldn't be there until about the same time so she devised a surprise for Jackson. She had previously gone to a dollar store and picked up some decorations, balloons and candles. Carrie hurried out to her car and collected them from her trunk where they were safely kept from being discovered. Busily she blew up balloons and posted a congratulations banner above the doorway. Festively she decorated the table and counter, complete with candlelight. The take-out arrived just as Jackson was coming from the bedroom. Carrie answered the door, took the bags of food, and met Jackson in the kitchen. "Surprise!" she yelled. "Wow! What's all this?" Jackson asked with obvious approval. "Oh, just a little something to celebrate your success so far and for future triumphs. The food is here so let's eat." Carrie put the food on platters and in bowls and then carried them to the table where nice dinnerware was placed and silverware set. The candles were lit and soft music was playing in the background. After dinner, the two of them found themselves lying on the sofa next to each other. Carrie had her back to Jackson but felt his strong arms embrace her. She felt secure and safe. Carrie gently asked, "Jackson? What plans do you have for your future?" Carrie felt the warmth of his breath against her neck as he responded. "That takes some thought, Carrie. My life plans have taken many unexpected turns and hills. I reluctantly think about my future in fear that it will change drastically from what I would like to see happen." "What would you like to see happen?" she kept inquiring. "Oh, let's see. I would like to continue my tennis career, get married and maybe have a couple of kids. I would like to find a way that I could make a difference in people's lives." "You have already accomplished some of your goals. You make a difference in my life and so many others. And, your tennis career is just beginning. As for the other things that you want to accomplish, well, that's not really up to me." Carrie responded while giving Jackson a hug with her arms covering his. "Don't be so sure you have nothing to do with my goals and dreams. You have everything to do with them. You are so much a part of my life that I can't see a future without you." Jackson gently and romantically kissed the back of Carrie's neck and held her tight. They were both so relaxed that they fell asleep until the alarm in the bedroom woke them up the next morning.

Frantically, Carrie and Jackson woke up and managed to ready themselves for the day. Carrie rushed home to change and freshen up while Jackson dressed in clean tennis attire and grabbed all his gear. By the time he reached Carrie's apartment she was ready and waiting on the sidewalk for him. They scurried off to the club with adrenaline flowing in Jackson's veins like a river. Jackson was stoked! He couldn't remember when he had been so excited and felt so prepared for an event. Arrival at the club was similar to the day before with crowds, reporters and many tennis players all vying for the same outcome. Jackson was again scheduled to play on court three. He wasn't superstitious, but caught himself thinking that this might be his lucky number or an omen. Jackson laughed and shook off the idea as absurd. He checked his schedule again to make sure he had his bearings and kissed Carrie good-bye at the intersection of the two hallways, one that led to the observer stands, and the other that led to the courts. Jackson stopped at the doorway this time to stretch his arms and shoulders. The ice he had applied the night before had been a tremendous help. Once he felt that he had stretched enough he pushed through the doors and deposited his supplies and gear on his bench. The same routine was then conducted where he was introduced to his opponent. This had not varied before any game and beginning of a match. Jackson didn't recognize this player as he did his first, but didn't discount the player's exceptionable ability because he wasn't familiar with him. This time his opponent won the spin and opted to serve first. Jackson chose the near end of the court to receive. Jackson stared at the player on the opposite end of the court intently as he sat in the middle of his side waiting for the player's serve. He watched as the first serve grazed the net. The player lost a serve to the 'let' as that was called but had one more chance. Jackson saw the ball coming at him like a bullet and it bounced once and then twice. Jackson pushed with all his strength to get his chair over to the side of the court to return the serve. His racket barely caught the ball as Jackson hit it with his powerful forehand, sending the ball into the back side court of his opponent. He was out to a great start, leading the set by two games to zero. He won the first, second and the third set giving Jackson another victory and another match. All that was left was the championship match. The officials gave the players a thirty-minute break before the championship match was to begin. Carrie took advantage of the break to visit Jackson and give him some words of support and encouragement. Jackson had played a total of three matches with at least six games per set and three or more sets per match. He was showing some signs of fatigue. Carrie took hold of Jackson's arms and looked at him directly. "Jackson! You can do this. You're strong and talented and the most persevering human on earth! I have complete and utter faith and confidence in you. And, that's all I have to say. No, wait. One more thing, I love you."

 Jackson hydrated himself and did more stretching but did it with no one around. He wanted to have quiet to clear his thoughts and think mentally about the game. He clasped a white hand towel and wiped his face and neck. The feeling of the towel was rough and exfoliating. Jackson tossed the towel in to a bin designated by the club for dirty laundry. He wheeled over to the bench and slowly picked up his racket. Jackson performed a tension check by bouncing the fatty part of his palm against the strings to feel the bounce created by the tension. It felt really good and for a moment it brought Jackson back to the first time Joe had introduced him to tennis and stringing rackets. It had been a fulfilling journey and Jackson had made many memories to keep near and dear, and lasting friends that he could never forget. Jackson quietly expressed to himself the gratitude that he owed to God for giving him these blessings and opportunities. For a brief second he flashed over his life and realized how many times his life had been spared. Now he wanted more than ever to make his life count for something.

The observer stands were more crowded for this match than any of the others. The officials had allowed reporters into the arena. This didn't bother Jackson, he was used to reporters and news media attention. Jackson met his opponent and proceeded to the racket spin, which he won. He chose to serve, his strongest feature and his advantage. The player he was against was strong and talented. Jackson struggled to return his serves and lost the first game. He mentally did a silent adjustment to his attitude and got a second wind. He came back ravaging the next five games and winning the set. The following game and set wasn't won easily, in fact Jackson lost the set. That put he and his opponent tied at one set each. The next set went to Jackson and the following went to his opponent, making the score tied again at two sets each. They battled game after game and when they reached the end the score was six games to six games. A tie breaker commenced and the tension was high. Evenly matched, the two players volleyed for long periods of time putting the audience on edge. The score teetered back and forth from one player to the other, when finally, Jackson had the add-in advantage with the score at fifteen- fourteen. The crowd and courtyard was engulfed in an eerie silence and sweat dripped down Jackson's temples. He tried to wipe it off with the shoulder of his shirt. Jackson took his time after announcing the score before he served. He concentrated mentally and envisioned his serve whizzing with speed and strength over the net and landing out of the reach of his opposition. It was if everything turned to slow motion. Jackson watched his toss soar above and behind his head like he had done many times. He felt the grip of his racket as he grasped it tightly and dropped it behind his right shoulder. Jackson imagined his strength being like a combination of a shotput thrower and lifting 400 pounds of weights. He swung with all his might and lowered his head to watch the ball speed like a flash of lightening over the net and swiftly bypass the opposite players racket, unreturnable. Jackson had won! He had won the match and the whole tournament! Carrie was jumping up and down in the observer stands and throwing all rules of etiquette out the window by screaming to the top of her lungs. Photographs were being flashed at a rapid succession and you could hear the hundreds of clicking sounds as the cameras' shudders were released. Jackson sat his racket on his lap while he basked in the moment and excitement. When he finally picked it up, he noticed he had three broken strings. His last serve not only broke records for speed but also broke his racket.

Chapter Seven

FAME, FORTUNE, FAMILY

"Jackson! Mr. Jackson Montgomery. How do you feel about being ranked number five in wheelchair tennis?" The paparazzi followed Jackson everywhere. It was hard for him to have any privacy. After winning a few dozen tournaments, located from Los Angeles to New York City, Jackson found himself acquiring a moderate fortune. It became necessary, for his safety and Carrie's, that he hire a personal bodyguard to accompany him to the tournaments. He was six-foot five and weighed over 350 pounds. His name was Rex. No one but Jackson knew his last name. It was kept confidential. Jackson hired Rex because of his credentials: he was an ex-Marine who had gone into law enforcement and worked as a security guard part time. Rex was local and came highly recommended and that's all Jackson needed to make it happen. Rex had a black, Jeep four-wheel-drive that he used to accompany Jackson to his tournaments. He never rode with him because there wasn't room, and besides, Carrie felt uneasy around Rex.

Jackson spent time re-inventing his old charity that had been neglected since he couldn't play golf. This time it became a general athlete's scholarship that included both golf and tennis. Jackson was headed to the club for a ribbon-cutting ceremony. Several dignitaries would be attending and of course there would be a lot of press coverage. Carrie would be by his side where she felt comfortable. Both vehicles pulled up to the club and Rex parked, with permission, beside Jackson in a handicap stall. Rex wore a black suit, white shirt and dark tie. His shoes looked like shiny black vinyl and the complete outfit, including the sunglasses he wore, gave him the appearance of a government spy or FBI agent. It didn't bother Jackson; he ignored it. Jackson was dressed in a suit also but not black. It was a dark blue pin-striped with a wide lapel. His light blue shirt was complimented by the dark blue and red paisley tie he wore. Everything matched and fit perfectly; that was Jackson's style. He even donned an expensive pair of cufflinks on his shirt sleeves. Jackson went everywhere looking like a millionaire. No wonder he needed a bodyguard.

The administration at the club had built a wooden platform that covered the steps. The ramp to the left of the stairs was still available for customers to enter the clubhouse. There were blue and red banners strung along the edge of the platform and tall standing potted plants on each end. Jackson thought the plants resembled trees. Chairs were evenly placed on the concrete area in front of the steps with press accommodations located on each side of the audience. Jackson got a few butterflies in his stomach when he glanced at the number of chairs set up. He guessed there were at least two hundred or more. Jackson hadn't been expecting that many, but was pleased. He rolled his wheelchair to fit just behind the podium that had been set up for the speakers. Carrie took a seat next to Jackson and Rex stood in the background.

The crowd gathered and settled in their seats. Time came for the dedication to begin. Joe Fielding gave background information about the charity and an introduction to Jackson Montgomery. "I cannot begin to tell you how amazing this young man is, words do not justify a description." Joe began. "He is a decorated war hero who served his country with pride in the United States Marine Corps and after he was wounded, came home to become a hero in the sport of golf. He rose to the title of Professional Golfer and was a success in the PGA. He not only accomplished that unforeseen feat but he learned to water ski and snow ski with only one leg. I am honored to call this man my friend. He is truly a hero. His car accident did not stop Jackson Montgomery from forging forth with valor. You now know him well as one of the stars of wheelchair tennis. Mr. Montgomery does not hoard his wealth but uses it to help others. He is one of the most generous people I know. Ladies and gentlemen, I give you Mr. Jackson Levi Montgomery." A huge applause ensued, accompanied by a standing ovation. The crowd quieted and sat down as Jackson wheeled up to the podium, which had been lowered for him to speak. Jackson was a little teary-eyed when he began and it took a few minutes for him to regain his composure.

"First let me thank Joe Fielding for that remarkable but exaggerated introduction. I have just done what I needed to do, nothing special. There are so many people who have played a big part in my success: The Marine Corps who molded me into a disciplined human being, the hospital staff who gave service unselfishly to care for my needs, my sports fans who offered encouragement whenever I slumped even a tiny bit, my family and friends who gave unconditional love to me every single day, and Carrie who has changed my life for good and forever. I would not be here without all of these support groups. I especially want to thank God for my abundant blessings; and have made it my calling to pay it forward as much as I possibly can. That is why I am dedicating The Montgomery Athlete's Support Association to accomplish that cause, to help pay it forward to deserving and qualified athletes that need an extra boost or help to accomplish their dreams." Another boisterous applause erupted and lasted several seconds. As the crowd died down, Jackson pushed his chair over to the side of the podium where a large fat ribbon was strung across the front of the platform.

Joe handed Jackson an oversized pair of scissors and Jackson cut the ribbon, making this historic dedication complete. Cameras flashed and reporters rushed to the front of the platform to interview Joe and Jackson. Rex had to stand in front of Jackson and keep the press at bay. The ceremony dragged out for a while as Jackson accommodated a few reporters and journalists. The crowd dwindled and Jackson turned to Carrie. "Are you ready to go celebrate?" Carrie was standing next to him and felt herself pulled down onto Jackson's lap. Jackson usually was against public displays of affection, but on this occasion he really didn't care what people thought. He hugged Carrie tightly and gave her a long intense kiss. When he finished he cupped her chin in his hand and said, "Carrie I love you beyond words. You are my light and my life." Carrie was crying tears of joy and returned Jackson's sentiments. She stood up and started to walk down the ramp, looking over her shoulder to make sure Jackson followed and Rex, of course.

They came to the bottom of the ramp and started toward the cars when they were stopped by a young man. He was well dressed and looked like he was about in his twenties. Politely he addressed Mr. Montgomery. He reached in his suit to grab something and as he did Rex instinctively moved in front of Jackson and put his hand on his gun. The young man carefully removed an envelope from his suit coat as he said, "Whoa, take it easy. I was given two hundred and fifty dollars to deliver this to Mr. Montgomery. I'm not here to cause problems or hurt him in any way." Jackson took the envelope from the man and then bombarded him with questions. "Who gave you the money and envelope? Do you remember what they looked like? Which way did they leave?" The young man began answering Jackson's questions. "I don't know his name. It was a man, one man and he was average height, dark hair, brown eyes and he was dressed in a tuxedo. I thought that was weird. He left in that direction." The young man pointed directly behind him toward the parking lot. "Stay here while I read this message," Jackson sternly said as he raised his eyes and glared at the man.

Jackson slowly pulled a folded piece of paper from the envelope and carefully opened it up. He was used to unknown situations with booby-traps involved. The paper was creased into four squares and was covered with a message written with cut out letters from a newspaper or magazine. The letters were different colors and sizes. Jackson read, "Have five hundred and fifty thousand dollars transferred to the account below by three p.m. tomorrow or have your dealings with John Remington exposed. You can join him in prison." Jackson was totally taken off-guard and surprised by the note but managed to ask the young man to leave his name and a way to be contacted. "Am I in trouble?" The young man fearfully asked. "No, you're not in trouble but I need to be able to reach you if my lawyer needs to ask you any more questions. Go ahead, you can leave now." Rex had taken his hand off of his revolver and was now vigilantly scanning their surroundings to make sure there wasn't another threat waiting. He asked, "Mr. Montgomery, are you all right sir?" "I'm fine, Rex. Let's go get in the car. I am going to make a stop by my lawyer's office. Carrie, you're welcome to come or I can take you home." Jackson's voice sounded concerned and a little fragile. "No, I want to come with you," she replied with haste.

Both vehicles arrived at Mr. Herchek's office thirty minutes later. Rex was sent ahead to notify the lawyer of their arrival. Jackson and Carrie waited in the car for a signal that meant they could safely go into his lawyer's office. "I can't believe all of this." Jackson was still numb from the recent encounter. He mumbled a few more statements, "I did not have anything to do with John Remington's business dealings, except for the real estate. How can I be blackmailed for something that is nonexistent? This is crazy!" "Jackson, we will take this to the lawyer and the authorities. Everything will work out. It will be okay." Carrie was her usually supportive self and was as shocked at the situation as Jackson. Rex opened the outside door of the office and motioned for them to come in. He stood straight and reached out his hand to hold the door for his boss and his boss' girlfriend. Jackson pushed through the door, went down a hallway and entered a plush office. The receptionist greeted him. "Mr. Montgomery, Mr. Herchek is expecting you. Go right in, sir."

"Jackson! What trouble is brewing now?" his lawyer pushed the desk chair he was sitting in away from his desk and plopped a stack of folders in front of him. Jackson took the paper and envelope from his suit jacket and handed it to his lawyer. Silently, he waited for Mr. Herchek to read the message. His lawyer took hold of his glasses and held them in his fingers and the paper in the fingers of the other hand. He nervously swung his glasses back and forth. "This is serious my friend, really serious! *Do* you have any dealings with, or knowledge of Mr. Remington's organization?" "No! Absolutely not! All I did was sell real estate." Jackson retorted. "What about the money put in accounts on the Cayman Islands that you told me about?" Jackson's lawyer wanted to be thorough and not miss any details. "I put some of my money in a joint account that I had opened with Vanessa but I rarely used it, only for deposit. Vanessa and her father told me they were transferring funds to his charity organization. I knew nothing about the Cayman Islands until after we were divorced." "Can you prove any of this?" was his lawyer's next question. "Vanessa's signature was on all of the transactions. I really didn't keep track because I stupidly and naively trusted her. Her father had given me a great job and he seemed to be honest, a man I could trust and he was also my father-in-law." Mr. Herchek concluded that the best thing would be to take the note to the authorities and let the detectives decide what to do with the blackmail money. Next stop was the police station and Jackson was extremely uneasy about the whole plan and situation.

The police station looked ominous and forbearing. Rex was required to leave his handgun at the front desk. Jackson asked to see Officer Vargas Gonzales who was the detective that had been handling other investigations for him. An officer went in the back and brought Detective Gonzales out to see them. Gonzales motioned for them to follow him to a back room where there was more privacy. They entered a room that had a large rectangular table in the middle with metal chairs on each side. Jackson thought it was an interrogation room. It even had a one-way window on one wall facing the table. "What can I do for you Mr. Montgomery?" Gonzales said as he sat himself down in one of the chairs. Mr. Hercheck took over the conversation after introducing himself. He showed the note to the detective and explained some vital details of Jackson's alleged involvement with Remington, and offered explanation as to why Jackson knew nothing about Remington's dealings. Mr. Herchek was also prepared to offer proof of this evidence. Detective Gonzales listened carefully but was not surprised about the situation.

"It seems you've had a few run-ins lately with associates of John Remington. First the break-in to your home, then the tire slashing and now this. It's concerning. I think someone wants you silenced and they're determined." Jackson felt that was obvious but respected the detective's take on his predicament. "What do you suggest I do about the blackmail money and the demand to have the money transferred by tomorrow?" Jackson wanted some quick answers. At times he wasn't very patient. "I have an idea." Detective Gonzales stood up and called another officer into the room. "Put this note in evidence and brush for fingerprints. Then trace the account number to the bank where they want the money transferred, immediately." Gonzales turned to Jackson, "We will trace the account and stake out the bank where it is located. You make the transfer and we will have a plain clothes officer there to apprehend the person that makes the withdrawal. I think we are dealing with amateurs, so this should go as planned." "And what if it doesn't?" Jackson's anxiety began to surface. "You just make the transfer deposit Jackson. Let us worry about the rest. We will keep you updated. Stay near your phone for the next couple of days, at least until you hear from me." Detective Gonzales leaned over and shook Jackson's and his lawyer's hand and tipped his hat in respect at Carrie.

Jackson, Carrie and Rex arrived at Jackson's home and quietly and somberly went inside. Rex asked, "Mr. Montgomery, I can stick around for a while, if you would like." "Okay, Rex. That sounds good. Make yourself comfortable and at home." Jackson was relieved to have some extra protection right now. Carrie insisted on staying in the guest room and said she would stay until the blackmail money was picked up and the blackmailer apprehended. She put her things down on the sofa and then directed a question to Jackson and Rex, "Can I get you a Coke or water?" Rex said that he was fine and Jackson requested a cold Coke with lots of ice. Carrie hurried off to the kitchen and returned to the living room. By then Jackson had transferred to the recliner and welcomed the cold drink. He guzzled down the whole glass full in three or four swallows. Jackson was extra thirsty and nervous. He kept going over the plans for the next day in his head with trepidation. Carrie quietly sipped her cola, pulled her legs up and bent her knees onto the sofa and looked at Jackson with a combination of love and concern. It was getting late and Jackson let Rex leave and go home. Before Rex left, Jackson asked him to return early the next morning. Jackson fell asleep in the recliner holding on to his empty second glass of Coke. Carrie carefully removed the glass from his hand. Then she put it in the kitchen, turned the lights to a faint dim setting, and covered Jackson with a throw blanket that was draped over the back of the sofa. Sleep came rapidly to Carrie. She was exhausted from the intensity of the day's events.

Jackson had awoken early without disturbing Carrie while she slept. He was finishing his shower and getting dressed when Carrie was startled awake by the phone ringing. Jackson answered the call. She overheard his side of the conversation. "Yes, I'm ready detective. It's early and the bank hasn't opened yet, but I will get it done as soon as they are. The fingerprints on the note were a match to who? Oh, I see. Thank you. Yes, my body guard will be returning this morning. Carrie is here with me. We'll be fine. Thanks again." Carrie jumped out of bed and quickly dressed. She borrowed a pair of Jackson's sweats and a t-shirt. As she headed for the kitchen she pulled her long blonde hair into a ponytail and secured it behind her head with an elastic. She was barefoot and a little out of breath when she walked around the doorway and stopped abruptly. Carrie was inquisitive to Jackson about the phone call that he received earlier. "It was the detective making sure everything was in place and I was ready to do this. He also said that they matched the fingerprints on the note to a man who is in the system for armed robbery. He told me he could tell me more details about it later." Jackson seemed unusually calm and nonchalant. "Okay then!" Carrie stated. "Are you hungry? Do you want some breakfast?" She totally changed the subject abruptly and on purpose.

Jackson and Carrie were at the table eating breakfast when Rex arrived. "Mr. Montgomery, I am going to check the perimeter of the house and windows to make sure everything is secure." Rex looked at Jackson for his approval. "That's great Rex. Check the garage while you're at it, please." Carrie cleaned up from breakfast and Jackson moved the phone over to the table where he could reach it more easily. Jackson looked at the clock on the kitchen wall. It was nearing nine o'clock when the bank would be open. Jackson pulled out his wallet and checkbook and held it tightly and stared at them both. Carrie came and sat softly down at the table. She didn't want to disturb Jackson's train of thought. The silence was broken when Jackson expressed himself, "This isn't going to get much easier if I keep putting it off. So, I might as well do it right now!" Jackson picked up the phone and speedily dialed his bank. He sat still while it rang.

"Hello, this is Jackson Montgomery and I would like to make a transfer to the following account. Yes, I have my credentials." Jackson then gave the bank information to verify his identity. "I need to transfer five hundred and fifty thousand dollars to the following account: 67490600000295039. Yes, that's correct. This needs to be done immediately please. Thank you. Thank you very much." Jackson took a deep breath as he hung up the phone and looked at Carrie across the table. "It's done. Now we wait."

Three o'clock came much too quickly for Jackson. He had passed the time by having a lunch that Carrie prepared, a turkey club sandwich and some raw vegetables. Jackson sat stalwartly by the phone after lunch, tapping his fingertips in a nervous rhythm. Carrie had been trying to keep the atmosphere light and calm, and was successful until the doorbell rang at 1:15 pm. It startled everyone and especially put Rex on high alert. He held his hand out to Carrie messaging that he would answer the door and for her to stay back, out of sight. Rex slowly and carefully opened the door with his left hand while resting his right hand on his revolver. A reporter stood in front of him and insisted that an interview be granted. Rex relaxed his stance and sternly told the reporter that Mr. Montgomery was unavailable and shoved the door shut on the pushy reporter. He informed Jackson about the incident but Jackson didn't seem to be focused on anything else but the phone.

It was a usual day at the bank with a moderate amount of patrons there to do business. The bank's façade consisted of two large ceiling-to-floor glass windows with the bank's name and hours of operation printed in black lettering close to the doors. Two heavy revolving glass doors were situated in between the large windows and were the only entrance and exit to the bank. Four tellers were seated behind a thick, plastic barrier that stopped three inches from the counter. This allowed transactions to be conducted without too much inconvenience. Several beautiful paintings hung on the walls and a massive clock hung on the wall behind the tellers. To the right sat several desks that were work spaces for the loan officers. Each had a phone and a cylinder of pens sitting on top. There was a middle-aged man waiting at one teller, a mother with a young child at another teller and a young college student at a third teller. The teller in the middle was free and raised her head to glance at one of the revolving doors. A tall woman delicately pushed her way through one of the revolving doors and entered the bank. She immediately walked toward the middle teller. The woman was well dressed and wore a two-piece satin white suit. Her hair was covered with a light weight scarf that tucked behind her neck. Large dark sunglasses covered her eyes and her hands were adorned with white gloves. She was already tall but her high heels made her appear even taller than usual. The woman wore pale-pink frosted lipstick and was the complete essence of high-society glamour. She stepped up to the counter and removed her gloves which she draped over her large black-vinyl hand bag.

She pulled out a small piece of paper from an outside pocket of her handbag and pushed it under the glass barrier. "I would like to withdraw the amount written on top of the paper from the account written below it." she said. The teller politely responded, "I will need to see your identification, please." The woman opened her bag and pulled out a driver's license and a credit card. The teller glanced down at the cards and then up at the woman. "For this amount I will have to get the bank manager's approval. I'll be right back." The teller turned and went into the manager's enclosed office and shut the door. The woman started to get fidgety and looked in the direction of the manager's office frequently. Little did she know that a sting operation had been set up. The teller gave the manager the code that they had discussed with the police earlier and the manager called the plain clothed policemen that were posing as loan officers. He was careful not to make eye contact with the suspect. When the teller returned, she bought some time for the police by typing on her computer and telling the woman that she was putting the transaction through. "Ms. Remington, we just about have the transaction complete. I'm sorry it has taken longer than expected." "Just hurry!" the woman impatiently responded.

A plain-clothed officer had made his way behind her and reached out to grab her arm. She was startled and tried to jerk her arm away, but the officer had his handcuffs out and started reading her rights to her. "Ms. Vanessa Remington you are under the arrest for black mail and attempt to do physical harm to Jackson Montgomery." Another officer joined him and the officers escorted Vanessa outside and put her in a patrol car that was now waiting in front of the bank. The officer driving the car radioed ahead and let the precinct know that the subject was apprehended. Vanessa was booked into the county jail with her fancy clothes and her snooty condescending attitude. The author of the blackmail note and her accomplice was arrested and booked into county jail.

The phone rang at Jackson's home and caused everyone there to hyper start their nervousness again. Jackson rapidly picked up the phone. "Hello? Yes. This is Jackson Montgomery." "Mr. Montgomery, this is Detective Gonzales from the third precinct. I wanted you to know the sting went as planned and Ms. Vanessa Remington has been arrested for black mail and physical threats." Jackson hung his head and sighed. A distinctive silence followed before he said anything. "I was hoping that she wasn't involved, but apparently she was involved more than we all suspected. Then whose fingerprints were on the note?" "It was a local criminal she had hired again to do her dirty work. He has a record for convicted armed robbery and assault. We will continue to have a patrol car drive by your house for the next forty-eight hours just to be safe. Keep your bodyguard close for a few days. We're hoping this will die down now that we've made an arrest. Any questions, call me at the precinct and you try and have a nice day, sir." "Thank you detective. I will, and you the same." Jackson placed the receiver on the phone base and looked over at Carrie. "It's over. I think it's finally over! They have arrested Vanessa. She has been involved with everything. I should have known. Like father like daughter. Now she can visit 'Daddy' and share a common interest-criminals put in prison." Carrie came over to Jackson's wheelchair and wrapped her arms around his shoulders. "I'm sorry it had to end like this Jackson. It must be extremely hard and frustrating for you." "Yeah, I'm sorry it had to end this way too, but I feel like I should have seen it coming." "How? How could you predict the future on how someone you once loved could betray you in such a despicable way? You are not responsible for any of this. The Remingtons are! They are a greedy, selfish, and cruel family that act like the mafia. You are just lucky to be rid of them." Carrie was worked up and her body language told the story of how concerned she still was for Jackson.

The next few weeks held vital court dates for Jackson. He was called to the witness stand to testify on more than one occasion. The courtroom was full of supporters, friends and reporters. Cameras were allowed for these proceedings. The bailiff called for all to arise as the First District Judge entered the room. When everyone was seated, a courtroom officer escorted the twelve-member jury to their seats. The jury was diversified and ranged from young adult to elderly, and various races and occupations. Gender seemed equal when Jackson surveyed the jury stand. The prosecution went first with an opening statement and the defense followed. Jackson was the prosecution's prime witness. Jackson's heart began to pound as he was called to the witness stand. He rolled up to the witness stand and pulled his chair in front of it. He raised his right hand and took an oath to tell the truth and nothing but the truth. Jackson had a brief flashback. The last time he had raised his hand to be sworn in was when he joined the Marines and that to him was a more pleasant situation than the one he found himself in presently.

As the prosecutor approached, Jackson turned his head toward Vanessa. A cold steel-like glare met him; the same one that had followed him from his entrance into the courtroom to the witness stand. It was awkward and uncomfortable for him, but Jackson persevered. Jackson was asked questions about his marriage and his relationship with Mr. Remington. As uncomfortable as it was, he was able to tell about Vanessa's cruelty and threats. Vanessa was convicted by the jury of extortion and black mail but not attempted murder. That charge was thrown out of court for lack of evidence. She still was sentenced to fifteen years in prison with a right to appeal. Jackson figured she would appeal but it would take some time and that would give him a break so that he could breathe easier. The Remingtons had already zapped him of his energy and focus. Now, he could finally turn his focus and energy back to the two most important things in his life- Carrie and tennis.

Workouts at the club increased and Joe scheduled more tournaments, an especially important one down in Atlanta, Georgia. Jackson prepared for the flight down to Atlanta and asked Carrie to accompany him. The airline made accommodations for Jackson's wheelchair and special attention was given to his tennis equipment. The couple sat side by side on the flight down, Carrie seated next to Jackson's wheelchair. They talked about everything but tennis. Carrie felt that was refreshing. In the middle of the flight, Carrie caught Jackson off guard, "Jackson, why don't we plan a trip to Ohio and you can meet my mother and brother? We can plan it around one of your tennis tournaments if you'd like. They are anxious to meet you." Jackson didn't know what to say to Carrie; he wasn't thrilled about meeting family. He didn't want them to think less of him because of his condition. But Jackson knew how important this was to Carrie and he would do almost anything for her. "Sure, that sounds like a great idea." His speech was slow as it exited his mouth. "When do you want to make this important event happen?" Carrie's excitement showed as she turned to face Jackson and poured out the plans to him. He could tell she had been planning this for a while. Two weekends after this tournament was the magical scheduled event. Jackson gripped the arms of his wheelchair tight as the plane landed. Jackson heard and felt the landing gear touch down on the runway. There was a slight jerk and gravity threw him forward as the pilot applied the brakes of the aircraft forcefully until the plane had slowed drastically. They started to taxi to the terminal and everyone was instructed by the flight attendants to remain seated with their seat belts fastened until the aircraft came to a complete stop. Jackson looked at Carrie with an exasperated look on his face. "Now, we get to wait."

Jackson was allowed to exit the plane first and was accommodated again. The airline was gracious with their customer service. Jackson and Carrie made their way to baggage claim and retrieved their luggage. An airport worker offered to assist them to the outside of the airport where they could hail a cab. The taxi was quick to pull up to the curb and the driver jumped out to assist Jackson with his wheelchair after he had transferred to the front seat. The cab driver put his chair in the back next to Carrie. She didn't mind; she was overcome with excitement and didn't feel inconvenienced at all. Jackson instructed the driver to take them to the Grand Hotel located in downtown Atlanta.

The cab driver was paid more than he charged, as was customary for Jackson to do. He and Carrie waved for a bellhop to help them with their luggage and then checked into the hotel. Jackson had reserved two rooms, side by side. He deeply respected Carrie's conservative values. They had arrived midmorning and had time on their hands, so after they settled in, they decided to go explore and get some dinner.

Jackson had twenty-four hours before tournament time and he was going to take advantage of the time he and Carrie had together. Jackson had carefully planned a special dinner at an expensive French restaurant and had made reservations prior to their arrival. He gave a bellhop a tip to go to the gift shop and buy flowers. Jackson was going to surprise Carrie. Jackson was dressed in one of his best suits and wore his signature cufflinks on his shirt. He held the bouquet of roses on his lap and wheeled over to the door that connected their rooms. Jackson knocked. "Are you ready? Can I come in?" "Give me just a minute." Carrie responded. Jackson patiently waited, which was not one of his strengths and finally the door opened revealing Carrie who looked magnificent. She wore a long black evening gown with simple straps and a V-neck. Material scooped down her back and loosely gathered in a half-circle just below her shoulder blades. A beautiful and dainty gemstone necklace was around her long neck and earrings that matched the necklace decorated her ears. Jackson had never seen her look as beautiful as she did tonight. He took hold of her hand and gently kissed it, then handed her the flowers. "These are for you." He said. "Oh Jackson they are beautiful and my favorite color. Let me find something to put them in." Carrie looked over her room and spotted a vase sitting on one of the tables. She put water in it and then arranged the yellow roses to her liking. She hoped that she hadn't destroyed a valuable artifact or done something unacceptable by using what looked like an expensive vase.

They arrived at the French restaurant right on time for their reservation. Jackson was treated like a king, just like he was back home. On their way to be seated, Carrie noticed the string quartet over by the dance floor. She thought to herself, "This is amazing! A dance floor! I love to dance!" Then she stopped her thought process when she realized the capabilities of her partner. Carrie shrugged it off as not important. The host sat them at their table and suggested something on the menu for them to try. They both ordered *Flam de Poisson,* which was flamed broiled fish with a special butter garlic sauce. Water was all they had to drink and Carrie had the waiter put a lemon in her water. She claimed it made the water taste better and disguised the mineral taste. Jackson loved her little quirks; that's what made her unique and special to him.

When they finished their meal, and before desert was served, Jackson put his napkin on the table. He pushed over to Carrie and held out his hand. "May I have this dance?" Carrie was speechless but managed a surprised "of course". Carrie wasn't sure how Jackson was going to accomplish this but she had a lot of confidence in him and felt he could manufacture unexpected miracles. Jackson rolled his wheelchair onto the dance floor and took both of Carrie's hands in his. He instructed her to stand on his feet and hold on to the arms of his wheelchair. "Don't worry, you won't hurt me," he laughed. "I can't feel anything in them." "Are you sure about this?" Carrie asked. "Never been surer." Carrie took her high heels off and then cautiously stepped on to Jackson's feet and bent down slightly to take hold of the arms to his chair. The music began to play and Jackson rolled his wheelchair around the dance floor, swaying and swerving with the beat. Soon a crowd was gathered watching the couple who were mesmerized with one another. The dance ended with them giving each other a big kiss as applause broke out around them.

After a few dances, they found themselves back at their table. Jackson ordered their desert, Crème Brulee. The candlelight reflected off and made Carrie's face aglow and her eyes sparkle. She had caught Jackson watching her for long intervals all evening. "Jackson, you are staring at me." she declared. "Can't help myself. Being with you now transcends any perfect moment I could ever imagine. You are absolutely beautiful always, but tonight you are radiant." The waiter arrived and placed the custard dishes of Crème Brulee in front of them. Carrie picked up her fork and was about to take a bite when she abruptly stopped. She looked down at her desert and in the middle of it was a carefully placed diamond ring. She gasped and looked across the table. "Jackson!" Jackson responded immediately, "I can't kneel down on one knee but the sentiment is there. Carrie you saved my life and brought me back to an existence that I love living. You have been there for me and you are my best friend. I want to share every day with you forever. Carrie Langston, will you marry me?" Carrie squealed a loud "yes" and jumped up from her chair, ran over to Jackson and gave him a huge hug and then a long passionate kiss. Jackson reached across the table and pulled the ring from the desert. He wiped it off with his cloth napkin and then placed it slowly on Carrie's left ring finger. Cheers and applause followed from the tables full of restaurant patrons. Important journeys begin at unexpected moments in time.

Jackson played better than usual at the tournament in Atlanta. He went on to win and made the local and national news. The officials clocked his serve at 148mph, a new wheelchair tennis record. This was also in the papers, complete with a large picture of Jackson serving in the beginning of the sports section. He went away from Atlanta with two special memories and a renewed vigor that he welcomed home like an old friend. When they landed at the Denver Airport, there were more paparazzi then usual there to greet them. Jackson was starting to become annoyed at all the attention. Rex had dropped Joe off at Jackson's car and Joe drove it over to passenger pickup. He loaded their luggage in the car and Jackson transferred to the driver's seat. It wasn't until they were on the highway home that Joe anxiously blurted out, "Well, I hear congratulations on in order!" "How did you know? It just barely happened a couple of days ago." Jackson was surprised. "Oh, I read about it in the Atlanta newspaper. It was also on the local news station. You can't get away with anything in public Jackson. Don't you know that by now?" Joe let out a laugh and reached up from the back seat and slapped Jackson on the shoulder. "Anyway, I am happy for the two of you. Have you set a date?" Jackson smiled and looked over at Carrie then rolled his eyes. "That's up to my fiancé. And we haven't had time to discuss it yet. Don't worry Joe. We'll keep you updated!"

Jackson was working out at the club the next day with Joe. They were on their second set when the receptionist walked in and interrupted them. "I'm sorry to disturb you gentlemen but there is a camera crew out in the lobby. They say they represent Tennis Magazine and would like to talk to Mr. Montgomery." Jackson thanked the receptionist and motioned for Joe to go with him to check out the situation. Jackson was still in tennis attire and sweaty as he approached the crew. He wiped his hands and face off with a towel he had on his lap and shook hands with apparently the person in charge. "Hello Mr. Montgomery. It is a pleasure to meet you. We are representing Tennis Magazine and have been following your career success. We would like to get your permission to film you while you practice and do an article featuring you in our magazine. If that would be all right?" Jackson looked at the heavy duty cameras two of the crew members held and the notebook and pen the person that spoke to him held. The man with the notebook also had a still camera draped over his shoulder. "I am honored," said Jackson. "This is kind of intimidating. I'm nothing special to deserve this kind of recognition." "Oh, but you are!" the man with the notebook replied. "It is only a select few that make it into our magazine to be featured. And you have been chosen to be one of the select few. It is we who are honored Mr. Montgomery." "I don't see how I could say no. When do you want to start?" Jackson questioned. "Right now would be good if that works for you?" The man with the notebook motioned for his crew to get ready and they followed Jackson and Joe back to the court.

Back at the court, the two men were instructed to play their sets and the match as usual and to try and ignore the cameras, especially not to look at them. The crew was organized and professional, which is what Jackson expected from them. Jackson was able to show off his monstrous serve and playing ability at a level that was unprecedented. A crowd of viewers gathered in the stands and Jackson began feeling like this was a tournament match rather than practice. Joe was enjoying himself and pushed Jackson to his limits and beyond. Jackson improved every time he played Joe because Joe was able-bodied and challenged Jackson's skills. They finished the match and both of them hurried over to the water bottles sitting on the sidelines. The crew manager approached Jackson and Joe. "Congratulations gentlemen! That was a fabulous display of all around talent. My editor will be pleased with our results. Mr. Montgomery we will notify you when the article is run and we'll send you a copy of the magazine. We will send one to you, also Mr. Fielding. Thank you both for this wonderful opportunity." The camera crew and manager left the club and Jackson and Joe headed for the showers.

Jackson couldn't wait to call Carrie and tell her of this surprising and wonderful event that he had just experienced. He explained every detail and every move taken. Carrie was elated and could hardly contain her excitement. "You keep coming up with more and more reasons for us to celebrate Jackson!" "What's there to celebrate?" Jackson teased. He could hear her whisper something negative but couldn't make out what it was. "I'm teasing you. Do you want to go out and celebrate tonight?" "I thought you would never ask." Carrie ended the conversation by telling Jackson he could pick her up at seven.

Carrie sat down in the passenger bucket seat of the car and buckled her seatbelt. "Where are we going tonight? The usual?" She was referring to the steak and lobster restaurant where they had their first date. "Nope. I'm expanding my horizons. We are going to a highly recommended Chinese restaurant." Jackson looked over at Carrie to see her reaction. "Jackson? Are you kidding? I thought you didn't like anything about Chinese food?" Carrie was in shock. "I don't, but I figured its time to move forward and leave the past in the past. This is one small way I feel that I can do that. Is that okay with you?" "Of course." Carrie replied. "Let's go have a chopstick lesson!" They pulled up to the restaurant and had the valet park the car. When inside Jackson realized that it was a traditional Chinese restaurant where the guests typically sat on the floor. Jackson quietly went over to the hostess and asked if they could accommodate a wheelchair at a table. "Of course Mr. Montgomery. There is a room this way please. It has a table and a chair for the young lady." Jackson couldn't help but wonder how the hostess knew who he was as he and Carrie followed her to an extra small room that was decorated in mostly red and gold with Chinese lanterns hanging in each corner. There were vases made of Jade on an ornamental table against the wall. Chinese art featuring mountainous scenery was painted in pale water-colors on the back wall. At first Jackson cringed a little and had to fight back bad memories. He eventually settled in to his new adventure and relaxed. Carrie and Jackson ordered, with Carrie's direction and suggestions. Jackson looked at his food and glanced around to find the silverware. "Oh, you use these." Carrie held up the set of chopsticks laying on the side of her dish. Jackson ripped the paper off his sticks and held them up in front of his face. He thought to himself, "I handled worse than this in Vietnam. I can certainly do this!" He watched Carrie carefully as she maneuvered the chopsticks with ease. Jackson studied her method for a few minutes and bravely made an attempt. All of the food he picked up with his sticks fell back on his plate before he could reach his mouth. Carrie couldn't help but laugh. "Oh, I see how this goes. You're really enjoying watching me be humiliated. Aren't you?" Jackson flashed a big smile in Carrie's direction and chuckled sarcastically. "Well, it is quite entertaining." They both laughed and continued to enjoy one another's company. Jackson eventually got the hang of using chopsticks and was able to finish his dinner which he surprisingly liked.

The weekend sauntered in and Jackson made creative plans which would enable him to take advantage of this time. Thursday afternoon he gave Carrie a call before she went to work at the hospital. "Hello, beautiful! I'm wondering if I could interest you in a trip to the mountains this weekend. The fall colors are incredible this time of year." "You're not suggesting that we are going camping are you? Cause if you are, I need more notice." "No not camping yet. I thought we could go up to Aspen and take in a good restaurant, see the shops and stay in the lodge." "That sounds great! When would we leave?" Jackson responded, "I already know you have Friday off from work so I thought we could leave late afternoon after you get some sleep. Pack a small bag for the weekend and I'll pick you up at 4:30." Carrie agreed and so far Jackson's plans were going smoothly.

Carrie tossed her bag in the trunk of the car along with Jackson's and promptly joined Jackson in the front seat. The drive across the city was uneventful and somewhat boring but as soon as they started up the mountain the view became a canvas of colors and contrasts. Yellow quaking aspen trees spread unevenly at the base of the mountain and dark green pines reached their way to the skyline. Majestic rock cliffs hung on the edges of the canyon walls that lacked foliage but made up for that lack with a design of grays, browns, dark-iron-colored and white rock formations. Traversing alongside the highway and the mountain's bottom edge was a clear river whose water smashed into rocks to form rapids along its journey. A few miles up the canyon, the shrubbery and brush exhibited bright colors of orange and red. Mother Nature had orchestrated a perfect canvas painting for all to enjoy.

They entered the quaint ski village and made their way to the lodge, which was made of large pine logs and a roof that resembled old pottery. Jackson made a call to the local restaurant that was highly recommended to him to make reservations. They took some time to settle in their rooms and then walked to the restaurant which was only a couple of blocks away. It was a chalet-style building with a cobblestone entrance in front. The awning that covered the doorway was an inverted V-shape and had scalloped edges. Windows were small sections divided by strips of wood. The name of the restaurant was *Der Württemberg* and was carved from wood, painted light blue and hung over the top of the awning. As they entered the restaurant, the faint sound of an accordion playing greeted them, and a host seated them at a table in the center of the dining room. The table was massive wood and the chairs were similar. The servers in the restaurant were cordial and accommodated Jackson's wheelchair.

Neither Jackson nor Carrie had ever experienced German food and struggled to find something on the menu that they could understand. Jackson waved for the waiter to come to their table. "This is our first time here. Is there something you could recommend?" "Of course Mr. Montgomery." The waiter smiled at Jackson as if he was a long-lost friend. Carrie smiled at him too and shrugged her shoulders because she knew what he was thinking. "How does he know me?" The waiter had recommended *Roulade* which consisted of thin strips of meat slathered with mustard and filled with bacon, onions and pickles. This meal progressed into one of the more interesting dinners they had experienced in a long time. They both had mixed feelings about the food, but kept an open mind in the spirit of adventure.

Jackson and Carrie spent the rest of the evening window shopping and visiting a select few shops. The atmosphere of the village was unique to Aspen and character flowed from every corner. The night air cooled quickly and Carrie wrapped a bulky sweater around her shoulders and put a light-weight coat around Jackson's. Often while they were strolling along the cobbled walkways Carrie would randomly give Jackson a big hug and tell him how much she loved him. On one occasion Jackson caught her arm and pulled her around to his lap and then wheeled over closer to a window of one of the shops. "What do you see? Look in there and tell me." "A bakery?" "That's right and we can't go back to the lodge without a piece of Bavarian cheese coffee cake. Come on let's go!" Jackson started to push toward the door, "Wait! Give me a chance to stand up." Carrie navigated off his lap. "Oh, but I so like having you in my arms and near me." Jackson laughed.

The store was an unusual bakery where its walls were lined with German pastries and cakes along both side walls and in front below the cash register in a glass case. They were enjoying the inviting smell of the baked goods when a voice from behind the register called out to them, "Can I help you?" she said with a thick German accent. "Yes. We would like two pieces of your Bavarian cheese coffee cake and two Cokes, please." Jackson thought the middle-aged women was delightful and had a contagious smile. "Are you two newlyweds?" she asked. "Uh, no, not yet. Why do you ask?" Jackson was curious about her question. "Because you look so much in love like a lot of newlyweds that come up here to Aspen." The woman giggled and handed them their cake and drinks. Carrie thanked her and the couple sat down at a white rod-iron table in the middle of the room. It was Octoberfest and the perfect time to visit Aspen. Carrie and Jackson sat in the bakery and watched the people outside while they enjoyed each other's company and their Bavarian cheese coffee cake.

All the way home Carrie quizzed Jackson about wedding plans- where, when and who to invite. They had just decided on a December wedding when they rounded a familiar corner on the highway. Jackson pulled off the side of the road. "Jackson, what are you doing?" Carrie looked over at him and noticed he was upset and tense. "Is this where it happened?" she gasped. Jackson sat silent for a few minutes and then slowly began recounting what he remembered of the experience. He stared in front of him at the road and the embankment that was at its edge. He heard tires squealing and then loud sounds of metal smashing against the rocks and ground and glass breaking as he mentally experienced the car roll over and over until it landed upside down. Smoke and gasoline fumes burned his eyes and choked him; making it difficult to breathe. Jackson remembered drifting in and out of consciousness. He recalled the feeling of a liquid substance running down his forehead and cheeks and the panicked feeling he had when he realized he could not feel his legs. Last thing he remembered was the sound of a saw cutting metal and someone pulling him out of the car and placing him on a stretcher. Everything went dark after that. Jackson felt uncomfortable with his memories. This is one he would often wish to forget. Carrie reached over and took his hand but didn't say anything. She quietly listened and looked at Jackson with concern and support. When it appeared that he was through talking about the experience, she asked, "Are you okay? Do you want to leave or do you want to stay a little longer?" "No. Let's leave. I've seen all I want to see." Jackson replied. "Is this the first time you have been up here since the accident?" With Jackson's response of yes, she gently said, "This must be really hard for you." Jackson didn't say anything else and sharply turned onto the highway and sped ahead.

Carrie realized, after their trip to Aspen that she only had a couple of months to plan a wedding. She first wanted Jackson to meet her family, so plans ensued for a trip to Ohio. The plans worked around a tennis tournament in Dayton that weekend. Scheduled itinerary was to play the tournament and then spend three or four days with Carrie's family in Bellbrook. Carrie made the call to her family to give them a heads up and the date of their arrival. Reggie answered the phone in a gruff voice, "Hello?" "Reggie this is Carrie. I've got some exciting news! I'm engaged to be married. His name is Jackson Montgomery. He's been a professional golfer and now is a professional wheelchair tennis player. He is amazing and the love of my life! There's so much more and I will tell you all about everything when we get there for our visit." Carrie was talking so fast Reggie barely understood what she said.

"So, he's in a wheelchair? How do you really feel about that?" Reggie sounded more than concerned. He truly wanted his sister to be happy. "Do you know what you're getting into?" Reggie was upset as he tried to offer words of caution even though he didn't know Jackson. "Reggie, I know exactly what I am getting into and I love Jackson very much and want to marry him. You don't need to worry or be so concerned. We will arrive the last weekend in October for a tournament in Dayton and then come to the farm and stay three days. Sound okay?" "Yeah, sure. I'll tell mom that you are coming. She will be excited to see you and your fiancé." Reggie told his sister goodbye, slowly hung up the phone and thought to himself, "That guy better be worth it or he'll answer to me!"

Jackson and Carrie arrived at the Dayton International Airport Thursday evening the last week of October. They were both familiar with the routine that was expected when they went to tournaments. It was usual for them to stay at a nice hotel and go to dinner the night before the tournament. Dancing was always included in their entertainment and they calmed each other by just being together. Jackson was up early on the day of his matches, ate a good breakfast and called Carrie to be ready to go early. Carrie quickly grabbed a bagel and juice from the café downstairs and hurried to eat it before the car arrived to pick Jackson and her up. They scurried out the heavy hotel doors to a black limousine that was parked in front. Rex had flown in late the night before and was not only Jackson's body guard but acted as his chauffer. Rex jumped from the car and walked fast over to Jackson and then pushed his wheelchair over to the side of the car's middle seat where he transferred in. Rex then opened Carrie's door on the opposite side for her and lastly put the wheelchair and Jackson's tennis equipment in the back section of the limo. "Ready, sir?" Rex looked in the rear-view mirror as he asked Jackson for further instructions. "Yes. Please take us to the Dayton Evergreen Country Club on 8800 East Northshore Drive." "Yes sir," was Rex's reply.

Jackson worked hard for each set that he won. He was off today and he really didn't understand why. The tournament dragged on and each set was a nail biter. His second match was barely won in a tiebreaker 17-14. At the end of the day Jackson was exhausted and talked to reporters sparsely. Even though he was lucky and won the tournament, Jackson berated himself for not playing his best. For the first time tennis was not priority number one and at the front of his thought process. He was thinking about so much more-Carrie and meeting her family. Jackson couldn't bear to be judged negatively and his greatest fear was that Carrie's family wouldn't accept him. It was odd that after everything that Jackson had accomplished in the public eye and how much the public had accepted him, he still had an unquenchable thirst for the acceptance of Carrie and her family. Jackson felt he had always been prepared to meet his fears but this was different. He felt vulnerable with his weaknesses exposed.

The drive from Dayton to Bellbrook, Ohio was beautiful and was a country road not interstate. Fields of corn and barley passed by them like frames in a motion picture. Every few miles a large red barn sprung up surrounded by a white picket fence. Some of the barns had giant American flags painted on the side denoting a definite sense of patriotism in the area. There was little traffic and the ride was relaxing, which was a good thing because the car was a rental and Carrie had to do all the driving; Jackson couldn't without hand controls. Carrie met up with a bulky sized tractor crawling along the side of the road a couple of times. She became expertise at swerving out around them and not needing to slow down. Driving through Bellbrook, Carrie took on the role of tour guide and was upbeat about showing Jackson the sights. Bellbrook was considered to be a medium-sized town to Carrie but definitely a small town by Jackson's standards. Bellbrook consisted of four traffic lights, three gas stations, two banks, two grocery stores, and several shops located along both sides of the main street that ran through town. Carrie's farm was located on the far outskirts away from city-center.

Carrie turned off the small road down a dirt covered lane and drove toward the farmhouse. The sound of tires transitioning from tar to dirt was obvious and loud. The house was a large white two-story farm house that had a porch that extended around the entire front of the house. A double-seated swing hung from the ceiling of the porch. Two bulky patchwork pillows invitingly sat on the swing. Reggie stood just above the front steps with his hands on his hips. His head cradled a cowboy hat that shaded his sunburned face. The jeans and the plaid shirt he wore were accented with a leather belt and a large silver belt buckle. His boots were worn and scuffed from hard work and his arms and shoulders were strong and broad. Reggie chewed on a toothpick and glared at the approaching car.

Jackson and Carrie pulled up to the steps and turned off the engine. Carrie got out of the car and greeted her big brother with a "Hi, can you give us some help?" Reggie was obliging and lifted Jackson's wheelchair out of the backseat and unfolded it next to his car seat. He bent down and shook Jackson's hand. "Howdy. I'm Reggie, Carrie's brother and I presume you are Jackson?" Jackson reached out to grasp Reggie's hand, "I am and glad to meet you, Reggie. Carrie has told me a lot about you." "Well, it can't be all good, I guess! Do you need help?" Reggie stood ready to help Jackson with his wheelchair if he needed it. "No thank you. I've got this. I will need some help to get up the stairs though, if you don't mind?" Jackson had transferred to his chair and secured the arms while carrying on the conversation with Reggie. It took more effort for Jackson to push the wheels of his chair on dirt than on sidewalk or pavement but he managed to whip around to the stairs quickly and without effort. He turned the wheelchair so he faced away from the stairs and the wheels were against the first step. "Do you know how to lift a wheelchair upstairs?" Carrie immediately intervened.

"Why don't you talk me through it?" Reggie looked at his sister with confidence. "Okay. Grab the handles securely and tip the chair back on the edge of its wheels toward you. Now pull hard and gently move the wheelchair onto the next step. Then repeat the process until you are on the porch." Navigation was a success and Jackson breathed easier. Reggie picked up their luggage and showed them inside. Conveniently, there was a guest room on the main floor with a bathroom attached and a wide enough doorway that his wheelchair could be accommodated. That's where Jackson would stay. Carrie stayed upstairs in a room that she grew up in. There was an additional room built onto the back of the house and another bathroom. This is where Mrs. Langston stayed. She had fragile health but was alert and sharp. She greeted them in the living room as they entered. "Hello and welcome! It's so good to see you Carrie and nice to meet you Jackson. Both of you make yourselves at home and let me know if you need anything." Carrie acknowledged her mother and Jackson respectfully thanked her for her hospitality.

Dinner was a delicious home cooked meal complete with pork chops, mashed potatoes, gravy, applesauce, corn on the cob and homemade rolls. Jackson couldn't remember the last time he had a home cooked meal. He was even more surprised to find out Reggie had done most of the cooking. The family sat around the table for hours telling stories about Reggie, Carrie, and their dad. Discussions were made with details about Jackson and Carrie's encounter of when they met, their courtship, and engagement. Jackson was grilled by Reggie on his background, beliefs and upbringing. Reggie was a normal protective older brother and Jackson could relate to how he felt. Jackson was humble and didn't talk about his accomplishments much but Carrie would jump into the conversation and fill in the gaps or add her version with more details. Jackson felt comfortable with Carrie's family and relaxed in their home. He had a calmness come over him and a sense of acceptance that he hadn't felt in a long time. All of them cleared the table and cleaned up after dinner. Jackson tried to help without awkwardly taking up a lot of space in the kitchen.

The next day was planned the evening before and Carrie was duly excited as she rose early and prepared for the day. After breakfast she and her mother headed for Dayton to pick out a wedding dress that would be shipped back to Denver for the wedding and reception. Hurriedly they swept their handbags up and Carrie gave Jackson a peck on his cheek. "Bye! You boys have fun today!" Carrie called as she ran out the door to catch her mother who was already in the car. "You too!" Jackson called back. He then looked over at Reggie who was shaking his head and laughing. "I've never seen my sister this happy, Jackson. Thanks to you." "She is my whole world and I am deeply in love with your sister. I promise I'll take good care of her Reggie." Jackson got somewhat serious. "How about we kill some time?" Reggie asked. "What do you have in mind?" Reggie responded with the suggestion that he take Jackson over to the golf course and clubhouse and give him a tour. Then they could grab a burger and a Coke. "That sounds great!" Jackson grinned and turned his wheelchair toward the door. "I'm going to need some help getting down the stairs. You basically do it the same way as coming up only lift the chair one step at a time slowly down to the bottom." Jackson looked at Reggie for a confirmation of his instructions. "I've got this!" he said. Jackson squinted his eyes and flinched a bit as Reggie bumped his chair down each step with a slight jar. He was relieved to be at the bottom. The rest was an easy task for Jackson.

The golf course was typical of a smaller town or city. Fairways were well kept and sand traps raked with precision. The greens resembled outdoor carpet and were lighter than the grass in color presenting with a light shade of Kelly green. A few trees lined the course and a small pond was in the middle of the ninth hole. Reggie took Jackson on a tour by way of a golf cart. Jackson basked in bucket loads of memories as they navigated through the fairways. He really missed walking them and feeling the thrill of tee-offs. When they ventured into the clubhouse Jackson noticed there was no gym or tennis courts. It was small and matched the character of the town. "This is really nice Reggie. Do you play golf?" "Thanks. I try my best at golf but I am definitely a beginner. Are you ready for that burger?"

Reggie took Jackson to an old mom-and-pops hangout across town. It was dated by the looks of the front. Faded turquoise paint covered the façade and old sliding glass windows attached to the countertop pickup area. Worn out black vinyl letters blanketed the menu which had a layer of clear plastic on top of it. The menu was simple and consisted of burgers, home-style fries, onion rings, hotdogs, drinks and shakes. Both Reggie and Jackson enjoyed the biggest burgers available with everything on them, an order of onion rings with plenty of ketchup and a Coke. Jackson ordered a thick chocolate shake as a desert. For a moment, Jackson felt like he was back in high school. The two of them conversed for what seemed like hours and they soon noticed they had lost track of time.

Meanwhile, Carrie and her mother had arrived at the bridal shop and were exploring it, looking for her perfect gown. The shop was located in a quaint area of town and carried an old Victorian look. Two large glass windows settled on both sides of the front door. Displays of wedding dresses, shoes and accessories were carefully laid out in each window. Wooden flower boxes lined the outside edge of each window. The front door was painted a cream color and had an oval–shaped piece of glass in its center. *Rose's Wedding Boutique* graced the glass in a bold Victorian style of writing. A large brass doorknob welcomed patrons and as it turned, a small tinkling sound came from a bell when anyone entered the shop. Inside were several dresses placed on manikins and a wall of veils in a variety of shapes and styles, an area where shoes were sold, and fitting rooms along a back hallway. Many dresses were hung on racks in the front of the store.

Carrie was mesmerized and somewhat overwhelmed as she stood just inside the front door. She was a simple person and wanted her dress and her wedding to be in that perspective. A middle-aged woman greeted them, "Can I help you ladies?" Carrie hesitated as if to convince herself this was real, "I am looking for a wedding dress more simple and tailored, rather than big and lacey. And, a simple veil." "I think we can help you. Come over here," the woman gestured for Carrie to follow her to the racks of dresses along the wall. Carrie passed over almost every dress she looked at until three caught her eye. She went to the fitting room to try them on and couldn't ignore the butterflies she was feeling in her stomach.

Each one found Carrie coming out to a full-length mirror and slowly turning around examining the fit and look it gave her. Discouragement sat in when she rejected two out the three she had chosen. Then the last one made her face light up and her eyes widen as she twirled in front of the mirror. The gown was made of a light-weight white knit material and hung in a conservative A-style from the bodice. The sleeves were three-quarter length bell shaped with a delicate slit on the outside from three inches below the shoulder to two inches above the sleeve edged. Around the below-the-collarbone neck laid a circular collar that fell flat against the dress. It had small scalloped edges with tiny pearls and rhinestones appliqued along its edges. A very small and barely noticeable sweep-style train hung down the back of the dress. "Oh, it's perfect!" Carrie exclaimed. Carrie went on to select a shoulder-length veil made of thin soft netting with scalloped edges to match the neck of her wedding dress. The scallops were appliqued with tiny pearls and rhinestones. A white comb allowed the veil to be placed securely in the hair with the veil flowing down the back of the neck. Simple white pump-style shoes were Carrie's choice for footwear.

Carrie and her mother made arrangements after the fitting for everything to be shipped to Carrie's apartment in Denver and then they found a unique little café down the street. Discussing wedding plans over lunch was new to both of them. Pictures of the complete wedding outfit had been taken to share with Jackson when they arrived back at the farmhouse. She anticipated seeing the look on his face and the prospect of Jackson being more involved going forward. Carrie hadn't been able to discuss detailed wedding plans with Jackson because he had been so busy, but she was hopeful that he would participate more as his tournament schedule slowed down.

Chapter Eight

BEST-LAID PLANS

The doorbell rang and Jackson started to answer it when Joe burst through the entry way. "Jackson! Have you received your mail yet today?" "No, I haven't picked it up. Why?" "I'll go get it for you." "You have to see this!" Joe held a magazine in his hand and was flipping it around while he spoke. It took seconds for him to retrieve Jackson's mail. Joe shut the front door and swooped down on Jackson fast as he slapped the magazine in his lap. "Look at this, Jackson! This is incredible!" Jackson slowly picked up the magazine and looked at the front. It was Tennis Magazine and he said nonchalantly, "Okay, it's Tennis Magazine. So what?" "Turn it over Jackson!" Joe excitedly stated. Jackson turned the magazine over to see the full back cover featuring a picture of Jackson serving at a tennis match. It was a close-up view and you could even see details of his facial expression. "Now turn to page twenty-three." Joe hurriedly turned his magazine to page twenty-three and ruffled the pages as he turned them around to show Jackson. "It is a three-page article on you Jackson, from your beginnings to now. The article is well written and even features stats about your serving speed and technique." "I am speechless," Jackson said. "Oh, and it gets better. My sources tell me that there is a special about you on the channel nine news tonight." Joe grinned. "Your sources, huh?" Jackson reluctantly asked. "Yeah, I have sources and contacts in high places! Why don't you give Carrie a call and ask her if she wants to come over and watch the broadcast tonight? We can order Italian take-out, my treat."

Carrie was eager to accept the invitation to watch the evening news with Jackson and Joe. She wore something comfortable and casual. Carrie opened the front door and then knocked. "Hello, I'm here. Jackson?" "I'm in the kitchen. Come in." Jackson looked up from putting the take-out meal on plates to connect with Carrie's eyes. "What are you two doing? It smells good and looks even better." Carrie peered over Jackson's shoulder to scan the counter and look for the evidence of what she had smelled. "We are having Italian tonight, courtesy of Joe. Grab a plate and let's go watch the news." Jackson thought it odd that they were all excited about the evening news of all things. Carrie opened the refrigerator and quickly positioned three bottles of Coke between her arm and stomach. Then she swept her plate up into her free hand and headed for the living room. She turned and watched for Jackson to come around the corner. Jackson settled in to the recliner and Joe settled in to the sofa as they placed their plates of food on the table in front of them and used the remote to turn on the television.

It was toward the end of the national and local news that the sports section began and the anchorman came on and immediately started with the story about Jackson. They showed video footage and still pictures depicting Jackson's journey since his return from Viet Nam. Some photos had slipped his memory, until he saw them again. Jackson didn't get nearly as excited as Joe and Carrie. In fact, he didn't show much emotion, and quickly grabbed the remote control and switched off the television as soon as the program ended. Carrie glanced over at Joe and shrugged her shoulders. "What's wrong Jackson? I thought this would please you and get you excited." Jackson's mood rapidly changed as he responded, "All of this attention is making me crazy!

I don't deserve all of it and I have no privacy whatsoever." Joe joined the conversation and leaned forward toward Jackson. "Hey, buddy. Slow down with the self-sabotaging. You absolutely deserve *all* of the attention. Don't let it make you crazy. Embrace all of this as a Godsend. Look what a turn your life has taken since the accident. And as far as privacy goes; you can't be famous and extremely well-liked and have your privacy too. People love you and look to you for inspiration. You give so many hope; some that I'm sure you're not even aware of. So quit berating yourself. Think of it as a new mission to complete, Marine. You've got this!"

Jackson looked over at Carrie and she had tears in her eyes. "Carrie, I'm sorry, I didn't mean to hurt you." Jackson felt foolish for his outburst. "Jackson, it's just that I love you so much and it kills me to see you do this to yourself. It goes beyond being humble. And frankly, it is annoying to see someone as talented and blessed as you talk about themselves the way you do." Jackson was feeling attacked from all directions. His reply was defensive, "I know how lucky and blessed I am and I know I am good at what I do, but I get sick and tired of expectations from everyone. I can't seem to get away from it. I am not perfect and its time you all figured that out and quit expecting me to be!" The room grew quiet as the three of them tried to allow things to settle and cool down. Carrie picked up the dirty plates and silverware without saying a word. Joe finished his Coke and made an excuse to go help Carrie clean up. Jackson sat and felt guilty for blurting out feelings that he didn't have all the time. He knew Joe and Carrie were just trying to help. He rolled his chair into the kitchen and put an apology in motion.

Jackson and Carrie had an appointment for cake tasting the next day. They arrived at a renowned bakery in a quaint older section of downtown Denver. Its outward appearance was one of elegance and the displays in the windows were inviting. "Jackson, before we go in I have something for you." Carrie pulled a rectangular shaped flat object from her large handbag. It was wrapped in brown paper and tied with a piece of twine. "What's this?" Jackson said as if he expected her to tell him before he opened it. "I guess you'll have to wait and see." Carrie gave Jackson a comforting smile. He untied the twine and then carefully unfolded the brown piece of paper that it was wrapped in. Jackson grasped an eight-by-ten framed picture of the back cover where he was featured in Tennis Magazine. The frame was a dark ornate wood that matched Jackson's decor in his living room. "This is beautiful Carrie. You didn't have to do this for me." Jackson kept staring at the framed picture. "I wanted you to have something that would remind you every day of how amazing you are and deserving of praise. I love you, Jackson. Now let's go sample some wedding cakes!"

The shop owner greeted them cordially but business-like. He escorted them to an elegant room with several glass-topped tables positioned in each corner and the center of the room. The chairs were high-backed and armless. The back was an oval shape of plush golden velvet encircled by white and gold-trimmed wood. The seats were equally plush and padded and gave the chair a distinctive French provincial look. Long, white linen curtains hung from the windows and were gathered to the center side by an inch diameter gold cord; tied and with tassels dangling at the ends of the cord. A faint smell of baked goods floated in the air and the walls were covered with paintings featuring French bakeries and sidewalk cafes. Carrie and Jackson seated themselves at the center table. It had legs that resembled large white candy-canes resting on their hooks with the ends supporting the glass top. Carrie and Jackson reached for the white-linen napkins located just in front of them on the table and unfolded them on their laps.

Jackson thought to himself, "This is really fancy!" After seconds of entertaining that thought, the host caught his attention as he began to read the choices of cake and other desserts that the shop had to offer.

There was a variety, ranging from a simple double-chocolate fudge teared cake, a banana coconut and pineapple teared cake, a peanut butter caramel rum cake and a lemon-blueberry cheese vanilla cake. The host brought samples of each for Jackson and Carrie to taste. Sparkling water was served to quench their thirst. The cakes were served on china and the sampling forks were sterling silver. Jackson felt as if he was at a formal dinner and it was somewhat uncomfortable. He endured for Carrie's sake. She was enjoying every minute, like a child at a birthday party, excluding the candles. "I just can't decide!" Carrie exclaimed. "Which one do you prefer, Jackson? Here taste this one." Carrie scooped up a piece of the lemon-blueberry cake on her fork and navigated it toward Jackson's mouth, holding her opposite hand under the fork to catch any crumbs. "You're going to think I'm crazy, but I like the peanut butter caramel rum cake." Jackson gave Carrie a look of wanted approval. "Okay. Well, I really like that one too." Carrie's enthusiasm grew as they agreed on an important item for the reception. They discussed with the host about having a butter cream icing for color purposes and was told it was totally doable. Next stop was the florist.

The strong fragrant smell of flowers met Carrie and Jackson at the door of the florist's shop. There were three sections in front: one to the left with baskets and rows of different flower-types hanging on the wall, in the center were two sturdy shelves housing vases of all designs and sizes, and to the right towered three massive refrigerators with glass doors. The containers inside had several floral arrangements in vases with a price tag attached. Jackson and Carrie moved past the middle shelves and approached a half circle counter situated in a small corner of the room. A young woman in her twenties greeted them, "How can help you today?" She had a friendly smile, conversational green eyes and long red hair that hit just below her shoulders. Carrie quickly took over the conversation, "We need to order flowers for our wedding."

"Of course," the young woman replied. "Come with me to the back. We have a room with a table and chairs where you can sit comfortably while I show you samples of what we have to offer. Right this way." The woman opened a small swinging door at the end of the counter and motioned for them to follow her. They quietly went down a narrow, dimly-lit hallway and through an older wooden door that opened to a large room that looked comfortable but not ornate. The table was round and older, possibly an antique. Someone had taken time and patience by restoring its original beauty.

Picking out the floral arrangements took Carrie and Jackson much longer than choosing a wedding cake. Carrie couldn't make up her mind. Jackson was agreeable about everything and not so particular. The young woman who had greeted them when they first arrived sat next to Carrie and offered a few suggestions. Since the wedding was to be in December and they didn't want the traditional red, white and green color scheme, but still wanted it to be warm with a Christmas feeling, she suggested a simple white and gold color scheme with sprigs of green holly. Also, Carrie's favorite yellow roses could be blended in to the theme. After a couple of hours of debate and decision making, a design and theme concept was agreed upon. Carrie's wedding bouquet was to be arranged with white lilies, yellow roses and sparsely placed sprigs of holly. The boutonnieres were yellow roses with a sprig of holly on each side of the rose. Center pieces were long square frosted vases filled with yellow roses and white lilies. Green pine boughs served as table runners. There would be three Christmas trees set up that were different heights with tiny white lights, gold round and tear-drop ornaments, a wide gold ribbon garland and large gold ribbon bows evenly placed. There were white tree skirts that hugged each tree and white satin paper-wrapped gifts with gold ribbon would be under each. Carrie envisioned it all coming together more exquisite than she had originally imagined. Excitement grew as it started to feel real to both Carrie and Jackson.

The next few weeks Carrie and Jackson spent most of their time arranging the guest list and acquiring a venue for the reception. Things were chaotically busy and Jackson rarely thought about tennis. He made plans and reservations for their honeymoon which he was going to keep a secret. Plane tickets were booked and reservations made for a small village in Switzerland. The village, Einsilden, was cradled at the bottom of a small ski resort and was a mile away from a Montessori. Beautiful pine-covered, snow-capped mountains surrounded the village in a protective way. The streets were cobblestone and all the buildings had the look of Swiss chalets. The inn where they would be staying, was a family-owned bed and breakfast style quarters with log cabin décor throughout the whole building. A massive stone fireplace filled the main entryway and colorful soft chairs and sofas lined the wall. The main dining room was located to the right of a fireplace, which was shared with the entryway. Small log-style tables with wooden chairs spotted the floor and the table cloths were light blue with embroidered red flowers on the edges. Two walls of the dining room held large pane-glass windows that offered a postcard view of the mountains and clear blue sky. Upstairs were the sleeping quarters, complete with a feather bed and homemade ornate quilt. An older porcelain basin stood along one wall and fresh clean towels were folded and placed next to it. Bathroom facilities were down the hall and were shared with other patrons. Jackson made sure they were aware of his needed accommodations while making the arrangements for his and Carrie's stay. He found they had made renovations a few years ago to be able to accommodate wheelchair accessibility. This included an elevator and widened doors to all the rooms. Jackson was so excited to tell Carrie; he could hardly contain himself.

It was late fall in the Rocky Mountains. The air was sharp and crisp in the early mornings. Bright blue skies complimented the scarcely snow-capped peaks and a patchwork of rich fall colors covered their base.

This was Jackson's favorite season. He considered the weather perfect for a tennis match. In between wedding plans and business meetings for his charity, Jackson participated in several tennis tournaments and was at the top of his game. His tennis career was as vibrant as his surroundings. At home, trophies decorated the fireplace mantel and rested stoically on the wall shelves. Jackson was well-aware of their presence but never brought them to anyone's attention. It wasn't his way. This particular morning Jackson glanced at his collection as he hurried out the door. He had an appointment with the ecclesiastical leader who was going to perform his and Carrie's marriage. Jackson also had to obtain a marriage license. His mind was a spinning tornado of thoughts that didn't seem to calm at any time. He quickly threw on a light-weight jacket, grabbed his keys and locked the door behind him. He stopped for gas and picked up a Coke from a local drive through. The trip would take about an hour to reach his destination. More often than not, Jackson avoided having any kind of food or drink in his console while he was driving, but this time was an exception. All this thinking and decision making was causing a non-quenchable thirst to hover over him, and although he didn't drink much of it, the Coke strangely served as security just to have it there.

On his way to the meeting, Jackson's thought process went back and forth from wedding plans to observing the scenery and thinking how beautiful it was where he lived. The spiritual leader that he was meeting lived on a back secluded road lined by pine trees and greenery. Jackson approached the man's rambler-style home with anticipation and vigor. He was comforted when he noticed a ramp leading from the driveway to the front door. Jackson made note that having a ramp must mean someone living in the house had some sort of disability. Nervously, Jackson rang the doorbell. He seemed to wait for an uncomfortably long time before a grey-haired man in his early 70's slowly opened the door. "Ah, you must be Jackson Montgomery?" the soft-spoken man replied. "Yes sir. I am here to make arrangements for my fiancé's and my wedding. Carrie has recommended you highly and has the deepest respect for you. We would love it if you could perform the ceremony." "Well come in and let's talk." "Thank you Mr. Bennion." Jackson said as he pushed over the threshold of the door. "Please call me Brother Bennion, if you don't mind." The man's face seemed to glow and his eyes were gentle and kind. He was clean-shaven and donned an infectious smile that filled his face.

The two of them spent hours conversing about their stories of life and experiences that they had been through. Jackson felt unusually comfortable telling Brother Bennion things that he had only told Carrie. At times Jackson became tearful as he expressed emotions that he never before realized he had. Brother Bennion listened quietly and intently to Jackson, offering few comments. "I noticed your ramp outside. If it isn't too personal may I ask what it is for?" Jackson inquired. "My wife used it for a few years before she passed. *She* was also confined to a wheelchair." Brother Bennion became momentarily sober. They sat quietly with no information offered by Brother Bennion as to the cause of his wife's confinement. "Enough about me," the gentleman stated. "Tell me about you and your bride-to-be." The mood lightened when Jackson told about how he and Carrie met and fell in love. Soon the attention was brought to focus on the venue and reception. Jackson wanted to respect Carrie's wish to keep the wedding ceremony small and intimate with only a few family members and friends. Brother Bennion explained, "The space in the room where you'll be married is limited; so a small number would be ideal." Brother Bennion also went into detail about the procedures that took place in this special room and what was to be expected. This experience was fresh and new to Jackson and he was still acclimatizing to his new faith. They secured the date, place and time and cordially shook hands. Jackson left feeling calm and fulfilled. He had a sense of security he had never felt before.

He started home just as the sun began to set. It was so vibrant that it became distracting and Jackson had to make a conscious effort to focus on his driving.

The day after found Jackson and Carrie on another mini road trip. This time to view and secure the reception hall. Carrie sat on the edge of her seat and didn't seem to notice she was constrained by the seat belt. Exuberant anticipation filled the atmosphere of the car and Carrie periodically looked at Jackson and giggled. The reception hall wasn't too far away from Jackson's home and was a complete turnaround from the Lake Hills Country Club where he was married before. *The Logging Homestead,* as it was called, projected a look that matched the name that it had been given. Made of rustic logs, it stood majestically against the background of the breathless mountains. Large windows lined the front of the lodge and looked over a sleekly varnished wooden porch. The porch awning was held up by huge, round pillars and tiny white lights were wrapped around the banisters of the front stairs. There was a wheel-chair ramp to the right of the stairs. Both Carrie and Jackson thought it was perfect before they even saw the inside.

The couple made their way to the reception hall and dining room, which were more than satisfactory and then sat down with the manager in the dining area for lunch, his treat. The waiter brought a small appetizer out and placed it in the middle of the table. Jackson and Carrie stared at the basket. It contained whole, unshelled peanuts and they listened as they were instructed to throw the peanut shells on the wooden floor. Carrie's eyes widened as she chuckled and clenched her lips to fight back an awkward laugh. "Okay then," Jackson said as he quickly scooped up a handful of peanuts, sat them down in front of him and began cracking the shells. He popped several peanuts in his mouth as his eyes twinkled approval. "You seem to be a natural at this Jackson!" Carrie broke out in a quiet laugh as she covered her mouth. "Yup. I could definitely get used to this. It reminds me of Christmas time on the ranch. Mom would buy bags of nuts and have them sitting on the kitchen table like a smorgasbord that we could help ourselves to at any time. These peanuts are great, but I can't wait for the main course!"

Jackson had ordered a Porter House steak with a baked potato and salad on the side. Carrie ordered a simple Club Salad with a roll. The restaurant had a unique policy: if you could eat their 2-pound Porter House steak in one sitting, your meal was free. Jackson couldn't resist the challenge so he quickly got down to business. Carrie looked at Jackson curiously, "You *do* know that the meal is already free, right?" "Oh, I know but this sounds like fun!" Jackson's competitiveness was second nature. He even competed with himself! They relaxed and enjoyed themselves. It was so memorable that they made a pact that they would return to *The Logging Homestead* even after the reception had concluded.

Time sauntered by until the last tennis tournament before the wedding finally arrived. It was held in Atlanta, Georgia again. Jackson had been to several tournaments in Atlanta, but one stood out with a special memory. That is where he proposed to Carrie. Preparations were made and flights booked in advance. Jackson always paid for Carrie's ticket but now he also paid for Rex's. Rex consistently accompanied Jackson almost everywhere he went for security reasons. When they arrived, and after settling in their rooms, Jackson and Carrie headed toward the French restaurant where they had become engaged months ago. Rex followed them but hung back a little to give them some privacy. The street was quiet and dimly lit. Large buildings towered on both sides of the street and lent an echo effect to the sounds created by their walking. Lamps that resembled gas-light posts were located on each side of the door and a dark green- striped awning covered the entrance. Jackson and his beautiful bride-to-be approached the restaurant. Carrie was a few feet in front of Jackson and Rex was standing nearby, intently keeping watch. Rex turned his attention to the corner just a few steps from the entrance and noticed a medium built man wearing a black hoody and black plants. He was hovering on the far side of the lamp and awning. There weren't many people there tonight and Carrie turned to see if Jackson was coming behind her. Swiftly the man in black lunged at Carrie, grabbed her across her shoulders and drew a knife which he promptly put under her chin against her neck. Taken off guard, Jackson instinctively wanted to stand up and rescue her from this situation but he felt helpless. So he blurted out, "What do you want? Don't hurt her!" While Jackson nervously waited for a response, Rex had anticipated the potential problem and had quietly positioned himself behind the assailant. He softly approached the man not making a sound. Rex saw the terror on Jackson's face. Just as the man was about to state his demands, Rex grabbed his hand with the knife in it and slammed it against his own thigh, knocking the knife out of the man's hand. He deliberately pulled the man's arm around to his back and shoved him to the ground. Carrie broke away and ran to Jackson as he yelled for someone to call 911. It was not much of a struggle for Rex to keep the man subdued until the police arrived. Rex was ominously strong and unimaginably large and tall.

In minutes the flashing red lights of the patrol cars filled the night sky and their sirens slightly deafened the group on the sidewalk. Two officers cautiously exited their cars with guns drawn and pointed them at Rex. Alarmed, Jackson quickly shouted, "The man on the ground is the assailant! This man is my body guard." Jackson and Carrie watched as one officer asked for ID and another handcuffed the man in the black hoodie and escorted him to the patrol car. Jackson, Rex, and Carrie answered questions and the police took their statements. The three of them stood stone-like and without emotion while they watched as the patrol cars drove away with their lights flashing.

Jackson broke the silence by asking if Carrie was all right. When she assured him that she was, Jackson turned to Rex. "What the hell? What is going on Rex? What just happened?" Rex seemed annoyed at the question because he felt the answer was obvious. "I saw the man hanging out by the corner and he seemed to wait until you got closer and then he made his move. I have no idea who he is or why this happened, but I do assure you that you and Miss Langston are safe." "I thought I was through with this kind of crap. But apparently not!" Jackson looked at Carrie as he sighed heavily. "What do you want to do? Do you still feel like eating or do you just want to go back to the hotel?" "I'm ok" she responded. "I am not going to let some imbecile dictate how I am going to spend my evening. Besides, I am starving!" With that comment, they entered the restaurant and took one look at the dance floor. The memories of the night that Jackson proposed was healing and helped to fade the events of earlier.

Paparazzi swarmed Jackson at the upcoming tournament and reporters couldn't help but compete for microphone dominance. All questions were directed to the previous evening and the events that occurred at the French restaurant. Jackson waved most of them away as Rex cleared a path for him and Carrie. Once inside, Jackson found that playing tennis was cathartic and his stress level lowered considerably. It was incredible that he was able to concentrate on the tournament and actually win. Jackson was the epitome of perseverance.

For the next few weeks that's exactly what Jackson did, persevere. Patiently he endured a multitude of last minute wedding projects and details. He tried hard to make it look like he was invested in them. But reality was that Jackson really wasn't that picky. It wasn't that he didn't care, but he didn't have really strong preferences for anything. He was truly pleased with the whole wedding scenario like it was and couldn't wait to see how it would play out.

Jackson started to receive several invitations to speak at various events: special lectures, business conferences, high school graduations and university symposiums. Most of the time Carrie handled his schedule and booked him to speak, but now she was too busy with wedding planning to engulf herself in Jackson's business affairs. Jackson and Carrie decided to hire a personal assistant for Jackson, just until he and Carrie returned from their honeymoon. Jillette Ashford was interviewed by Jackson, Carrie and Joe. Miss Ashford was a young twenty-two-year-old who was working her way through law school. Her black, bobbed hair accentuated her ivory skin. She dressed business-like and wore mostly tailored, wool dress suits in conservative colors of greys and browns. Rex ran a background check on her for security reasons, which turned out to be squeaky clean. Daily check-ins were essential to coordinate Jackson's schedule and the wedding events. Jillette picked up the skills needed quickly; more than most. She was able to relieve the pressure both Jackson and Carrie were feeling. Time escaped existence and the holidays were soon upon them.

Jackson and Carrie were going to spend Thanksgiving with Jackson's family in Flagstaff. Carrie had only met them under dire circumstances and urged Jackson to let her see them in their own home environment. Carrie stared out the window of the 747 as it began its decent to the Phoenix airport. Everything was sunny and there was no sign of even a parcel of snow like back home. They acquired a rental car and began their trip to Flagstaff, which was two hours away. She amused herself on the way to Jackson's parents by taking pictures of the scenery from the window of the rental car. Rex was driving a large van-style vehicle with Carrie and Jackson in the back. Miles of rust-colored sand and cacti covered the landscape, and the warm sun aggressively beat through the window. Occasionally, Carrie would catch a glimpse of a few straggly looking trees. "What kind of trees are those?" she asked while quickly pointing to the side of the highway. "Those are Cedar trees, I think." Jackson gave Carrie a funny look. "Why are you so interested in the scenery?" he inquired. "Because," she said with emphasis. "It is different than anything I've ever seen and it is just beautiful!" Jackson couldn't help but laugh. "You actually think this desert is beautiful?" "As a matter of fact, I do!" Carrie retorted.

The scenery graduated from desert to small mountains covered with vegetation and evergreens. Jackson's whole family was waiting on the front porch to greet them. Mr. Montgomery Sr., Mrs. Montgomery, Samantha, and Rachel, Jackson's youngest sister, all stood on their tip toes waving exuberantly. Rex pulled the vehicle in front of the porch and before he came to a complete stop, all of them rushed and descended on the car. Excitedly, they began opening the doors and giving hugs before Jackson and Carrie could exit. Rex and Mr. Montgomery Sr. took care of the luggage while Samantha and Carrie managed Jackson's wheelchair. Rachel stood nearby clapping her hands and jumping up and down as she expressed her excitement. "I am so, so glad to see you big brother. Oh, yeah, and I am happy to meet you Carrie." "I am definitely thrilled to be here." Carrie flashed a grin at Rachel and moved forward to embrace her with a cordial hug.

Settling in was uneventful. Jackson's childhood home had been accommodated with wheelchair access years ago after the accident, in hopes that he would return to visit much more often than he actually did. It was evening and after a simple home cooked meal, Jackson's father built a fire in the hearth and they all sat around and shared stories, memories and pictures from albums the family had placed on the coffee table. Jackson took a secluded moment to turn his head and scan the scene, touring the itinerary of childhood memories he was finally able to remember. A sense of peace and contentment wrapped around him like a warm, soothing blanket and Jackson thought, "I have everything I need or could ever want right here in front of me. I am so blessed."

Jackson awoke early to the smell of his mother's baking and hearing a bustle and commotion in the kitchen. His mother was giving instructions to his sisters and Carrie to solicit help in preparation for Thanksgiving dinner. The lady of the house had been awake since 4:30 am. when she began cooking the turkey, making the dressing and rolls. She had already made several pie crusts the day before that would eventually be the home for pumpkin pie, chocolate cream, banana cream and lemon meringue pies. The smells were memory stimulating and drew Jackson into the kitchen. He smiled with affection when he saw Carrie with a large apron on, her hair pulled back into a ponytail, and flour brushed across her forehead. When she saw Jackson she smiled and gently reached up with the back of her hand to wipe the flour off. It was a good thing that the kitchen was extra-large so it could accommodate the women focusing intently on their individual assignments that contributed to the eventful Thanksgiving meal.

"Come on everyone! It's time to sit down. Dinner is ready!" Mrs. Montgomery smiled and waved her hands in anticipation as she placed dishes of vegetables, baskets of rolls, mashed potatoes, turkey gravy, dressing and candied yams in front of the family. Jackson's father carefully carried the turkey which was on a huge platter and set it in the center of the table. Per tradition, he proceeded to carve the turkey and when finished he sat at the head of the table and reached out his hands. "I'll say the blessing on the food." Jackson knew it as 'grace'. They all joined hands and reverently bowed their heads. After the prayer concluded, a strong 'amen' was said in unison.

Plates were filled to capacity. Jackson couldn't recall the last time he had eaten so much at one time. Amid the conversation, Carrie inquired, "What other traditions do you celebrate so robustly?" Jackson's father jumped at the opportunity to tell his story. "We have a tradition that takes place the day after Thanksgiving. My wife makes turkey sandwiches out of the leftover turkey and her homemade rolls. She fills a few thermoses with hot chocolate and we head for the mountains up above our ranch. We usually get a good load of snow here in Flagstaff. Believe it or not there *is* snow up here most of the time in winter months. When there is, we take our snowmobiles and when there isn't we take our trucks. Then we cut down our own Christmas tree, bring it home, and decorate it as a family." "Oh," gasped Carrie. "That sounds amazing!" Mr. Montgomery then turned to Jackson. "And, Jackson, we have a surprise for you. We have constructed a chair that fits on the back of the snowmobile and is complete with a seat belt to strap you in for safety. You can go with us, Son!" "Great." Jackson said reluctantly. "Sounds like being strapped to a bobsled. Can't wait." Jackson thought to himself, "Of all the things I have accomplished in the last couple of years, I think this might be the most challenging."

Morning crept over the mountain ridge and made the new-fallen snow gleam with brightness. Mrs. Montgomery was up before sunrise and had prepared all the essentials for the family outing. Eager to get an early start, everyone was dressed warmly and waiting in the living room for all to gather. Rex, Mr. Montgomery Sr. and Samantha had brought the snowmobiles to the front of the house. Jackson was pleasantly surprised at Rex's versatility. Rex had experience with snowmobiles and he would be driving one machine and carrying Carrie as his passenger. Mr. Montgomery had Jackson; Samantha drove with her mother on the back and Rachael drove with a long, black, flat sled that she dragged behind. Jackson needed help getting onto the chair attached to the back of the snowmobile. Once he transferred, he fastened the seat belt tightly and gripped the handles attached to each side of his chair. They were to help him with balance and increase his ability to lean into the turns the driver would make. Jackson was cautiously excited. It helped to focus on the tasks he had accomplished, namely waterskiing and snow skiing. He felt this would probably be a similar experience. The drivers covered their heads with a thick, warm stocking hat and pulled ski goggles down over their eyes. The high whiny-pitched roar of the engines started in sequence and the lead snowmobile driven by Mr. Montgomery, Sr. quickly pulled away from the rest. The track of the machine rotated rapidly from front to back much like the rotation of tires to propel them forward. Powdered snow blew slightly in Jackson's face and he felt the sting of the cold. Exhaust fumes occasionally pierced his nostrils but most of the time he breathed in deeply the clear fresh air of the mountains. Jackson had felt these extraordinary feelings before: when he became a professional golfer, when he learned to water and snow ski with one leg, when he became one of the first wheelchair tennis players, and now with this experience. He was emotionally overwhelmed.

The short journey up the mountain found Jackson sparring with childhood memories, both good and bad. He wrestled with thoughts of disappointment that *he* should be driving the snow mobile, not Rex. Jealousy seeped in and Jackson was surprised at himself for letting such an emotion enter his thoughts. He dismissed it as inconsequential. He did, however, think a lot about Carrie and how she was experiencing the ride. Imagination took over and he could envision her cheeks being blush-red from the cold wind and her face covered with a shiny dew from the blowing of the powdered snow. He could almost hear her laughter and at that moment Jackson resigned to his imagination and jerked himself back to reality.

Cutting down the Christmas tree was an observable activity for Jackson. He remained on the snowmobile and was amused as he watched Rex and his father wade through snow that hit their knees and flounder their arms to give them propulsion and balance. They were visibly winded when they arrived at a group of trees and turned to the family waiting at the snowmobiles for direction on the choice of tree to cut. Mr. Montgomery, Sr. pointed to several different trees and finally a unanimous voice fell on a perfectly shaped ponderosa pine that would make a splendid Christmas tree. After the tree was cut, it was tied to the long black sled that was behind the back of Rachael's snowmobile and secured. Everyone devoured the turkey sandwiches and hot chocolate that Mrs. Montgomery had prepared. Cold air makes one hungry and big appetites were not lacking among them.

Back at the ranch house, the afternoon and early evening were spent decorating the tree. Round and tear-drop shaped ornaments, large red bows and berry covered garlands were strategically placed on each branch. "Carrie, would you do the honor of placing the star on top of the tree?" Jackson's father's grin was wide and his teeth extra white against his sunburned and windblown face. "Me?" Carrie questioned. "I would love to." Jackson reached out and took hold of Carrie's hand as she stepped carefully onto the ladder. Stretching a bit, she pushed the star over the top branch and let the cord dangle in the back of the tree. Samantha plugged the star in and then as Carrie stepped onto the floor from the ladder she said, "Is everyone ready?" As the tree was lit the room glowed with a warmth of contentment and smiles of satisfaction were present on each of their faces. Jackson pulled Carrie to his lap. "I am so excited to put up our own tree and start making our own traditions. I never dreamed I could be as happy as I am right now with you." He then wheeled over to the doorway that led to the dining room. Attached to the top was a cluster of mistletoe. Jackson and Carrie didn't seem to know anyone else was around. Their gazes were soaked in to each other's being and the passion they felt in their kiss transported them to their own Shangri-La.

Chapter Nine

MARRIAGE AND MISTLETOE

"Just tell them NO!" Jackson forcefully replied to Joe who was on the phone with a reporter from the local news channel. "I don't want any reporters, journalists or paparazzi near or around the wedding chapel or the reception. PERIOD!" Joe covered the mouthpiece of the phone and asked, "Can't you just grant one or maybe two interviews?" "Who are you talking to?" Jackson inquired. "It's the young man who wrote the article about your journey, you know the one about after the war to now. Remember? He did an excellent job and was complimentary, but realistic about what he wrote." Joe answered. "Oh, I guess that an interview wouldn't hurt. It will have to be before the wedding because after the reception Carrie and I will be flying to Switzerland for our honeymoon." Joe turned back to his conversation with the reporter. "I'll have Miss Ashford, Mr. Montgomery's personal assistant, contact you this afternoon. Okay, your welcome. Have a good day." Joe hung up the phone and glared at Jackson. "Sometimes you're impossible!" Jackson nonchalantly turned his wheelchair away from his computer and pushed himself toward the kitchen. "I need a drink." Jackson rolled his eyes at Joe and shrugged his shoulders, demonstrating his aloof attitude.

Jillette had arranged the interview with Mark Buchanan for the following afternoon. Jackson requested that it be held at *The Logging Homestead*. He felt it was best to surround himself with a positive environment. Jackson arrived ahead of Mark and was seated at a table waiting for him. Mark made his entrance and cheerfully greeted Jackson and pulled up a chair. "Mr. Montgomery, I can't thank you enough for giving me the opportunity to interview you." "Please, call me Jackson. You already have first-hand knowledge of my life and that's personal." "Yes Sir." Mark respectfully replied. "Let's order something to eat before we get started," Jackson said as he picked up a menu and directed Mark to do the same. The waiter approached the table. He was dressed in casual jeans, a red-checkered flannel shirt, leather belt and swede leather shoes that resembled hiking boots. Jackson immediately thought of a 'lumberjack' when he saw him coming their way. The waiter addressed Jackson with well-deserved recognition. "Good afternoon Mr. Montgomery. It's a pleasure to see you again. What can I get for you?" Jackson was theatrical when he ordered his typical two-pound Porter House steak medium rare and Mark ordered their halibut special. The waiter returned in a few minutes and placed a basket of peanuts in front of them. Mark was astonished when he observed Jackson shell the peanuts and then throw the shells on the floor. His eyes glanced downward at the floor and then focused on Jackson with inquisition. Jackson gave Mark a spirited grin and continued eating the peanuts. The interview went on for an hour and a half with questions ranging from how Carrie and Jackson met and became engaged, to plans for the wedding and honeymoon. Mark included information about Jackson's status in the tennis ranks and his travels on the circuit. Jackson didn't seem to mind answering questions for Mark but was relieved when the interview was over. He waited until Mark left and then immediately called Carrie. It made him feel much more calm and relaxed to have a conversation with the love of his life rather than the media.

Jackson soon found himself rushing around his house trying to gather his belongings needed for the wedding and reception. Joe was there to help but seemed more frazzled than helpful. He constantly blurted out the check-list, which he had comprised, "Have you got your white tie? How about socks and a white belt? Oh, yeah, don't forget your tuxedo and cummerbund for the reception!" Jackson stopped Joe in the middle of his rambling. "Joe, relax! I've got this. It is all lying on the couch ready to go." "I know," Joe replied. "I'm just so nervous." Jackson gave Joe a perturbed look. "You're nervous? I'm the one getting married today! Look, I need you to pull yourself together, Joe. You're my best man and I need you to keep *me* calm!" "Yeah, yeah, okay Jackson. Sorry. I'll do better, I promise." Joe pulled his shoulders back, pushed his chin out, and fist-punched the air in front of and above his head, as if he was giving himself the 'charge' signal. Quietly he mumbled under his breath, "I've got this! Let me load everything in the car while you make a last check *just* to be sure you haven't forgotten anything." Joe whisked up the clothing and bags that were on the couch and briskly walked to the car, where he placed most of the items in the trunk. He hung Jackson's tux and white suit on a hook that was above and on the side of the back seat. Meanwhile, Jackson humored Joe and wheeled through the house visually scanning for items that might be left behind and systematically marked them packed in his mind.

The car was freezing, and both Jackson and Joe could see their breath as they talked. The sky was a bright, cold blue with lightly fallen fresh snow on the ground. Joe grabbed a snow scraper and jumped out of the car to clear the windshield of ice. Jackson was distracted in thought as he focused on the deep scratching sound the scraper made as Joe pushed it back and forth against the windshield. Joe brought some delicate snow flurries back in the car as he climbed in when he was finished. "Whew! It's cold out there!" Joe exclaimed as he breathed hard and rubbed his hands quickly together. Jackson countered with,

"It's a perfect day." He had a content closed-mouthed smile on his face as he put the car in drive and directed their course toward the sacred religious building and chapel where he would be married to Carrie. Clumps of snow fell on his windshield from the trees hanging overhead that had been weighted down from the evening's storm. There was a soft silence in the car. Jackson was thinking and Joe was gazing out the window. The silence was occasionally interrupted by the thud of the snow falling against the windshield, which prompted a quick brush of the windshield wipers clomping back and forth several times before stopping. Soon they were out of the trees and speed picked up as they entered a nearby highway. Snow flew from the hood of Jackson's car over the top and past his side windows. Nature was showing her quiet excitement.

Jackson's heart began racing and his stomach was doing noticeable flip-flops as they pulled into the parking lot. The majestic structure stood before him like a monument to all things sacred. The building was a light cream-color and large pillars guarded the front entrance. An enormous steeple balanced the center of the building and a golden statue of an angel was perched at the top. The sliding doors were trimmed in gold and the grounds were covered with undisturbed fresh snow. There were garlands of snow flocked trees that lined the sidewalk leading to the entrance. It resembled a majestic castle floating on a soft cloud. Jackson was carrying his white suit and white clothing he would be wearing for the ceremony and Joe exhibited a look of a well-to-do business executive. A tall, middle-aged man greeted Jackson, asked for some identification and then offered to show him to the groom's area. Another kind gentleman escorted Joe to a place he could comfortably wait for Jackson.

In the groom's area everything was ornately decorated with gold-trimmed white tables, a sofa made of smooth, teal-blue velvet and two large arm chairs that matched. The temple workers, as they were called, were quick to offer Jackson all the assistance he needed to be prepared for the event that was only moments away, his wedding. Jackson struggled a little with dressing in a suit, wearing a belt and a tie. It took him longer than most to dress and he felt the awkwardness of everyone being so concerned about his ability to take care of his own needs. Jackson knew they all meant well, but he didn't have time to focus on their concern as he was so nervous about what lie ahead.

He wouldn't see Carrie until they were at the wedding alter and receiving their vows. He imagined how beautiful she would look and basked in the feelings of love that he had for her. The time for the ceremony arrived and Jackson found himself wheeling into a slightly bigger- than- average room with white, velvet-backed chairs arranged in a half-circle. These chairs would seat the limited guests who were there to witness his wedding. Jackson scanned the room and made eye contact with his parents. They returned his glance with a loving grin of approval. Joe was seated next to Jillette and Carrie's entire family had made the trip. Jackson pulled up to one side of the alter and faced the opposite side. It was next to a velvet covered low step where he and Carrie would kneel across from each other to take their vows. There had been some considerable concern earlier among the temple workers that Jackson wouldn't be able to navigate kneeling at the alter; but Jackson stubbornly and emphatically insisted that he would be able to do it without help. Jackson thought to himself, "This is one time that I am going to complete this mission on my own, with only God's help."

Carrie walked into the room from a separate door than Jackson. She floated over to the alter, smiled at Jackson and looked at the officiator who then motioned for both of them to kneel at the alter across from each other. Carrie went first and nervously watched as Jackson pulled the right side arm off of his wheelchair and maneuvered to the edge so he could transfer himself to the small bench. He made sure his wheels were locked and he used his strength and determination to reach out and grab the top of the other side of the alter and carefully lower himself down. Carrie instinctively reached out to give Jackson her hand in assistance, but his look of independence caused her to withdraw it and rest it in front of her. He then positioned his legs with one hand to a kneeling position; alternating the hand and arm he used to steady and support himself and accomplish this difficult task. Jackson concentrated so hard on making this happen that he was unaware of his surroundings for a few minutes. But, Carrie was acutely aware of the situation. She could almost feel everyone in the room holding their breath and mentally offering their assistance to Jackson. She teared up as she observed Jackson's face become bright red with a fine film of sweat covering his forehead, cheeks and chin. Finally, Jackson was able to take Carrie by the right hand, as he was instructed to do, and intently listened to the officiator conduct the wedding ceremony with grace and dignity. The officiator counseled them to be kind to one another and love each other deeply and unselfishly. He advised them to always put God first in their lives and then their family. When the officiator mentioned the part about them being together forever, they both looked intently into each other's eyes, smiled faintly and squeezed each other's hands. Jackson took note of the mirrors that were strategically placed behind each of them signifying eternity. The mirrors displayed an endless reflection and Jackson thought of the endless love he had for his new bride. The most satisfying feelings and thoughts went through Jackson like exposure to the warm sunshine after being cold. Jackson placed the elegant, but simple ring on Carrie's finger and she did the same for Jackson. Jackson then slowly and meaningfully kissed Carrie and told her that he loved her. Jackson was out of breath and his arms ached by the time the ceremony concluded and when he went to transfer back to his wheel chair a couple of men rushed to aid him. Jackson waived them away signaling that he didn't want their help. Carrie patiently waited until Jackson had his side arm placed back on his chair and the brakes released and then assertively went to him and wrapped her arms around him tightly. "I love you so much Jackson, and I am proud of you." Jackson returned the sentiment, gave Carrie a quick kiss and then they both returned to their respective dressing areas to change.

This time Carrie traveled with Jackson to the reception center while Joe caught a ride with Jillette. It was dusk when they arrived and the sky was a burnt-orange and reflected on the snow. The sky was clear and gave the look of a water-colored painting. Carrie still wore her wedding gown, but Jackson had changed into his tuxedo and shiny black shoes. Jackson motioned to Carrie to stay put in her seat while he transferred to his wheelchair and then went around to Carrie's side of the car to open the door for her. "Wow! You're my wife!" Jackson proclaimed when he opened the car door, as if he was trying to convince himself. Carrie laughed and distinctly mouthed, "And, you're my husband." They both melted into the realization of belonging to each other for eternity and enjoyed being in the moment.

Tiny white lights covered the railing, the pillars on the porch, and trimmed the roof of *The Logging Homestead*. A greeter met the guests and directed them to the dining room where a meal was completed before moving to the massive room where Jackson and Carrie stood with Joe and Samantha, best man and maid of honor respectively. Three pine trees hovered in the corner and were donned with artificial snow on the tips of the branches, wide gold ribbon garland encircling the tree and white and gold glistening ornaments hanging from each branch. They added warmth and light to the reception room because of the enchanting and pleasant glow that was cast. Presents of various sizes, wrapped in white shiny paper and tied with gold ribbon surrounded each tree like a scarf in winter. A string quartet added a soft elegance as they played classical and Christmas music. It felt like Christmas morning, celebrating with family and friends and experiencing the joy of receiving just what you had dreamed of your whole life.

Jackson motioned to Carrie to lean down to him when there was a break in the crowd. "Have I told you in the last few minutes that I love you? I feel like I am in a transparent bubble and all I can see is you. I sense your warmth and I have vision of your joy. I take comfort in knowing you feel the same way." "You know I do, Jackson. This experience is magical and spellbinding." Carrie reached over and gave Jackson a hard squeeze being careful to not smash his boutonniere. The yellow rose with sprigs of holly stood out against Jackson's midnight black tux. Just as Carrie rose up to resume her position in the reception line, the bubble that Jackson had so romantically described to her suddenly burst. Carrie gazed in horror as her eyes pounced on the person standing in front of them. "Well, hello Jackson. You're looking good." The woman condescendingly nodded at Carrie. "Vanessa, what are *you* doing here? I thought you were in jail." Jackson exclaimed. "Thanks to Daddy and a good lawyer, I am no longer incarcerated thank you; and besides, I couldn't resist a good party." Vanessa had an underlying swagger that Carrie couldn't help but notice and it alerted her to exhibit caution. "You weren't invited Vanessa." Jackson distinctively stated. "You know I have always been a party crasher. And, I need to give my condolences to the bride." Vanessa's voice raised as she brought forward the glass of wine she had been holding out of sight next to her side and threw it in Carrie's face. Commotion ensued and multiple gasps and heightened conversation could be heard. It all alerted Rex, who was standing nearby and witnessed all of it.

Rex vigorously escorted Vanessa out and put her in a cab, warning her to stay away from Jackson and Carrie. He told her that if she came anywhere near again it would be considered a threat and the police would be called. Carrie slowly looked down in shock at her gown which was now wine stained and burst into tears. Jackson quickly assessed the situation, took Carrie's hand and softly said, "Come on, let's get out of here. He took Carrie to a back room where she changed into her regular clothes. "I'm sorry Carrie. I didn't see that coming! We can have your gown cleaned." "It's okay Jackson. Vanessa is a vile woman and you have nothing to do with what happened." "Oh yes I did. My involvement with the Remingtons was what brought us to this very situation and I am deeply sorry." Carry cupped his cheek gently and sighed, "If it's all right with you, I would rather head to the airport now instead of going back in there. The reception is almost over anyway and we have already cut the cake." "That's a perfect idea. Just give me a minute to change and I will tell Rex we are ready to leave." Both of them moved into hyper-drive. They were anxious to leave the reception and the potentially embarrassing remarks that might occur. Rex carried and loaded their luggage into the car and kept the photographers at bay. There were crowds of admirers, reporters, and joy seekers, even though there wasn't an invitation given nor their attendance planned. The crowd was like a swarm of bees and it was exhausting making their way through. Questions were yelled at and hummed around them.

Jackson and Carrie leaned back in their chair on Jackson's private jet. They were still holding each other's hands and acting as if no one else was around. They simultaneously lowered the back of their chairs and clasped their fingers together tightly. The attendant kept offering drinks and snacks but they ignored her and focused in on each other. Carrie and Jackson slipped into slumber quickly, aided by the exhaustion they were feeling from earlier. They were rested and breathed a sigh of relief as the plane touched down in the Zurich Airport. Their excitement grew as the sound of the tires screeching pierced their ears and they felt the jar of the massive machine become land bound again. As they descended from the plane, their noses were suddenly cold as they took in the crisp, clean mountain air. A tall man with a husky build was there to greet them at the baggage claim. He retrieved Jackson and Carrie's bags, placed them on a large cart, and greeted both of them. He had an accent as he spoke. "Mr. Montgomery, I presume? I am Johann and will be your driver and body guard for the remainder of your visit here in Switzerland." Rex had arranged ahead of time for a rental car and hired a well-vetted bodyguard to drive them around where ever they wanted to go. Rex emphasized that the Montgomery's safety was to be of utmost importance to Johann.

The first stop was the family owned bed and breakfast that Jackson had booked months before. Switzerland was everything Jackson and Carrie expected. The quaint hotel, chocolate shops, cobbled walk-ways and a myriad of small shops, plus the scenery produced memories that were branded into their thoughts. They absorbed the experience in its entirety, melting into the feelings of the Swiss culture, the unique architecture and designs and the unforgettable foods and pastries. Jackson couldn't resist taking home a token souvenir; one that would always remind them of Switzerland. So, Carrie and Jackson explored the village shops until they found the perfect fit, a Swiss clock shop. It had a small wooden exterior with two large windows on each side of the door. The glass was adorned with fancy gold writing that was written in French or German; they weren't sure. They couldn't understand or read either of those languages. As they ventured through the glass door trimmed with dark wood, a high pitched bell rang. It was the deep rich sound of a brass bell and not like a door bell. Jackson's eyes opened wide as his glance settled on the wall of different sized and variety of clocks. Some were cuckoo clocks with extravagant and ornate designs and others were simple time-keepers. All were made of wood and brass and were unparalleled from anything he had ever seen. Carrie wandered in amazement, carefully examining the ones that caught her attention. Then Jackson saw it. Toward the back of the shop stood a grandfather clock. The wood was rich and polished with a flat shine. The glass had beveled edges and was thick and hearty. Perfectly sculptured brass was woven throughout the clock's design. While Jackson sat admiring the masterpiece, the shop keeper quietly walked over and asked, "Would you like to hear it chime?" His accent was thick and hard to understand but his friendly smile invited Jackson to nod his head and say, "Yes, I do."

The shopkeeper was an older gentleman with grayed hair and beard. He wore a pair of spectacles on the edge of his nose. His cheeks were a rosy pink and his eyes a twinkling light blue. He carried a small beer-belly and his pants were held up by suspenders. A pair of baggy trousers complimented his gray-striped shirt. The keeper reached forth his wrinkled hand and placed the key in the slot to wind up the clock. He trembled as he worked and often looked up with a wide grin that pushed his cheeks up and made his eyes squint. Jackson listened intently for the chime while trying to drown out the tick tock of the hundreds of clocks running in random and different rhythms throughout the shop. The mesmerizing chime came and soothed Jackson much like classical music had done in his past. Twelve chimes filled the air and attracted Carrie to the scene. She gently placed her hand on Jackson's shoulder and halfway through the performance she whispered, "This is the one."

Jackson and Carrie spent considerable time trying to communicate with the shop keeper about their desires. He just kept nodding his head and in a thick German accent repeated, "Ja, ja." Carrie frustratingly asked, "Do you or anyone speak English?" The man reworded the question, "Ja. English?" He then turned and went to the back and opened a closed door. Soon a young, thin woman approached. The woman wore her long blond hair in a braid that fell against her back. Her eyes were the same light blue as the shop keeper and her cheeks just as rosy. Her dress was embroidered with beautiful flowers that were commonly seen in the Swiss countryside. She was carrying a bright colored towel and seemed to be drying her hands. "Hello, I am Beketa. He is my grandfather." She motioned to the man who had helped Carrie and Jackson and spoke with the same thick accent, but she spoke English well and was easier to understand. "Do you want to make a purchase?" "We absolutely do!" Jackson answered excitedly. Can you ship it to our home in the United States?" "Ja, we can do that. It does take a few weeks and is quite costly." The girl gave a look to Jackson that required a response. "That's fine. Time and expense is of no concern. We would love to purchase this Grandfather clock." "Okay," Beketa grinned. "Come this way and we can fill out the paperwork and get started." Carrie and Jackson celebrated their new-found treasure by having a special dinner in a nearby village restaurant before their preparation for their flight home.

The new Montgomery family's arrival home was festive to say the least. Paparazzi and reporters were lined up at the airport like vultures waiting for their prey. Cameras flashed with vengeance and gave competition to the bright holiday lights that were scattered all through the airport on the way to the baggage claim. It was assuring to have Rex meet them and escort them safely to their car. Rex wasn't one to initiate conversation so it surprised Jackson when he asked, "Was your trip acceptable sir. How did Johann work out for you?" "He was extremely skilled and professional. And, he was friendly. He showed us a lot of sights and shops to explore. Thank you, Rex for arranging everything. It made the trip much more enjoyable and we felt safe, knowing that Johann was there for us" "Your welcome sir, and congratulations to you both." Rex rarely smiled but Jackson could see in the rearview mirror that his face matched his tone of voice. Jackson mischievously thought, "Goodness, he has white teeth! I've never seen his teeth before." Jackson returned Rex's smile.

The couple arrived at Jackson's home one week before Christmas. Jackson asked Rex to hold the door open for him then motioned for Carrie to come to him. He pulled her down to his lap and proceeded to carry her over the threshold in his wheelchair. Carrie threw her head back and laughed as she clung to Jackson's neck. She slowly breathed in the scent of his cologne when she placed her lips next to his neck. Once inside, she briskly stood up and opened her arms wide. "Okay, enough play. We've got work to do!" "What? We just got home." Jackson wheeled closer to Carrie and asked, "What work are you talking about?" "Why, a Christmas tree silly. And all the decorations. I'll call Joe to come help if you don't mind?" Carrie had already taken off her coat and was starting to navigate the phone call. "Uh, sure. I don't mind." Jackson timidly said. Rex carried their luggage inside and put them in their respective rooms. "Will that be everything Mr. Montgomery?" Jackson reached in his wallet and took out two, one- hundred dollar bills. He placed them in Rex's palm as he shook his hand. "This is something extra for you. You do a great job and I want you to have a Merry Christmas." "Sir, this is too much. You already substantially paid me my wages." "I know. Just consider this a tip." Rex nodded his head, thanked Jackson, and closed the front door behind himself.

"Okay, kids! Let's get to it!" Joe briefly knocked and burst through the front door. "Oh, hi Joe. We'll have to do something about the way you announce your arrival. We *are* glad to see you though." Joe greeted Jackson with a big man-hug and gently turned to Carrie and asked if he could hug her too. "Of course. You're family. Are you ready to do this?" Carrie and Jackson had gathered their warm coats and gloves and were prepared when Joe arrived. Climbing in the car, they all headed for the nearest Christmas tree lot. Jackson felt it wasn't the same as cutting down your own tree like back home, but it was exciting for him and Carrie to start their own traditions. Carrie pushed Jackson's wheelchair through the snow at the tree lot. It was just deep enough that she struggled and then eventually turned it over to Joe. Jackson was particular about the tree he wanted and was grateful that Carrie had the same taste. Both of them abruptly stopped in front of a medium height blue spruce. It was symmetrical on all sides and they felt it was perfect. Jackson could smell the scent of pine as he watched the tree be cut. The workers bundled it with twine to keep the branches from breaking and to make it easier to load on top of the car. This was a challenge because Jackson's car was a convertible, but they managed and soon were on their way home.

Joe and Carrie moved furniture around to make room for the Christmas tree. Carrie invited Joe to stay and share in the tree trimming party with them. She also invited a few of Jackson's friends from the club over. Joe carried all the lights for the tree and for the outside in from storage, and Carrie cradled the box of newly purchased ornaments and sat it under the tree. Jackson was able to place the lower tree lights on and Carrie reached the higher ones. The lights were tiny and white and smothered the tree. Small red bulb lights were sporadically dispersed amongst the white. A beautiful Christmas tree evolved after the ornaments, garland and the star was placed on the top of the tree. The color scheme resembled Carrie and Jackson's reception, which pleased them even more. Carrie stood back from the tree with Jackson and the others to evaluate their work, and there was approval all around. Joe mentioned to Carrie and Jackson that they should come out onto the porch and see what had been done. Carrie slowly pushed Jackson over the threshold and into the night air. Lights were strung everywhere, on bushes, on windows, the roof and even on the trees. It made a spectacular Christmas village experience. Carrie clasped both of her hands and put them up to her mouth as she gasped. She teared up, which gave the scene a blurred effect. "How can we ever thank you?" She muddled through her tears. Joe sprang forward, "How about some of those freshly baked chocolate-chip cookies you just made and some hot chocolate?" "Okay. That works for me!" Carrie motioned for everyone to come into the kitchen and dining area. Not only was she gracious and humble about her talents, but she was also hospitable and treated all of her and Jackson's friends like family.

The first stage of the Christmas holiday was a success, thanks to caring friends; and now the next few days were spent shopping and wrapping presents. Carrie insisted that Jackson not be too extravagant with their Christmas because she was raised to be frugal. Even though she and Jackson had money, this concept was still engrained in her nature. But Jackson didn't intend on scrimping for Carrie, even a little bit. He had things planned for her that would be memorable and lasting. He thought about the Grandfather clock that they had purchased in Switzerland which, miraculously, was arriving two days before Christmas. Jackson had paid for a rush delivery but held his breath that they would actually follow through with the agreement. The Grandfather clock was only part of the surprise. And that's exactly what it was, a surprise. Jackson didn't tell anyone, even Joe. He waited until Carrie was scheduled for a day shift at the hospital, which was rare, but did happen on occasion.

Jackson put on his leather coat and gloves and made his way to his car. He was exuberant as he transferred in the car and warmed up the vehicle. He kept thinking about Carrie's gift and how she would possibly react. It had been snowing and the roads were wet and slushy so Jackson exhibited extra caution as he headed downtown. He had previously selected the gift from a high-end jewelry store and ordered it to be meticulously wrapped. Jackson was on his way to collect the gift and carefully place it under the tree so Carrie wouldn't suspect right away.

He drove for quite a few minutes up and down each row of the parking garage looking for a handicapped spot close to the elevators. He stopped in back of one and put his signal on hoping someone would approach soon so he would not block traffic. A young man, carrying an armful of packages and clasping bags with handles attached, walked close to the vehicle. He unlocked the car and trunk where he placed all the gifts he had with him. Then he jumped in, started his car, backed out and drove away. Jackson's blood began to boil and he gritted his teeth. His heart rate increased and his breathing was deep and labored.

He slammed both of his fists on the steering wheel. "That man could walk just fine. He was not handicapped! Why can't people think of those who really *need* the handicapped parking spot and not use it just for convenience?" Jackson was so hurt and angry that he teared up, but abruptly wiped his eyes and finished parking his car. He reached up and hung his 'handicapped' sticker on his rear view mirror, which was an item he noticed that the previous occupant did not have.

The heavy glass doors leading to the area where he found the elevator, were a challenge. His chair banged against the door several times before he was able to maneuver his wheelchair into the door space so that he could finally push through and open it. The elevator buttons were barely within his reach, and when he reached the inside of the elevator he exhaled deeply and with relief. Jackson's eyes were drawn to the small green lights above the elevator doors that notified the occupants what floor was on the other side. He was lost in thought as he waited for the ground floor to appear. Then a bell brought him back to reality and he pushed himself out into another enclosed area. Through two more glass doors and he was on the sidewalk.

Jackson looked up to see the light snowflakes float to the ground. Some of them touched his nose and cheeks and left a minute sensation of cold as they rapidly melted. Crowds of shoppers bustled by him. Many offered an awkward glare, probably wondering what a guy in a wheelchair was doing on the street in this weather. At least those were Jackson's thoughts. He glanced to his right and noticed a crossing walk about ten yards away. Jackson found himself subconsciously giving himself a 'pep-talk'. "You can do this Marine. Complete your mission."

Carefully and with caution, Jackson eased his wheelchair down a small sidewalk ramp that led to the road and crossing walk. The cement in the ramp was grated to avoid anyone slipping on the slanted walk. The light had turned green for the pedestrians to proceed to cross the street. Many people hurried by Jackson and even acted annoyed with him being there. His wheels slipped in the slushy snow and ice, so Jackson gave an extra heavy push to dislodge them from the pile of ice in which they had become imbedded. Panic set in as Jackson felt his wheelchair start to tip and become off-balance. Jackson felt the sting and painful sensation to his face as he planted cheek first on the ground. His face was burning and he had landed sideways causing his left shoulder to painfully throb. The smell of fumes from passing cars burnt his eyes and nostrils. He blew out the cold dirty slush that had found its way into his mouth. It had a gross taste of salt and soil. Jackson squirmed to try and right himself into a position that he could help himself, but to no avail. He cranked his head and neck to see if anyone was around that could help and caught a glimpse out of the corner of his eye of several people who had passed by him and were now reaching the other side of the crosswalk. Car horns sounded as they swerved to avoid hitting him. Jackson's thoughts went briefly back to Viet Nam and being in a foxhole where he felt equally as trapped. He started counting the men and women that walked right by him and didn't even ask if he was okay. It was disheartening. Jackson started to feel the freeze set in and he wondered how he would ever get out of this situation, when two men in their twenties stopped and asked if they could help him. Gratefully, Jackson accepted and the two of them lifted and tipped Jackson and his wheelchair to an upright position. "Are you hurt?" One of the young men asked. "Oh, just a few scratches and maybe a bruise or two; but I think I'm okay." Jackson brushed the watery sleet off the front of his jacket and sleeves as he said, "I can't thank you enough," Jackson reached out and shook both of the men's hands. "No problem, sir." One of them called out. "Have a Merry Christmas and, oh yeah, thanks for your service." Jackson immediately thought to himself, "How did they know that I'm a Veteran?" Jackson pondered that thought as he proceeded to cross the road along the crosswalk. The mishap with the fall didn't deter Jackson from completing his mission.

He arrived home later than planned and quietly slipped over to lay his gift under the tree. Just as he did, Carrie came from the kitchen. "What have you got there Mr. Montgomery?" "It's Christmas time Mrs. Montgomery. I am allowed secrets and you are not allowed to hear them." Jackson turned and faced Carrie head on and she gasped, "Jackson! What happened? You're scratched and bleeding on your face!" Carrie darted over to Jackson and turned his cheek with her hand to get a closer look at his injuries. "It's nothing. I just lost my balance in my chair earlier, but I'm fine. Two nice young men helped me out." Jackson did not want to worry Carrie with all the details of what actually happened. Then his attention was drawn to Carrie's Christmas cardigan she was wearing. It was extra bulky and moving! "Carrie, what's in your sweater?" Jackson looked up to see Carrie brimming with excitement as she slowly and carefully unbuttoned the cardigan.

A little wet black nose pushed and squirmed its way out, followed by two warm dark brown eyes. Long eyelashes blinked at Jackson and the black, white and brown long-furred animal began to whimper and bark. It wiggled until the puppy jumped out of Carrie's arms and landed on Jackson's lap. Paws were placed on Jackson's shoulders and a pink tongue bathed his face in rough, wet, puppy kisses. The dog was hyper-excited to be on Jackson's lap. "Surprise!" Carrie shouted through a giggle. "Merry Christmas, Jackson. She is a mixture of terrier and poodle." Jackson had both hands under the puppy's front legs trying to hold her still when he was able to get a sentence out, "What are we going to name her?" Carrie looked up and hanging above the door where they were standing was the mistletoe that they had carefully placed before their wedding. She bent down and tried to give Jackson a kiss but had a lot of competition from the puppy's kisses. "How about Mistletoe? Let's name her Mistletoe."

Chapter Ten

VENGEANCE FOR VALOR

Jackson sat in the back stage of a large auditorium, peering out around the curtain to watch and listen to the host announce his introduction. The lights pierced through the darkness across the stage and platform, and reflected on the microphone occasionally flashing a bright glare his way. He watched as a young student pulled the microphone close to the front of his mouth, cleared his throat, stood up tall and smiled as he greeted the audience. Jackson parted another layer of the curtain making a tiny crack enabling him to scan the audience that he was about to address. To his surprise, every seat was full and there were students standing in the aisles. The young man began, "Good afternoon everyone. I am Kenneth Hayes, President of the religious student association on campus and I am honored today to introduce our guest speaker, Mr. Jackson Montgomery. Mr. Montgomery is a retired member of the United States Marine Corps and served two tours of duty in Viet Nam. Decorated as a hero, he returned with an honorable discharge to be faced with the task of recuperating and rehabilitating from a serious injury that he received while saving another soldier's life. Becoming an amputee with a prosthesis leg, he went on to accomplish the miraculous feats of water skiing, snow skiing and touring with the PGA as a professional golfer. After his success, he was faced with paralysis caused from an automobile rollover that changed his life again. With fortitude and perseverance, he pioneered wheelchair tennis on a national level and built his own business from the ground up. Now, without any more delay, I present Mr. Jackson Montgomery."

As Jackson slowly but purposefully rolled onto the stage, he noticed the podium being lowered to his wheelchair level and then he turned his head, fighting the glare of the lights, and shockingly observed the entire audience rise to their feet with a deafening applause. It lasted several minutes before Jackson could begin to speak. "First, let me thank the University for the gracious invitation to share my thoughts with you today, and especially thank Kenneth for his complimentary, but hardly deserved introduction. Let me point out standing off to the side of me is my body guard who is here for security reasons but I don't want you to be alarmed." Jackson briefly paused, "Although maybe you should be because he is extremely good at his job." There was muffled laughter, which signaled to Jackson that the audience was more at ease with the situation. He continued.

"Early on in my lifetime, when I was your age and going to school at a University, I was faced with conflicting decisions, as many of you are today. I had dreams of becoming a doctor and was working my way through medical school. Then Uncle Sam beckoned me and I had to shelve my dreams to serve my country. Viet Nam was a controversial war at home and, what I thought to be a 'Godless' war over there. I saw atrocities that no human should ever have to witness. But I saw and felt the Vietnamese people's pain and suffering, and in that moment I felt I was doing the right thing." At that moment a boisterous chant came from the back, and four protesters raised their clenched fists as they shouted in unison, "Baby killer! Baby killer!" over and over. Three males were dressed in worn baggy clothing and had headbands tied around their foreheads to hold back their long straggly hair. All of the protesters held signs made from cardboard and poster paper and on some were painted a brightly colored 'peace sign'. Security quickly and unexpectedly dispatched several officers to the loud and obnoxious group. The men and women fought the officers by jerking away and falling to the floor with a refusal to stand up. Some had to be dragged out by two uniformed men. Jackson stared at the scene in horror. His thoughts took him to a dark place in his past. He felt again, the physical pain of every punch in the face he received from those who rejected the war. His heart sank as sorrow surfaced and forced a remembrance that he cared not to entertain. Rex whisked him off stage to a safe place and drew his weapon to a ready position. Jackson lowered his head and waited.

As soon as it was clear to return to the stage, Jackson confidently continued his speech. "I have always used my sense of humor when I have been in a tight situation; but, this was not humorous. I take my service to my country seriously and I respect the right for freedom of speech. I think it should be done respectfully, though. Not once did I feel my sense of humor surface during this whole ordeal, nor should you find it funny.

I remember when I lost part of my leg and how I used my humor to see me through the nightmare. I had been taught by my parents to be positive and to even use my humor growing up, especially when faced with a difficult decision or situation. Did I have regrets after Viet Nam for the action I had taken that brought me to that point? Absolutely not! A fellow Marine and a brother was able to go home to his family when the war was over and that thought also kept me going. Being positive and accepting of the decisions you make, sets a defined course for your life. I wasn't aware at the time, of the exact course I would be following but something that I can't explain, found deep inside my soul, caused me to pick myself up and continue on, living life to its fullest. Maybe it was something I learned as a youth and maybe it was the Marine Corps that instilled this driving force inside of me; this force that would prove to be a help and necessity in my future." The eyes of the students were fixed on Jackson and the air was still as they intently listened.

"There were days that I got in fights and days that I came home from work with my prosthesis boot filled with blood. I turned to liquor, smoking, and some drugs to drown my pain. I lost sight of dreams, family and purpose. Headed down a dead-end street, I sank deeper and deeper into depression. It wasn't until I redefined my purpose and discovered new passions, which I truly started to heal. I had friends that challenged me to literally go out of my comfort zone. They knew me well and found out early that I could not and would not resist a dare. I don't recommend that attitude to all of you; it could get you into serious trouble." Again the audience enjoyed Jackson's humor and the easiness of his conversation.

"There were steep and rugged mountains to climb along the way but when I reached a point of feeling success in my accomplishments, I experienced a sense of reward that I had never felt before. It spurred me on and drove my perseverance to new levels. I have been loved. I have been hated. Paparazzi have annoyed me and I have felt the sting of rejection and scandal. When I was in the accident that took my legs, the feeling and control below the waist, I was done. Tired, beyond description, I melted my way into self-pity. I went to rehab for the mere reason that my friends and family kept reminding me that I was a Marine and a Marine never gives up on his 'mission'. I really wanted to die but was too ashamed to admit it to anyone. I became careless with mixing my alcohol and medications. And then, I actually did die. I was revived to be brought back to big changes that I wanted to make. Getting my drug addiction under control was hard and it hurt. I was always sick; but I took it upon myself to give up all of my addictions, including drinking and smoking, at the same time, which made the process almost impossible. I felt God had and was punishing me for all the terrible things I did in the war and afterward. I felt that driving force and the voice that kept saying to me, 'Persevere, persevere. Keep going Marine. You haven't completed your mission.' I truly felt that by trying to be valiant, I had brought the vengeance of God upon me. No matter. It was still my duty to pick myself up and follow orders, to persevere and keep going. And that is just exactly what I have tried to do. I encourage all of you to find your purpose and invite your driving force into your lives. Set your course for a positive road and don't deviate. But, if you do, get up and keep going; complete your mission."

A standing ovation followed, with a boisterous applause echoing through the spacious auditorium. Several students rushed up some side stairs to gain access to the stage and Jackson. Rex was prematurely there to ward off any danger that might evolve. Students were hovering over Jackson with programs that they wanted autographed, which they provided him along with a pen or sometimes a pencil, whatever they had. A few just wanted to shake Jackson's hand and many of them, surprisingly, thanked him for his military service. Jackson had talked so long that he began to lose his voice and eventually had to excuse himself from the crowd. He turned his wheelchair to follow Rex off the stage as he cleared the way for Jackson to exit the building. Carrie was waiting by the door and greeted him with a warm hug and hard kiss. "Oh, Jackson. That was incredible! I am so proud of you!" "Thanks," Jackson said dragged out slowly. "I'm really glad that it is over. I don't like public speaking. Remind me to ask Jillette to down schedule speaking events for a while. I need to spend more time with my tennis tournaments. Those crowds are quite different and more tolerable."

A few days later Jackson received a letter. He had read several letters but this one stood out to him. It was from one of the university students that attended Jackson's speaking event. The student's name was Greg and it began, "Dear Mr. Montgomery, I want to personally thank you for sharing your story. You have changed my life. When I came to hear you speak, I was also struggling with drug abuse and decision making processes. I wasn't experiencing much success or feeling any purpose, like you described you felt in your speech. Thank you for saving my life and inspiring me to make some positive changes and start living. Sincerely, Gregory Thompson."

This was one of hundreds of letters that flowed in through Jackson's personal mail and business mail. Reporters had jumped on the story and capitalized on Jackson's popularity. Every tennis tournament he played in across the country had entangled conversations about his inspirational speaking engagements at various universities and high schools. Jackson was a well-sought after commodity. Carrie never tired of listening to Jackson speak, or watching him play at a tournament and Jackson kept romance alive and interesting by scheduling periodic 'get-aways' to undisclosed locations that only Rex was aware. Sometimes it was Mexico or the Dominican Republic. Or often, they would venture to Europe and absorb all they could of France, Italy, England and Greece. Extravagant? Yes! But Jackson had earned the ability to lavish and be lavished every minute he spent on this earth. No one judged him. Jackson didn't only spend his wealth on himself and Carrie, but also had a flourishing charity organization, racket stringing business and promoted free tennis lessons for the youth at the country club where Joe was manager. He contributed annually to the local youth golf and tennis organizations and gave generously to a myriad of community charities. He made sure that every penny he had earned was put to good use. The rehabilitation unit at the hospital where he recuperated, also benefitted from Jackson's humble gifts.

Jackson and Carrie were kept busy throughout the spring and summer months, attending tennis tournaments and speaking engagements. Sooner than expected, the holidays were upon them and they began spending more and more time with extended family. They had just returned from an early visit with Jackson's family where they found everything to be well. Everyone looked great and was prospering at their various projects and tasks. Samantha was doing particularly well in her nursing courses, drawing down straight 'A's, while also pursuing singing, which she loved and an active social career. Sam was living at the sorority house located on campus and called Jackson every weekend to keep him updated and to have, sometimes meaningless conversations with him. One night the call was different.

Jackson heard the phone ring and he wheeled over to pick up the receiver. He was expecting Samantha's weekend call and he smiled big as he answered. "Hi Sam!" Jackson began. Jackson tried to sort out what was being said through muffled words and alternating sobs and loud crying. "What? Am I hearing you right? It's okay Sam. Are you hurt? Have you spoken with the authorities? You hold on. I'll catch a flight first thing in the morning. I'll be there for you; don't worry." Jackson's demeanor changed drastically and was noticed by Carrie as she rushed into the room. "What's going on? Was that Sam?" she nervously asked. Jackson quickly turned his head toward Carrie and blurted out. "Sam was assaulted at the country club where she has been working this past summer. She is devastated and crying inconsolably. Mom and Dad were notified by the authorities and then she immediately called me. She's not hurt badly; the sheriff took her to the hospital to be checked. I told her that I would get a flight out and be there first thing in the morning. I need to call Jillette and get her on this right away." Jackson's sentences ran together as thoughts raced through his head. Carrie reached out and put her hand on his shoulder, trying to console him. "I am so sorry Jackson. Do you want me to go with you?" Carrie spoke with concern. "No, I will call you if I need you there. I will talk to Sam first. Just stay by the phone for updates. Do you think you could help me get a bag packed really quickly?" "Absolutely." Carrie stood up and headed for the bedroom, while Jackson tried to reach Jillette and have her ready his pilot and jet for the emergency trip. Jackson felt a combination of gut-wrenching nausea followed by severe head-ache producing anger take hold of himself. "How can I help my sweet sister?" he thought.

Jackson's stomach rumbled and quivered and his heart was pounding at an accelerated rate as he sat anxiously in the seat of his jet. He was like a child when he caught himself saying, "Why aren't we there yet?" over and over in his thoughts. Jackson pulled himself from his chair and had the attendant retrieve his wheelchair even before the aircraft had secured landing and came to a complete stop. Jillette had arranged for a car to pick up Jackson and a highly recommended body guard to be his temporary driver. Rex hadn't been notified in time for him to accompany Jackson to Arizona. Jackson was mostly on his own. Jackson spotted the driver waiting in a black, four-wheel-drive vehicle on the tarmac. He motioned for him to help load Jackson's bags and him into the car. The man quickly and rapidly complied sensing Jackson's urgency. There wasn't much conversation, only Jackson giving the man the address of the University Sorority House where Sam was staying. There was a dragged out silence as the vehicle smoothly transferred from one major highway to another while making its way through the maze of traffic. Jackson looked at the address he had clenched in his hand and jerked his head toward a brown bricked building across the street. He asked the driver to slow down so he could make sure they were in the right place. "That's it! Park in front. You can help me out, but I'll see my way in." "The driver cautiously responded, "Sir I'll have to go around the block and come back on the other side. The street is extremely steep. Are you sure you can manage?" "Don't worry about me, just park the car." Jackson retorted rather abruptly.

Jackson sat on the sidewalk in front of the sorority house. He cradled two dozen white roses in his lap. He felt the cool moisture from the flowers against his stomach and breathed in the fragrance of fresh cut roses. Jackson previously had the driver make a stop on their way at a local florist and buy two dozen roses for him to take to Sam. They had to be white. Jackson peered up the three sets of stairs that forged their way to the front door and he humbly admitted to himself that he indeed needed some assistance. "Hey, would you mind giving me a lift up these stairs to this sorority house?" Jackson addressed a group of young men coming from the fraternity house that was next door. One young man in particular observably took charge and motioned for the group to follow his lead. They all introduced themselves and when Jackson reciprocated, many of them reacted positively recalling that they recognized Jackson from sports magazines and the news. "Who are you seeing at the house?" one bravely asked. "My sister, Samantha Montgomery." "Samantha's your sister? She's awesome! We all know her and like her a lot. She's so lucky to have you for a brother." Jackson thanked the young men for their help. "I'm good. I can take it from here, guys. Thanks again." He mumbled to himself about the validity of the statement that one of them had made concerning Sam's luck to have him for a brother. He wasn't sure that right now he could help his sister and give her what she needed. Jackson stretched his arm up and rang the doorbell.

A rather tall young woman with long brown hair answered the door. She wore partially ripped and worn jeans, a light colored t-shirt and white boat shoes. She had strikingly deep chocolate brown eyes that twinkled with friendliness. "Can I help you?" She looked down at Jackson and paused before she asked, "Are you Jackson Montgomery, the famous wheelchair tennis player?" "I'm not so sure how famous I am, but my name *is* Jackson Montgomery. How do you know who I am?" Jackson asked. "I play tennis and I follow your story. It's incredible! Sam must be your sister. She talks about you constantly. Come in. Wait here in the foyer and I'll go and get her." The woman started to walk away and then turned back around to flash a huge grin at Jackson. He was astonished that so many college-age students knew who he was, and about his story. It was a great feeling, but at that moment Jackson reminded himself that it was not about him this time, it was about Samantha.

Samantha lunged at Jackson as soon as she was close enough and threw her arms around his neck. She began sobbing as she buried her face into his shoulder. "Oh, Jackson, I'm so glad you're here. You just missed Mom and Dad. They were here about an hour ago." Jackson gently pushed Sam off his shoulder and picked up the bouquet of flowers from his lap. "These are for you. You are beautiful and pure like these white roses. And you will always be that way to me. I love you Sam." Sam slowly grasped the stems of the roses scrunching the plastic wrap, making a loud sound. She pulled the bunch of flowers close to her nose and breathed deeply in, savoring the fragrance. Samantha looked at Jackson and stared as she mouthed 'thank you' while a stream of tears made their way from eyes to chin. "Let me find a vase to put these in", she said as she turned and walked down a long hallway. Jackson could barely see through the open doors what looked like a kitchen and dining area. He heard conversation as Sam entered the room. "Oh, wow!" One voice taunted. "Are those from your 'boyfriend'?" "Stop. He is not my boyfriend. He is my brother." Samantha replied. "Sure" the other voice said. "I don't know of any brother that gives their sister a dozen roses, let alone two for *any* occasion." Samantha threw her shoulders back and stoutly gave her response, "Well, mine does."

It was quite the feat to maneuver Jackson in his wheelchair, but Sam and a few of her sorority sisters managed. Once in the car Jackson turned to Sam, "Where would you like to get a bite to eat?" Jackson noticed Sam's demeanor changed when her face lit up. "You know the best places to go here, so you are in charge, my lady." Jackson lovingly smiled at his sister as his eyes started to tear up. "Um, let me see. There is a great steak house just south of the city and near the country club.

I know how much you love steak." "Is that the country club where you worked? Are you sure that won't bother you?" Jackson became serious again. "No, I'm sure. I'm okay." Jackson tapped on the driver's shoulder and gave him the name of the restaurant. "Yes, sir." The large man glanced in the rear view mirror and gave Jackson a nod of acknowledgement.

The restaurant specialized in Italian cuisine. Paintings of grapes and vines covered the walls, and black rod iron chairs and tables were elegantly set with burning candles in the middle. Jackson seated his sister. He treated her with the same respect as he had for Carrie. Jackson had his usual New York steak and Sam had Prime Rib. During the meal, Sam leaned in and said, "You know you don't have to show me all this fuss." Jackson stopped as he was about to place a fork full of steak in his mouth. "Of course I do. You were there for me in my darkest hours and I want to be here for you in yours. That's what family does, Sam." After a few minutes, "Sam, will you do me a huge favor?" "I guess, Jackson. It depends on what the favor is." Sam teased. "Will you please take me to the club and show me where you worked?" "Why on earth would you want to see where I worked? You're upset and it will just make you furious!" Sam's voice raised and her eyes widened. Then, she took a deep breath and paused. "Okay, but only if you promise that you won't do something stupid." "And why would I do that?" Jackson avoided answering her question.

Jackson instructed the driver to turn the lights off and stay parked in the parking lot. He also motioned for him to get his wheelchair and bring it to his side of the car. Jackson began to transfer when Sam squirmed in her seat and anxiously asked, "Where are you going?" Jackson didn't immediately respond. Eventually he nodded toward a dimly lit building with neon liquor signs flashing in the windows. "I presume that is where he works?" Sam's whole body began to shake. "Who? You mean the guy who assaulted me?" No response and notable silence set in. Sam caught a brief glance at Jackson's waist when he transferred into his chair and had noticed a bulge in his shirt. "Jackson, what have you got in your belt? Is it a gun?" "You stay here. I'll be right back," he sternly directed Sam and then turned to the driver. "You come with me." Sam fumbled to get her seat belt off and jumped out of the car. She ran toward Jackson but two large strong arms stopped her. "You need to stay here, miss. Do as your brother says." Sam squirmed and kicked, and finally bit the driver to pry away from his grasp, then desperately ran after Jackson screaming as she ran, "No Jackson! No! This won't help anyone. Please!" Sam reached out and jerked Jackson's wheelchair to a stop. Her strength against her brother's surprised even her. Lying on Jackson's lap was a revolver; one like he used in Viet Nam and Jackson wore a look of determination, unlike anything Sam had ever seen before. Sam jumped in front of Jackson's chair and bent down to his eye level. "Please! I know you mean well, but this will ruin everyone's lives- mine, Carrie's, mom and dad's and especially yours. You will go to prison and so will I for being with you. Please, I know you're angry, but can't you see that Jackson?" Jackson clenched his teeth like he was fighting self-control. His right hand wrapped around the handle of the gun and his pointer finger rested on the barrel readied for use. His other hand came up to his forehead slowly and cradled his head while he was deep in thought. Sam pushed through worst case scenarios in her thoughts while waiting for a reaction from Jackson. "Okay, okay," he said reluctantly. Sam let out a big sigh of relief after holding her breath. "Thank you, Jackson. I love you. Now put the gun on safety and let's go back to the car. You will always be my hero, but not like this."

Jackson spent the next few weeks hovering over Sam through phone calls from Denver. He spent considerable time in phone conversations with Sam and Carrie. Jackson called from a tournament when he had a break. Jackson couldn't get past the incident and was still talking about it weeks afterward. "Carrie, I know honey. I need to let it go, but sometimes I just can't. I keep seeing the women that I saw tortured in Nam and I did nothing to help them and now my sister has been hurt deeply and I want to do something. In that moment, I wanted to kill the guy. If he had been standing in front of me rather than Sam, I probably would have." Jackson vented to Carrie often and it was becoming an increased concern to her. "Jackson, you have always wanted to fix problems and change bad situations and I love you for it! But this time you can't change what happened, nor can you fix it. Let it go and love Sam like you always have. This will help both of you heal. Trust me. You know I am there for you whenever you need me." Jackson felt Carrie's genuine and deep love for him and he knew that Sam, Carrie and he would be fine.

It was Christmas time and Jackson and Carrie had adorned their tree with clusters of tiny white and red lights. The decorations hadn't changed much from the year before nor had the outside lights. Presents again blanketed the bottom of the tree trunk with only the color of the wrapping paper changed. Their home had a slight scent of pine and vanilla that welcomed guests at the door. Carrie loved scented candles and had them burning in every room when she was home. Carrie and Jackson's favorite way to spend an evening included a lit fireplace, soft background Christmas music, and a romantic table set with their best china and glowing tapered candle in the middle. Jackson had anticipated coming home one particular evening to Carrie's grilled halibut, fresh garden salad and baked potatoes; one of Jackson's favorite meals.

Jackson swung open the door with a high level of concern. He had earlier received a call from Carrie about Mistletoe. She had jumped up on the coffee table and devoured a whole pound of chocolates that Carrie and Jackson had received as an early Christmas gift. Mistletoe was vomiting and lethargic when Jackson arrived. "Have you called the vet?" Jackson hurried over to the sofa where Carrie sat holding their little dog and comforting her by stroking her soft multicolored fur coat. "She feels hot, Jackson. The vet said to bring her right in. Oh, Jackson she could die." "Come on, let' go. I'll get her carrier." Jackson and Carrie didn't waste any time carefully but quickly driving to the veterinarian hospital a few miles away. Mistletoe still remain unresponsive and quiet. Jackson's heart melted with worry. He remembered Mistletoe's wet puppy kisses and her hyperactive way of greeting him when he arrived home each day. Carrie had tears rolling down her cheeks and she lifted Mistletoe up to her cheek and gave her a gentle hug and kiss. "It's going to be okay, sweetie. We love you. Please stay with us." "How is she doing?" Jackson excitedly asked. "No change." Carrie quietly commented. Jackson immediately pulled on the hand held accelerator of the car and increased their speed. All was a blur, traveling to the animal hospital. Lights brushed by like quick, short strokes of a painter and Jackson couldn't recall the journey once he arrived. Mistletoe was rushed into the hospital by a caring assistant who gently cradled the pup in her arms. Carrie handed the dog to the assistant with, "take good care of her." She stayed behind to help Jackson out of the car, but then realized he didn't need her help. Once inside, the assistant came out to periodically update them both on Mistletoe's condition.

Finally, when the Veterinarian approached them, Carrie and Jackson began to fear the worst. "Is she okay? Will she live?" Jackson was urgent with his questions. The doctor explained, "She is very ill. We have her on IV fluids and have pumped her stomach to remove the residue of chocolate in her system. Now, we need to wait. She is strong and appears to have been in excellent health before this incident, so her prognosis is encouraging. We will be keeping her for a couple of days to monitor her closely. Do you have any questions for me?" The doctor glanced at Carrie first and then Jackson. "Is she in pain or does she have any discomfort?" Carrie slowly and quietly asked. "No, she has neither pain nor discomfort. We have given her a sedative to help her rest and we will monitor her closely and keep her comfortable." The doctor turned toward the clinical area as Jackson spoke out a loud, "Thank you, Doctor."

Jackson and Carrie returned home to try and get some rest, but neither one of them could sleep. Carrie was up several times during the night. "Are you okay?" Jackson sleepily asked as he raised his head from the pillow to get a glance at Carrie. "I can't sleep at all! I am so worried about Mistletoe. You would think she was our child." Carrie began to pace and bite her nails, one of the minor flawed habits she had developed. "She is part of our family so of course you're worried. I am too." Jackson made the effort to turn on his side and face Carrie so the conversation didn't become muddled and hard to hear. "I didn't think I could get so attached to an animal. But she has definitely stolen my heart." Carrie continued. "Do you think she will be all right, Jackson?" "I certainly hope so. We just need to think like she will be and have faith. Do you remember the day you brought her home and hid her in your sweater?" Carrie laughed, "Oh, yes! She wouldn't hold still and made my sweater bulge so she wasn't hidden very well." "She pounced on me and lavished me with puppy kisses and she still does. That's one of the things I love most about Mistletoe. I kind of like having her around." "Me too." Carrie countered. "We're both still up and can't sleep so let's go in the kitchen and have breakfast. Then later we can go to the hospital to check on Mistletoe." Jackson started to get out of bed and transfer to his wheelchair. He told Carrie that he would meet her in the kitchen in a few minutes.

French toast and bacon were served up with some freshly squeezed orange juice. Carrie was an excellent cook and was constantly surprising Jackson with her myriad of talents. Breakfast was silent, lacking the laughter and conversation that was usually present when Jackson and Carrie had their meals together. When finished, Carrie told Jackson to go get dressed while she cleared up the table. Jackson thanked Carrie for breakfast and turned toward the bedroom. Carrie cleared the table but did not take the time to do the dishes. She piled them beside the sink, wiped her hands on a dish towel, and hurried in to get dressed. They were both anxious to find out Mistletoe's condition and the tension was palpable in the air.

Jackson pushed through the entrance with the glass sliding doors, followed by Carrie. They informed the receptionist that they were there and requested to talk to the Veterinarian that was in charge of Mistletoe's care. Carrie heard a high-pitched short bark and looked over toward the hallway. There stood the doctor holding Mistletoe. "I'll do better than that. Would you like to see your dog?" Mistletoe began squirming and panting as soon as she recognized her family. The doctor tried to contain her but failed. The little dog bounded from the doctor's arms and vigorously ran toward Carrie and Jackson. Jackson could hear her claws tapping lightly on the tiled floor as she ran. Mistletoe leaped onto Jackson's lap. A procession of tail-wagging, wiggles, jumping up onto Jackson's chest and wetting his face with love kisses pursued. Jackson and Carrie couldn't stop petting her and scratching under her chin, which was something she loved. "Okay, okay girl. I'm glad to see you too! Let's go home!" Carrie received the discharge orders and instructions for Mistletoe's care and she and Jackson, and of course, Mistletoe headed home. It would be one of the best Christmas celebrations that Carrie and Jackson would experience together even before they were married. Married with Mistletoe, what a great combination!

Christmas morning found Carrie and Jackson waking to Mistletoe barking and pouncing on their bed. She had become the alarm clock and was consistently on time. Mistletoe could sense the unusual excitement of the day and was more aggressive with her wakeup call. "Good-morning girl! Merry Christmas. Should we go see what's under the tree?" Carrie didn't expect an answer, but Mistletoe barked her approval immediately in response to Carrie's question. Jackson slowly opened his eyes and moaned, "What time is it?" "Time to get up! It's Christmas morning Jackson." Carrie took hold of Jackson's upper arm and shoulder and moved him back and forth to help him wake up.

It wasn't long before they were sitting in their pajamas in the living room. Jackson had lit the tree and Mistletoe was barking and chasing her tail in front of it. "Carrie, look over there by the fireplace." There stood the majestic Grandfather clock that had been purchased in Switzerland and the chimes on the hour filled their home with warmth. "How did you get it in here without me knowing?" She excitedly asked. "Oh, I had some help. It was delivered while we were at the hospital with Mistletoe, so I called Joe, and he and Rex came over, and brought it inside and signed for it." "Are you pleased?" "I am so pleased. Thank you, Jackson." "There's more," he said as he reached down and picked up a small package that had been hidden from Carrie. "Here. This is to remind you of our wonderful adventures and the love that has bonded us together." Carrie rapidly ripped the paper off and quickly opened the small, but beautiful box. It was red-velvet and looked expensive. Carrie's eyes widened and she gasped, "What is this, Jackson? I thought we were going conservative on presents this year." The joyful look on her face indicated her approval and consent to bend the rules she and Jackson had set down to follow. Carrie carefully picked up the item with her index finger and thumb and pulled it up into the air to examine it more closely. It was a sterling silver charm bracelet with a charm that represented everywhere she and Jackson had been during their courtship and marriage. It even carried a tiny nurse's cap with a red cross on it representing the hospital where they had met two years ago. Carrie didn't have words right away. She covered her mouth with her delicate hand and began to sob. "I'm sorry. Don't you like it?" Jackson looked at Carrie with a startled expression on his face. "Oh, yes Jackson. Of course I do. I love it! I'm just being emotional and sentimental, that's all." Carrie leaned over and cradled Jackson's neck in her arm. She pulled him toward her and gave him a long passionate kiss. "I love you Jackson."

Jackson opened his gifts from Carrie. He was equally surprised. Carrie had cleverly disguised the boxes so Jackson couldn't guess what they were. She also broke the rules by purchasing a Rolex watch and the other a new state-of-the-art tennis racket. She had to elicit Joe's help with the racket. She knew Jackson was particular about his tennis equipment. Mistletoe jumped in and out of the wrapping paper that was on the floor and showed her approval with her barking. The morning faded away quickly and after breakfast Carrie and Jackson flew to Arizona to visit family. Good food, thoughtful gifts, and laughter filled the environment in Jackson's parents' home. Sentiments of love and appreciation were given and hugs exchanged. Jackson and Carrie didn't want to leave. The Montgomery's home was contagious and gave a comforting security to them.

Jackson and Carrie were only able to stay for a day at the Montgomery ranch. Work was beckoning Carrie and Jackson had to prepare for another tennis tournament that was going to be held in Georgia. It was two days after Christmas and fresh fallen powder snow covered the yard. It glistened in the sunlight and its reflections were blinding. The sky was a steel cold blue and clear for miles. The sun was yawning and stretching over the horizon. Dawn had entered the atmosphere and there were scattered early morning sounds throughout. Carrie woke to Mistletoe pawing at her shoulder and whimpering uncontrollably. "What's wrong girl?" Mistletoe laid her chin on Carrie's arm and whimpered again. "Jackson. Something's wrong with Mistletoe." Carrie waited for a response. Carrie turned over nudging Mistletoe off of her arm and shoulder. She turned toward Jackson and was horrified as she recognized a sound that she was too familiar with at the hospital. Her medical knowledge identified it as the 'death rattle', a gurgling sound someone makes when they are dying and trying to breathe. "No! No! Oh no Jackson. Come on wake up!" She violently shook Jackson but did not get a response. "Jackson!" Carrie screamed. "Please wake up!" Carrie instinctively felt for a pulse on Jackson's carotid artery. When she didn't find one she frantically began CPR. Carrie was using all her strength to do chest compressions. Jackson was a large man with sculpted muscle mass on his upper body. Carrie managed to grab her bedside phone in between sets of breaths and compressions to call 911. She could hardly control the sobs and crying as she spoke with the dispatcher. "Mrs. Montgomery, continue CPR and we will have help there right away." The voice of the dispatcher was reassuring. Carrie continued CPR and silently offered up many prayers in Jackson's behalf.

Carrie thought her panic and grief were playing with her imagination when she heard a voice. It was Jackson's and spoke to her clearly so she could recognize it. "Carrie. Carrie. I love you beyond this life. You must let me go. I have completed my mission. Stop Carrie. Stop." Carrie struggled with what she had heard and passed it off as hallucinations caused by trauma. She shook her head and squeezed her eyes shut tight in hopes it would bring her back to reality. "I can't. I can't! I can't let you go!" She uttered over and over while still maintaining the rhythm she had established with CPR. The voice came again and said the exact same thing. Paramedics barged through the door and called out to Carrie. "Back here." She shouted. The medics took over the CPR and lifted Jackson onto a folding stretcher that they carefully maneuvered down to the ambulance. "Where are you taking him?" Carrie nervously inquired. "To the Veterans Hospital, ma'am. You're welcome to ride with him in the back." "Thank you." Carrie said as she climbed in the back of the ambulance. She stared at Jackson all the way to the hospital. She intently watched as the medics attended to Jackson's needs. Carrie knew from her medical knowledge that the situation was not good and that Jackson was fighting for his life. The voice that she had heard during CPR was haunting her. "What if it was truly Jackson and this is not what he wanted?" Carrie berated herself. She wondered if she had selfishly done what Jackson didn't want.

The ambulance traveled with lights flashing and speeding down the freeway. When they pulled up to the emergency doors of the hospital, several trauma doctors and nurses were waiting. Carrie stood by and watched as they rushed Jackson into the hospital. A nurse approached Carrie. "Come with me. I'll show you where to go." Then the nurse gave Carrie a strange glance. "You look awfully familiar." "I work here." Carrie responded with somberness. "Oh, I see. Is this your husband that we just brought in?" "Yes, it is. We've only been married for two years." The conversation ended as they both arrived at the ICU and Carrie was directed to wait outside Jackson's room. She took that moment to notify his family and Joe. Carrie's eyes were fixed on Jackson through the glass that divided her from the love of her life. Jackson was put on life support and heavy machines were ushered in and out of the room. She recognized the machines and knew they were conducting tests for viable life activity. Nighttime approached and settled in outside and at the hospital. Carrie refused to leave Jackson's side.

She looked up from his bedside and saw Joe standing outside the room. Carrie opened the door and fell into Joe's arms, sobbing uncontrollably. Joe wrapped his arms around her and pushed her face into his shoulder to muffle the sounds of her cries. "What happened?" Joe finally asked. "I woke up and he was gone, Joe. He was gone. I did CPR on him but he wanted me to stop." "What do you mean by 'he wanted me to stop'?" "He spoke to me Joe. He told me to stop and that he had completed his mission. But I didn't listen and kept going and even called 911. What have I done?" Carrie cried harder and her face became soaked in tears. "I'm not sure. I wasn't there." Replied Joe. "But you know him better than anyone, Carrie. I'm sure you did the right thing." "The right thing for me or for Jackson?" Joe stayed around until the next morning. He had assured Carrie that Mistletoe was being cared for by Rex and that he would call or stop by and check on her often.

In the early morning hours, Joe had moved to a waiting area to stretch out on a sofa. Carrie was still cemented at Jackson's bedside. She had hardly eaten or drank anything for hours. The nurses tried to encourage her to eat and to keep her strength up because the next few hours would be draining on her emotionally and physically. Carrie had a bottle of water with her and she nibbled at the food the staff brought her but she really didn't have an appetite. She fixated on Jackson and his care, and asked a slew of questions each time a physician entered the room. Carrie leaned back in her chair and stretched her arms above her head when she noticed Joe outside the room. He was motioning her to come to him. "Carrie, Jackson's family is in the waiting area. They are anxious to talk to you." Joe took Carrie by the arm and escorted her to Jackson's family.

It was a tearful and emotional reunion. They all had a lot of questions and Carrie only had answers for a few. Carrie explained in detail what had occurred and even included Jackson speaking to her. "That sounds like Jackson." Mr. Montgomery Sr. stated as he nodded his head. "We just saw both of you a few days ago and he looked great!" Jackson's mother wiped her tears from her eyes. "I can't believe this is happening! After all he has been through and accomplished!" Samantha was angry and shocked. Rachael stood by her mother and held her hand tightly. "They will only let two visitors in the room at a time and they have to be family." Carrie said with love. At that moment Dr. Zyaire miraculously approached. "I heard it was Jackson that they had brought in through the ER. And, I wanted to be involved in his care. So I am here, but not to deliver any good news." Dr. Zyaire took his hands out of his pockets and began using them to convey the words he needed to speak to Carrie and Jackson's family. "We have done an EEG which is a test to determine brain activity. Jackson's was negative. He has no brain activity and is essentially being kept alive artificially by a respirator. His heart is beating but he is not consciously breathing or thinking on his own. I am so sorry. You will need to make the decision to maintain life support or remove it. I will be back. I'll give you some time with each other." Dr. Zyaire had tears in his eyes as he turned and walked away from the group. All of them stood stoically and silently. No one wanted to be the first to break the silence. Carrie looked at everyone and then said, "Respectfully, I acknowledge that all of you have known Jackson longer than I have and I realize this decision should be mostly yours. But in saying that, I can't help but recall Jackson speaking to me and asking me to let him go. I feel Jackson wouldn't want to be kept alive to only exist in a vegetative state. I feel he would want all of us to let him go." Jackson's mother burst into tears and Samantha hit the wall with her fist. Mr. Montgomery Sr. hung his head and said, "Carrie I think you're right. Jackson wouldn't want this kind of life-a life with no quality. How do you feel Samantha?" he added. "I don't know. He's fought so hard to live. Why won't he fight now?" "I don't care that he thinks his mission is complete. What about his mission with us?" Samantha clearly was distraught and not able to contribute to the decision that had to be made. Mr. Montgomery Sr. summoned a nurse to go and get Dr. Zyaire.

Dr. Zyaire came toward them. He hadn't changed much in looks since Carrie had first met him when Jackson was in rehab. He wore the same brown-colored pants and dress shoes with a button-down shirt under his lab coat. Glasses now were cradled on his nose and his hair had greyed all over instead of just at his temples. "Have you made a decision?" Mr. Montgomery Sr. spoke on the entire family's behalf. "Yes. We want to take him off life support. We feel this is what Jackson would want." "Okay, all of you follow me and you can come and say your good-byes before we begin." Dr. Zyaire kindly motioned them to walk with him to Jackson's room.

Dr. Zyaire brought the family into the room and said he would give them some privacy while he stepped out into the hall and made arrangements for some staff members to be there for the extubation. One by one Jackson's family tearfully approached his bedside. His mother caressed his forehead and his father ruffled his hair. Samantha grasped his hand and pleaded with him to not go. Rachael was lifted up to give her brother a sweet kiss on the cheek. Carrie put her cheek next to his and then took his face in her hands. She couldn't kiss him because of the ventilator tube but she covered his hands with meaningful kisses. Carrie tried to hold back the tears as she told the love of her life good-bye. "I love you Jackson. I will see you soon. You wait for me and we will spend eternity together. I'm letting you go, not because I want to, but because you want me to and I love you. Good-bye my love."

Carrie nodded at the medical personnel in the room and one nurse gently removed the ventilator tubing from Jackson's airway. The family watched as his chest rose one time and then stopped. The monitor showed his heart still beating but slowing at a rapid pace. Silence came and the monitor showed a straight line where once there was a regular sinus rhythm of a beating heart. Dr. Zyaire looked at the clock. "Time of death 11:45 am."

People stood in long lines that were blocks long at Jackson's memorial. There were many that Carrie and Jackson's family didn't recognize, and some that were life-long friends. The memorial services were held in a large cultural building to accommodate the crowds. It was a beautiful and memorable service. Jackson's father spoke and Samantha sang one of Jackson's favorite hymns. Joe read his eulogy and Rex his obituary. Jackson's memorial services and burial were respectfully covered by the local news channel and the paper. The city was saddened and the nation mourned with close family and friends. Samantha struggled the most, and needed medication to help control her depression, and Carrie functioned in a fog-like daze. So many flowers filled the cultural hall that it made Carrie nauseous. She spent considerable time in the restroom throwing up. At one point in time, she questioned if it was really the flowers, but then dismissed her concern rapidly. It might even be something she ate; she really wasn't sure.

The memorial convoy of the hearse and several hundred cars proceeded to the cemetery at crawling speed. Jackson's gravesite was on the top of a hill that overlooked the countryside. He was being buried in Denver because the majority of his career and relationship successes had taken place in Denver. The hearse pulled up to the gravesite where Carrie, Jackson's family, and Joe were seated on padded chairs that encircled the grave. Carrie's mother and her brother, Reggie were there to support Carrie and Jackson's family. The first to approach the gravesite was two straight lines of Marine soldiers. They were dressed in the Marine blues that Carrie recognized from Jackson's military picture. Each of them cradled a rifle in his hand that rested against the same arm. With precision, the Marines walked in unison matching the swing of their arms and the distance they would step. When they came to the edge of the grave, one Marine would make a sharp turn to the left and the next to the right until a line was formed at the edge of Jackson's grave. There was a space left for the casket to be brought forward. Carrie and the rest of the crowd respectfully took a standing position as more Marines lifted Jackson's casket from the hearse. It was covered with an American flag and Carrie heard the soldier's commands as they moved forward slowly and precisely until they lowered his casket onto some silver piping that held the casket above ground until the services were over. The Marines that lowered the casket and the ones standing in the line with their rifles sharply saluted and then stood at attention. An officer graced the occasion, took the microphone, and announced the gun salute.

Carrie wanted to cover her ears during the salute and she couldn't help but think about the times that Jackson had told her war stories about gunfire and how it triggered him. As soon as the Marines finished their gun salute, those standing by Jackson's casket neatly picked up the flag and folded it triangularly and tucked in the ends. One Marine saluted the commander and handed him the folded flag. Then the commander slowly walked over and stood in front of Carrie. He presented the flag to her while thanking her for her husband's valiant service and dedication to his country. He then saluted Carrie and placed the folded American flag in her hands. The commander and the other Marines immediately walked over to the hearse and stood at attention. Carrie could still smell gun smoke from the rifles that were fired, and it stung her nose. She reached up to rub her nose with a handkerchief when the Bishop came to the microphone. It was time to dedicate Jackson's gravesite and to pray for it to be protected from the elements. Everyone bowed their heads and then in unison at the conclusion said, "Amen."

Carrie felt people come from behind and offer condolences by placing their hand on her shoulder. She was grateful but still struggled with the fact that this was real. She felt like they should be talking to someone else, not her. A dark feeling of numbness and disbelief hung over her, and she had the sense of fogginess like when one is drugged. Samantha cautiously approached the casket and then turned to Carrie. "Do you think he would mind if I took a flower?" "Of course not." Carrie managed a smile for Sam. The funeral home had placed a bouquet on the casket after the Marines removed the flag and Samantha wanted one of the roses. Roses were Jackson's favorite flower. Carrie absorbed every smell and sound and she photographed for her memory the scenes that she had witnessed that day, never to be forgotten. She had been fumbling with a worn, silver metal object that she rubbed between her fingers. She glanced down and carefully observed the detail. It had grooves cut into the surface which gave it a striped look. Some of the grooves were worn down and could barely be seen. It was Jackson's cigarette lighter that he had in Viet Nam. He had hung onto it to remind him to live life to the fullest and to remind him who he was. Jackson was a proud Marine who believed in completing missions where he was called. Carrie rubbed her thumb against the lighter and then turned it over. She slowly rubbed her thumb over the inscription engraved on the surface. Tears trickled down her cheek as she read, "THIS MARINE WILL GO TO HEAVEN BECAUSE HE SPENT HIS TIME IN HELL!"

THE END

www.ingramcontent.com/pod-product-compliance
Lightning Source LLC
LaVergne TN
LVHW011815060526
838200LV00053B/3787